WHAT THEY ARE SAYING ABOUT

REEL PEOPLE

What a great aid to writing your book REEL PEOPLE has been for me. A cast of strong, coherent characters is the basis of all truly good films—and the hardest thing for writers to master.

Nothing I've ever read has been as helpful as your analysis.

Finally, an aid to screenwriters, beginning or veteran, that gives us a handle on the mysterious process of character creation. Now when there's something "off " about one of my characters, I've got a way to put him back on track. Not only that, but it's a real treat to read: instructive, engaging, and fun.

Don Roos, Director/Screenwriter
BOUNCE, THE OPPOSITE OF SEX

REEL PEOPLE is a very thorough study of film personas—a fascinating look into the psychology that lies behind a wide variety of character types. It relies on in-depth research and is a valuable aid to any screenwriter.

David Parfitt, Producer
*SHAKESPEARE IN LOVE, WINGS OF THE DOVE,
THE MADNESS OF KING GEORGE*

REEL PEOPLE is an insightful analytical tool, invaluable not only to writers, but also to anyone looking to better understand characters, and for that matter, possibly themselves. Dr. Gluss has chosen excellent examples from films to illustrate his points, achieving the exceptional feat of making the reading as entertaining as watching the characters on screen.

Dump your shrink and buy this book!

Gary Levinsohn, Producer
SAVING PRIVATE RYAN, THE PATRIOT, PAULIE

Through careful research, clinical experience, and a prodigious knowledge of cinema, author-psychotherapist Dr. Howard Gluss has written a book both scholarly and entertaining. Rich in detail, his fascinating treatise surveys memorable personality archetypes depicted in film—what they represent, why we celebrate them, and sometimes even make them our metaphors for living. The author has given us a big helping of new knowledge, seasoned with spicy facts, humor and nostalgia.

This is a reading must not only for movie-makers and movie-lovers but for anyone interested in the creative process.

William Luce, Author
THE BELLE OF AMHERST, BARRYMORE

It's all in one place now—and film and television writers have Dr. Howard Gluss to thank! REEL PEOPLE is a wonderful and fascinating tool to help writers deepen their—and by extension the audience's—experience of their characters . . . it makes you want to write as well as run to the video store.

Richard Kramer, Producer/Writer
TALES OF THE CITY, ONCE AND AGAIN, THIRTYSOMETHING

Although conflict and structure are difficult aspects in their own right, it's the creation of believable and sympathetic characters that is by far the hardest. REEL PEOPLE not only points out many ways to make the process easier, but makes them easy to remember through wonderful anecdotes.

David Zucker, Writer/Director/Producer
AIRPLANE!, NAKED GUN, RUTHLESS PEOPLE

What a fine read this is. Highly informative and instructive, REEL PEOPLE makes what industry folk refer to as "development hell" considerably less hellish. This is an indispensable tool for those of us who are not writers, but wish to serve and support their work in the very best way possible.

Chris Chase, Producer
WALT DISNEY ANIMATION

REEL PEOPLE

REEL PEOPLE

FINDING OURSELVES

IN THE MOVIES

HOWARD M. GLUSS, Ph.D.
WITH SCOTT EDWARD SMITH

CONTENTS

III — The Workplates

DEDICATION

To storytellers.
Past, present, and future.

To Phyllis and Lonnie Smith.
Now and always.

ACKNOWLEDGEMENTS

for inspiration: Dee Bridgewater, Ph.D.

for movie-smarts: Garth Twa

for advocating: Stephen Greenfield and Chris Huntley
at Screenplay Systems

for making things happen: Frank Joseph

for making sense of it: Karl Monger

ABOUT THE AUTHORS

HOWARD M. GLUSS, Ph.D. is currently in private practice in Beverly Hills and is a Psychological Consultant for film and television production. A former student at the Banff School of Fine Arts and the American Conservatory Theatre, Dr. Gluss holds, in addition to his doctorate in Psychology, dual degrees in Drama and Communications Studies. His unique and valuable background in both the arts and psychology has made his expertise invaluable on matters of not only story and character, but the very nature of the creative process as well. Dr. Gluss has been called upon by directors, writers, actors, and producers to assist in bringing to life their most inspired creations. To facilitate interest, he has created *KeyLight Consulting* and the *KeyLight Seminars*. Dr. Gluss prefers eleven rows back from the screen, seats on the center isle, and fervently believes it is unforgivable to miss the previews.

SCOTT EDWARD SMITH has a broad-based, twenty-five-year history that includes Broadway, Las Vegas, national tours, film, and television. He has worked within the studio ranks as an executive and experienced his own personal development hell as a writer for television and adapting novels into screenplays for Warner Bros. and 20th Century Fox. He is the co-creator and producer of *KeyLight Consulting* and the *KeyLight Seminars*. He continues to write both fiction and nonfiction.

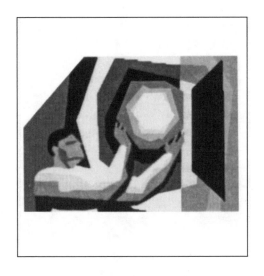

For more information visit our website:
www.KeyLightCompany.com

Reel People can also be accessed at
www.screenplay.com

FOREWORD

AUTHENTICITY. IS IT too much to hope for? The therapist in his office is not unlike an audience in a darkened movie theater. In a world of stolen moments and fleeting images occurs a journey of discovery. Figuratively and literally in the dark, the therapist and the filmgoer encounter a world of illusions—a place assembled from clandestine personas and enveloped in polished, well-crafted facades. All for a glimpse of what *might* be real. The therapist, like the filmgoer, enters the dark unsure of the success or failure that awaits.

From the first flicker of light on the silver screen to the final fade out of Hollywood's latest premiere, those who make movies work hard to create a world in which the events we are watching are really happening. Talented actors abound, as do elaborate sets, costumes, special effects to dazzle . . . the bottom line is there is much to convince you that what you are seeing is real. Despite such deliberation, it can be a rare and glorious thing to find authenticity in the central characters.

Why are the psychological personas of the characters that inhabit many films so often deficient of basic truths? In the ensuing rush of technical wizardry and creative genius, what is often curiously forgotten (or avoided) is looking straight into the eyes of the character and challenging them to tell the truth.

Reel People has a common ground with the films herein cited. They have successfully (arguably, some better than others) brought to vivid life a personality and used it at the heart of the developing story. It is not a special effect, a convoluted plot point, or a studio's multi-million dollar ad campaign . . . but the character that leads us. With the films examined in *Reel People*, the creators have been careful to make sure that the characteristic traits are not merely quirks, but ultimately the story. And if it were not for these defined traits, the story would not play out as it does. The plot will be defined by the character's actions.

It is essential to the dramatic structure of the story that the character is who he is.

There are many psychological theories used to approach and understand the human personality. These numerous avenues have foundations in widely disparate disciplines. Cognitive Behavioral, Psychodynamic Psychology, Gestalt, Existentialism, and Jungian theory are just some of the bases from which the psychologist may choose to work. Cultural, socioeconomic, and educational factors certainly come into play. And not to be underestimated, the aging and raging debate over *Nature v. Nurture.*

Nurture is of primary importance to the creative artist. Nurture concerns itself with outside forces that become internalized and determines how an individual will act. The action of, and reaction to, such forces is the why and how that explains a character's responses to stimuli. It is the source of the character arc. This, by the way, lends itself ideally to the business of storytelling. The exploration of the roots of these responses provides the creative artist with a viable backstory.

Faced with an array of information, the creative artist (as does the therapist) must search for the best way to create or explain a comprehensive behavioral pattern of the character (person) in question. There is little doubt that you will be better able to predict your character's actions and motivations through a greater understanding of the character's psychology. However, psychological theory should not be used as a rigid set of rules; instead, it should serve as a set of guidelines. Rather than forcing an interpretation of behavior onto a character, you should allow the character to lead you into the realm of theory. Familiarity with psychological theories will allow you to have a richer understanding of the human condition and the development of personality structures. This richer understanding will allow you to take greater creative chances, to be bolder in your choices.

Look at it this way: in order to create a complex, believable character, you must embrace both the character's strengths and weaknesses. An understanding of theory will allow you to do just that. *Casablanca*'s Rick Blaine is not so much remembered for his third-act patriotic efforts as he is for being a misogynistic, cynical loner—an original antihero redeemed by discovering his ability to love. Batman (*Batman*) did not become a superhero superstar because he was rich, handsome, and possessed ultra cool devices. He became immortalized because he was the Dark Knight. The psychodynamic underpinnings of his youth—the savage murder of his parents before his own eyes—is ultimately what caught our attention. It is unquestionably the basis of what makes Bruce Wayne tick. We relate to Batman not because he saves the day (or night, as is usually the case), but because we recognize the immeasurable pain he experiences.

You must feel comfortable with allowing your character the freedom to lead you—much like a patient leads his psychologist —down their own unique path of self-discovery.

With this in mind, it is probably not surprising that, when a psychologist first meets with a patient, he shares much in common with the creative artist at the outset of developing a character. Similar to the psychologist, the creative artist may know very little about his character. How does he react in a given situation? How does she function in a relationship? Why does he choose a certain partner? What was her childhood like? The creative artist and the psychologist are both interested in understanding human nature; and you can never fully understand the personality formation of any character unless you first understand his formative experience. Everyone, fictional or not, has a maturation level that determines his ego strength, his susceptibility to psychopathology, and the prefiguring of his life choices.

It's also valuable to note that the human psyche has many facets and you may not always be creating psychopathological characters. Not every movie has a knife-wielding mass murderer or egomaniacal tyrant. As with most things in life, there is a continuum at play. For example, two individuals with the Histrionic Personality Disorder can behave in manners as different as night and day. Someone wins at everything for attention, whereas another fails at everything for that same attention. To a greater or lesser degree, we all have such tendencies as narcissism, paranoia, obsessive-compulsive drives, and periodic depression. A character need not be pathological to be analyzed. Psychodynamic theory not only describes the characters on the outer fringes of sanity and society (the Hannibal Lecters/*Silence of the Lambs*, the Norma Desmonds/*Sunset Blvd.*), but also the characters that are merely troubled (Harry Caul/*The Conversation*), Carly Marshall/*Blue Sky*).

Furthermore, many people not only function quite well on a day-to-day basis, but also actually achieve great success because of personal behavior attributed to a specific disorder (Melvin Udall/*As Good As It Gets*). The nuances of psychological theory come into play with story characters just as they do with real people. Instilling this element into a fictional character serves to make them interesting and layered.

Within the realm of clinical practice and psychiatry, a theoretical assessment known as the *Diagnostic and*

Statistical Manual of Mental Disorders (the DSM) has been established. It is best described as "the language," a common ground that enables all therapists to speak with one another with some sense of understanding within the profession. It creates for the multitude of doctrines an international diagnostic language. Amongst its many assessments, the DSM has identified dozens of disorders. These disorders are categorized under such divisions as: eating, mood, childhood, anxiety, substance-related, psychotic, and personality. A complete list of these disorders can be found in Part Two: The Mental Disorders.

It is the last of these (the Personality Disorders) that serves as the basis of information presented in *Reel People*. This book presents and analyzes eight major personality types. Each chapter will offer films both classic and contemporary that depict the specific personality type being presented. The diagnostic criteria information found in *Reel People* (and gathered from the DSM-IV) is that of the American description as opposed to the European description, the ICD-9. Of the ten recognized personality disorders, seven (those most commonly seen in daily life and on the screen) were chosen. The eighth chapter of *Reel People* relates to the Masochistic Personality. The Masochistic Personality (by DSM-IV standards) is not actually a personality disorder at all. Regardless, it is a psychodynamic personality style often portrayed on the screen and, therefore, it has been included.

Immediately following the Introduction, there is an abridged definition for each of the eight personalities to be presented in *Reel People*.

It is important to reiterate: personality disorders need not be psychotic. What's more, it is perhaps best not to think of these personalities as *disorders*. The connotation plays heavy on the interpretation that something is horribly wrong when in fact the condition is more problematic than debilitating. The truth is, it's more of a *personality order*—a series of (severely) recognizable and correlating conduct responses. The key to understanding might be as simple as noting how the clinical phrasing of the diagnostic criteria for each of the personalities begins: *"A pervasive pattern . . ."*

What it suggests is something more complex than the Average Joe . . . an overwhelming commonality in the patterns of behavior.

It is important to mention that in the choosing of cinematic examples for *Reel People*, the emphasis was not on whether or not a film character fit the rigid diagnosis of the DSM-IV. Instead, examples were chosen to highlight a specific personality characteristic. For instance, Blanche Dubois is listed as Histrionic, although some might argue she is Narcissistic. In diagnosing characters it is more realistic to look at a combination of personality attributes. A person with a Narcissistic Personality may also portray Borderline and/or Antisocial characteristics, but in doing so will most likely prove less Schizoid (having a personality marked by extreme shyness, secluded intent, and an inability to form close relationships).

Above all, remember: although *Reel People* will draw from many theoretical sources, it is not meant to be an exhaustive overview of psychological study. Rather, it should serve as a practical guide for the individual found somewhere along the boundless plane of creativity. Proclaiming categorically a specific personality type onto a character is not the purpose here—most psychologists will tell you that in real life you can't—because the human psyche is much more complicated than simple definitions. Even the highly regarded DSM comes with a cautionary warning against such actions. If you understand the nuances that exist between the personality types, the opportunity to successfully create a true and honest portrayal will exist.

Here now is the best advice I can offer: the real value in using this book is in looking at various personality styles and combining characteristics to form a unique characterization. Art—as in real life—finds that these individuals rarely fit stringent characterizations. They are rather a combination of many different elements that form an individualized personality. As with all psychological theories, these personality styles should be used as a method for attempting to understand personality, but not as a basis for diagnosis.

These definitions should spark creativity and debate, not limit it.

It should also be noted that throughout *Reel People* (as a form of reference), dialogue from many films has been quoted in the hope of highlighting a specific point. The quotes from dialogue are taken from the film and not the original screenplay—and in many instances they are slightly paraphrased. It is with the highest regard (and deepest regret) to the author that this may have occurred. Welcome to Hollywood.

A closing thought and two confessions: First, this is *not* a "How To Write" book. Not for anyone writing anything. There is a surplus of scholars and insightful readings to instruct in the actual and formidable task of writing a story. Furthermore, in the case of *Reel People*, it would most likely be assumed it was created to serve the writer. With hope, it does. The aspirations, nevertheless, are much greater than that of the singularly courageous author. From first inception to last page, the intent of *Reel People* is to serve the creative artist. Not only writers, but also actors, directors, producers—anyone who might be involved in the process of telling a story. The hope here is that all individuals who contemplate the theories presented in this book will better serve the stories they are telling.

The second confession I must make is that I am in love with the movies. This love is neither a teenage angst nor a fond-yearning love. It is a lustful indulgence. It's the type of love that is blind and fool hearted. The type of love that forgives the bruising mistakes, bad intentions, shabby behavior, and sees only good in the object of desire. Admittedly, I will leap in front of (and take a bullet for) *Citizen Kane* just as quickly as I will for *Citizen Band*. There will be no cruel intentions in the diagnosis of films. There will be no bitter treatise of resentment for disappointing a loved one. Around the world are tables to sit at if you have nothing good to say regarding what is undoubtedly one of the most dynamic, engaging, joyous, and influential art forms in history.

Ultimately, if *Reel People* should serve you, then I have admittedly and selfishly served my own personal indulgence for the silver screen. If these pages inspire to better storytelling, then I will most happily sit in the dark and listen to the tale.

—H.M.G.

INTRODUCTION

FOUR POINTS FROM THE AUTHOR

Prior to reading the Personality Chapters or exploring the Workplates, it will be beneficial to consider the following four points as they relate to the fusion of psychology and the creative arts.

POINT ONE   MIND-CHANGE

A phrase you will find tossed about on these pages is **psychodynamic psychology**. Psychodynamic is a term going back some 100 years and reflecting concepts drawn from diverse schools of thought. Note the two components:

Psycho—having to do with the human mind
Dynamic—having to do with change

MindChange. The "dynamic" element was first used to stand in opposition to "static." Very quickly it was taken up to define "functional" rather than "organic." It is a way of thinking—not only about a patient but also about the relationship between patient and therapist. Psychodynamic psychology is a tributary to the psychiatric community that puts a great deal of attention (not to mention credence) on the product of **conflict and deficit**. The individual suffers from a *deficiency and conflict* in his or her psychological framework.

In essence, modern psychodynamic psychotherapy focuses on three areas of development:

- The interpsychic conflict of the patient
- The difficulties in maintaining a cohesive self
- The impact of early primary relationships

For many psychodynamic psychologists, the interpsychic world is one of internal conflict among the ego, the id, and the superego. The **ego** can be defined as the part of our personality that helps us make decisions, integrate reality, and maintain our psychological defenses. The **id** is the unconscious aspect of us assigned to discharge tensions between our sexual drives (libido) and our aggressive drives. The **superego** represents our moral values and our internalization of our societal and parental values. When all three aspects of our personalities battle amongst themselves the results can cause anxiety. In order to cope with this anxious state the individual may then develop psychological defenses. Some of the more prominent defenses include **repression** (the expulsion of unacceptable thoughts into the unconscious), **displacement** (undesirable wishes and thoughts that are attached to one source are displaced onto another), and **somatization** (painful feelings are communicated through physical ailments). As an individual matures he attempts to gain mastery over his drives and integration of various aspects of his personality.

The reduction of tension can also be viewed in the context of relationships (infant-mother dyad). As children develop they learn that drive reduction and integration can also be achieved by seeking relationships. How the child then internalizes these early relationships will have a major impact on his or her adult development. If a primary caregiver was experienced as hostile and non-loving, a child may then experience most intimate relationships with a sense of paranoia and trepidation. On the other hand, if the atmosphere of child rearing was one of love and nurturing, the child may then develop into an adult that is capable of having mature loving relationships.

In order to manage difficult childhood rearing situations the child may also develop defense mechanisms in addition to some of those already mentioned. One of the most prominent defense mechanisms developed in early childhood development is **splitting**. The world may become polarized into good and bad. This defense is based on a need for safety. The world must be divided into strictly good and bad experiences in order to integrate the good parts of the early maternal relationship and ward off the bad aspects of those same relationships. Unfortunately, the end result is usually one in which the person is weakened and growth is difficult.

In addition to developing a theoretical model for understanding interpsychic conflicts and maternal relationships, the psychodynamic psychologist will look at the external world of the individual and how external relationships help the individual in developing a sense of self-esteem and self-respect. Many times our responses to individuals in our environment will aid us in maintaining a sense of happiness. Our environment may validate us or we may have a dissimilar experience. If validation does not occur on a consistent basis our ego may experience a disintegrative quality that will fill us with anxiety. Many times an individual's hunger for drugs or alcohol will be an emergency attempt to ward off the disintegration of his or her sense of self. This fragmentation can occur on a continuum from anxiety to severe paranoia and panic.

Furthermore, the psychodynamic psychologist will attempt to understand a patient's life story by listening to his or her dreams, fantasies, fears, hopes, impulses, wishes, self-images, and perception of others. Similar to the creative artist, the psychologist must learn what is unique about each patient if they are to develop a comprehensive understanding of character.

POINT TWO   PSYCHIC DETERMINISM

An important factor in psychotherapy—as well as storytelling—is **psychic determinism**. This is a principle that states that symptoms and behaviors are external manifestations of unconscious processes. Although most of us prefer to think that we go through our daily lives as we wish, the basic psychodynamic principle is that each of us is a character living out a script written by our unconscious minds. Our major choices in life (our relationships, our careers) are not random chance or luck. Unconscious forces fundamentally shape them. Luke Skywalker (*Star Wars*) was not simply a bored teenager stuck in an isolated-galaxy-far-far-away farm life. There was a destiny tied to great psychological machinations. When human behavior becomes markedly symptomatic—when psychopaths eat their victims' hearts (*Silence of the Lambs*), when extramarital one night stands "won't be ignored" (*Fatal Attraction*)—the limits of free will become quickly apparent.

By delving into the character's early childhood experiences, you can establish a template—a strong foundation from which you can chart a character's evolution. Choice of career, types of relationships, and communication styles can all be traced back to a character's development during formative years.

This concept (that the past is tied to the future) cannot be stressed enough. Within the psychological community's diagnostic criteria of the personality disorders presented in this book, most of those definitions include the phrase, *"and present from early adulthood."* These personality disorders are honed and refined over many years. They are experts in the nature and manner of their behavior.

POINT THREE   CORNERSTONES

The sphere of the neonate's perception is a tight one and the development into a viable and distinguishable person is unmatched in both quantity and quality in the whole of a human's lifetime. The universe of an infant can be as small as a mother's nipple, and the feelings toward it, then, fill the whole universe. These first perceptions—as trite as they may seem to a fully formed adult who has to worry about mortgages, the intricacies of the stock market, and the incomprehensibility of, say, love—are the lode stones of our awareness and stick with us throughout life. Without question, all that comes after—the ability to integrate into society, the strength of our egos—is laid atop these primitive cornerstones.

The reason these cornerstones are so crucial is that all humans are born prematurely—the gestation period of a baby human is 21 months. This gestation period is due to an evolutionary give and take—we can't have both the big brain of a Homo sapiens and pass through a female human birth canal. So, ingeniously, a compromise was reached—we're born helpless and still gestating. The relationships with the outside world—the tiny universe of the nipple—are as vital to proper growth as nutrition. Our arms would not form correctly in utero without the adequate nutrients . . . neither do our personalities without the adequate nurturing during the vital first years of life outside the womb.

Developmental theory addresses human growth as the complex process that it is. Growth is a series of transformations, similar to a primordial cell dividing to create new life forms. Each stage of development is viewed as evolutionary and each stage becomes increasingly more complex. With each stage there is a sensible order—no stage can be skipped, and the preceding stage most often determines the one that follows. Evolution demands that new cells must take on a new responsibility to gain the next rung of the ladder. The stages of personality development must also exhibit growth in a new direction (i.e., maturity).

For the creative artist attempting to understand the evolution of his characters over time, developmental theories provide sophisticated insight into character psychology. The understanding of human development is essential for the creative artist if he is to understand how characters may change over time (as well as how and why they remain the same). Many psychodynamic theorists have centered on the first years of childhood development in order to differentiate between normalcy and psychosis.

Perhaps of greatest importance, the theories and very name of Sigmund Freud have entered the modern argot. His body of work has been extremely influential in all spheres of life. His ideas have shaped modern literature, music, drama, cinema, and art. The concept of the unconscious mind has proven to be one of the emblematic ideas of the 20th Century.

Freud used the metaphor of a cave in his original formulation of his theory of the unconscious mind. Outside the cave is the conscious mind. This is the realm of everyday consciousness and thoughts—where everything, seemingly, is relatively accessible to constant awareness. When you first enter the cave, you encounter the preconscious mind—the part of the mind where thoughts are below the surface of immediate awareness—yet with little trouble the individual can access them. But deep within the cave lies the unconscious mind, the region of our soul that harbors thoughts that are unacceptable or incomprehensible to the individual. These thoughts are not easily brought into awareness. The unconscious, the preconscious, and the conscious systems of the mind compose what Freud termed the **topographic model.**

Psychological illness, or psychopathology, is often believed to be the result of repressed memories of distant, early (and usually disturbing) events. The unconscious selectively forgets the things that are too painful or objectionable for the conscious mind to acknowledge. This is especially true with the repression of sexuality (Freud believed) and this repression was connected with the development of neuroses. The banishment to the dark recesses of the back of the cave of these highly troubling or inappropriate feelings can prove a tremendous battle. When a character has a great deal of repressed material, the battle to keep those terrible things safely hidden and cordoned off with defense mechanisms can lead to complex, irrational, and even seemingly insane behaviors.

Anyone familiar with Jungian archetypes or the insights of Joseph Campbell and *The Hero of a Thousand Faces* will recognize this cave business and its relationship to film and storytelling.

POINT FOUR THE PAST AS PROLOGUE

The past always serves as prologue. William Wordsworth's statement that "the child is the father of the man" describes it aptly and succinctly. Childhood experiences play the central role in the formation of adult personality. Although the process of personality development always involves the subtle and ongoing interplay between an individual's inherited traits and the environmental factors that shape those traits, it is impossible to overestimate the effect of early childhood relationships on psychological well being later on in adult life. It is also hard to overestimate the effect of a flawed childhood on adult psychopathology. Psychiatric illness can often be traced to just how good (or how bad) the relationship between the child's temperament and that of the parenting figure was during the early phases of life.

In the movie *Shine*, young David Helfgott is alternately encouraged and upbraided by his overbearing father. He can never be quite sure if he'll be thrown against a wall or be drawn up into the old man's ursine arms for a crushing embrace. The father is a survivor of the Nazi camps and is ruled by survivor guilt. He pushes his son to limits that horrify David's teachers, yet when David wants to strike out and pursue unquestionable success, the father refuses to let him go. When David insists, he is excommunicated. Throughout the film, the father has a constant litany for David: "No one will ever love you as much as I do." David believes this—he has to—but what he hears and what he experiences is very different. He winds up institutionalized, unable to fathom the intricacies of a mature, adult relationship.

The psychologist is trained to see that, through the way the patient relates to him, his behavior and responses actually symbolize some deeper processes. He must ask himself what the patient's relationships really symbolize, what aspects of the past are being replayed in the present. The creative artist must go through a similar process, though working the other way around: creating a puzzle as opposed to solving one. Whereas the psychologist has a fully formed "character" with whom he must get to the root of things, the creative artist needs to start from the roots, establish a clear understanding of what motivates the character and what behaviors will spring from this basis. He must constantly ask himself what the character's behavior actually represents.

THE PERSONALITIES

AN OVERVIEW

The following are the Personality Disorders included in *Reel People*. They are defined by the *Diagnostic and Statistical Manual of Mental Disorders* (the DSM). The diagnostic criteria information found in *Reel People* (and gathered from the DSM-IV) is that of the American description. Although these are clinical definitions, they are presented to inspire creativity, not limit it.

The Histrionic Personality

> A pervasive and excessive emotionality, theatricality, self-dramatization, and attention seeking behavior. Beginning by early adulthood and present in a variety of contexts.

The Antisocial Personality

> A pervasive pattern of disregard for and violation of the rights of others. Most significant is the substantial lack of remorse for the crimes that they commit. They also often exhibit an inability to control their violent impulses. They erupt without warning.

The Paranoid Personality

> A pervasive distrust and suspiciousness of others such that their motives are interpreted as malevolent.

The Narcissistic Personality

> A pervasive self-centeredness—an all-encompassing grandiosity about themselves, their achievements, and their

place in life. Along with this exalted self-centered behavior, there is also a discernible lack of empathy and a sense of entitlement that blinds them to all needs except their own. Beginning by early adulthood and present in a variety of contexts.

The Borderline Personality

A pervasive pattern of instability with interpersonal relationships, self-image, and affects, and marked impulsive behavior. Beginning by early adulthood and present in a variety of contexts.

The Obsessive-Compulsive Personality

A pervasive pattern of preoccupation with orderliness, perfectionism, and mental and interpersonal control, often at the expense of flexibility, openness, and efficiency. Beginning by early adulthood and present in a variety of contexts.

The Schizoid Personality

A pervasive pattern of detachment from social relationships and a restricted range of expressions and emotions with regard to interpersonal settings. Beginning by early adulthood and present in a variety of contexts.

The Masochistic Personality

An individual whose personality exhibits the need for suffering, complaining, self-damage, and self-deprecation. The masochistic is not defined by the DSM as a mental disorder.

I

THE PERSONALITIES

The Histrionic
The Antisocial
The Paranoid
The Narcissistic
The Borderline
The Obsessive-Compulsive
The Schizoid
The Masochistic

PRIOR TO READING THE NEXT CHAPTER
IT IS RECOMMENDED THAT THE FOLLOWING
FILMS BE VIEWED:

A STREETCAR NAMED DESIRE
MY FAVORITE YEAR
BLUE SKY

A LIST OF FILMS PERTAINING TO THE
HISTRIONIC PERSONALITY CAN BE FOUND
AT THE END OF THIS CHAPTER.

THE HISTRIONIC PERSONALITY

He won't kill himself. It'd please too many people.
—Roscoe Karns/Charles MacArthur, Ben Hecht,
Charles Bruce Milholland

B LANCHE DUBOIS, a wrung belle recently and rather rudely deposed from her Southern plantation, Belle Reve, arrives penniless in New Orleans. She takes *A Streetcar Named Desire* and descends upon her sister, Stella ("Stella for star"), and her new husband, Stanley Kowalski. Blanche seems to live in a highly vaulted fantasy world of grand manners and opulence, a world that is decidedly at odds with the shabby hovel in which Stella and her working class husband have made their home. Blanche lives by the misty light of her fading charm, a glow that surrounds only her these days, and tends to baffle those around her. At first, the frivolous, flirtatious Blanche amuses Stanley. Later, he is repelled when he realizes that she honestly believes her own distortions and fantasies. She cannot manage to focus on the reality that her life has crumbled around her.

Alan Swann is a blustering, turbulent, troubling movie star of yore who drunkenly swashbuckles his way into the life of Benjy Stone in the 1982 comedy, *My Favorite Year.* Born Clarence Duffy, he has sold his soul and the twinkle in his eye to the movie studios—sold it for a life of ongoing theatrics. He has become, without a doubt, Alan Swann. As Alan, the applause (at least in his own ears) never fades. He takes full advantage of the ability to publicly ride the roller coaster of his turbulent emotions and the whims of desire. He is a movie star at all times and never hesitates to abuse the rights and privileges thereto. He is ceaselessly provocative though he seldom seems authentic. It seems an act as he seduces any woman within arm's length without regard to any prior alliances—hers or his own. He charms, he does not try to deceive. He is the first to list his many faults. He gets away with avoiding responsibility through the fawning complicity of those around him. Any relationship that does not involve melodrama (and that does not allow him to hysterically express his emotions) he avoids.

In *Blue Sky*, Hank Marshall, a major in the U.S. Army, must cope with his wife, Carly, who, as he puts it, "always has to take everything right over the edge." A wiggling, jiggling sex kitten, Carly changes her hair color as often as movie magazines change their covers. Her erratic behavior, her smoldering, inappropriate seductiveness, her tantrums when she goes on a rampage destroying government property, have forced the Marshall family to change bases as frequently as the seasons. Carly fancies herself a dancer in the mold of Tempest Storm, though she is unable to make the distinction between being on stage and not. Even though she has a penchant for performing one-woman USO shows at home for visiting battalions, she loves Hank. She calls him "Daddy."

THE MOTHER LODE

When it comes to digging up the eccentric Histrionic, a near century of film excavation has unearthed nothing short of a gold mine. Storytellers have exhumed a rich world of complexities and inspiration from which to craft realistic and engaging personalities. This is due in no small part to the fact that the appearance of the Histrionic Personality is widely seen across cultures and age groups. They are everywhere, seldom go unnoticed, and have proven to be the meat and potatoes of some of the greatest films ever made. And where movies are concerned, we are talking about a wildly varied pride of films—from the eloquent grace of *A Streetcar Named Desire* to the urban rough *Dog Day Afternoon*. It includes such characters as the deft and drunken Arthur (*Arthur*) and the sexual strutting Joe Buck (*Midnight Cowboy*). The Histrionics' story has been told in everything from *All About Eve* to *Rocky Horror Picture Show*.

One of the interesting side notes is how cinematic history has chosen to remember these characters. Perhaps here, more than any of the other personality styles, there appears to be a direct connection between the Histrionic and that cherished little man, Oscar. Academy Award nominated and/or award-winning performances are (even by Hollywood standards) excessive. Taking home statuettes for their interpretations of Histrionic characters: Vivien Leigh (*A Streetcar Named Desire*), Jessica Lange (*Blue Sky*), Shirley MacLaine (*Terms of Endearment*), Diane Wiest (*Bullets Over Broadway*), Liza Minnelli (*Cabaret*), Barbra Streisand (*Funny Girl*), and Jean Hagen (*Singin' in the Rain*).

Equally impressive is a nominee list that includes such notables as Ronee Blakley (*Nashville*), Leslie Ann Warren (*Victor/Victoria*), Rosalind Russell (*Auntie Mame*), Anne Bancroft (*The Turning Point*), and Meryl Streep (*Postcards from the Edge*).

For the men, nominations graced Peter O'Toole for his Histrionic field day as Alan Swann in *My Favorite Year*; Paul Newman for the brooding Brick in *Cat on a Hot Tin Roof*; Chris Sarandon in *Dog Day Afternoon*; and Dudley Moore for *Arthur*. William Hurt (*Kiss of the Spider Woman*) took home the gold.

Writers, directors, and producers have also been served well by the Histrionic. At the center of Academy Awards nominations for Best Writing and/or Best Picture, such films as: *All About Eve, Terms of Endearment, Dog Day Afternoon, Bullets Over Broadway, Cabaret, Arthur, Cat on a Hot Tin Roof,* and *Kiss of the Spider Woman*.

THE HISTRIONIC VS. THE NARCISSIST

The characteristics to be discussed in this chapter define not only the Histrionic Personality but (with a few variances) the Narcissistic Personality as well. This is because these personalities (along with the Borderline Personality) belong to what is identified as a **cluster**. A cluster refers to the fact that these clinical renderings share many of the same traits. Separating one from the other in a film or in a developing story (let alone diagnosing them) can be a daunting task.

With the Histrionic and the Narcissist we find many overlapping qualities. There are also distinct variations. What qualifies a Histrionic such as Margo Channing (*All About Eve*) from a Narcissist such as Norma Desmond (Gloria Swanson in *Sunset Blvd.*), or Sally Bowles (*Cabaret*) from Joe Gideon (Roy Scheider in *All That Jazz*), is that Histrionics will generally distinguish themselves by displaying a greater degree of warmth and empathy. This is something uncommon for the oftentimes cold and manipulative Narcissists, who are frequently noted for a pattern of grandiosity, a need for admiration, and a lack of empathy. Histrionics behave with great similarity, but most often they do want people to genuinely love them (and will commonly fight it out for the existence of a relationship). Although perhaps formidably self-centered, they usually exhibit true (if hidden) concern for others. Narcissists, on the other hand, are rarely interested in someone else's point of view. Narcissists adhere to the concept of being loved by others, but know little of the feelings inspired by a sense of love. For the Narcissist, what will be most important are their needs and what they consider to be from others: *due respect.*

Pervasive and excessive emotionality, theatricality, self-dramatization, and attention-seeking behavior primarily define the Histrionic Personality. The Histrionic is easy to recognize as a personality that is as vivid and notable as it appears to be unstable. Although very much a generalization, a good rule of thumb is the following:

- The Histrionic Personality will be found in lighter fare—comedies and romances

- Narcissists generally play out in dramas, mysteries, thrillers, and black comedies.

You will find that Histrionics do occasionally appear in dramas—sometimes with great results (such as *Blue Sky, Streetcar Named Desire,* and *Kiss of the Spider Woman*). The same doesn't hold true for the Narcissistic character. They rarely show up as the protagonist of a comedy or romance. The reason for this is that Histrionics (despite their overwhelming quirks) are likable. At times they can be lovable. By their very nature, it's hard (if not impossible) to warm up to the Narcissist. To set off creating a comedy or romance with a Narcissistic Personality as the protagonist is to head down the proverbial hard road to travel.

THE BIG PICTURE

In psychological studies (and as suggested by the history of films) the Histrionic Personality is diagnosed most frequently in women. This doesn't mean that you can't find the personality disorder in men. You can and do. In men, the behavioral expression may be influenced by sex role stereotypes at both ends of the spectrum—from macho to femme. You see everything from the self-confidant stud, Alan Swann (*My Favorite Year*), to the drag-fitted Frank-N-Furter (*Rocky Horror Picture Show*). They can incorporate behavior ranging from that of the mock male bravado of a Joe Buck (*Midnight Cowboy*) to the excessive diva display of Michael Serrault's priceless Albin (*La Cage aux Folles*) and Nathan Lane as Albert in *The Birdcage*.

The behavior of the Histrionic Personality has the air of seeming less than authentic and frequently melodramatic. This is true not only in their outbursts of unearned rage, but also in their happier moments. They may react inappropriately, both in context and intensity. Blanche Dubois seems pathetic as she acts as though she were a spring debutante, stringing her sister's husband with a feather boa as he tries to discuss the very real matters of finances in a New Orleans slum. Alan Swann, in a rare (though undeniably grand) and seemingly contented moment, confides to Benjy that, "I can't tell where the bogus [me] ends and the real [me] begins. Nothing about me is as it seems to be."

Histrionic behavior displays manipulation, repetition, and provocation. Histrionics can be intensely sexual and view themselves as sex objects; their sexuality is often the sole measure of their self-worth. They appear as the eternal gamins, the vixens, the minxes, the flirts, and the studs. They tend to have a fluid self-concept and regularly rely more on their appearance for social acceptance than they do their accomplishments or more stable achievements. Blanche tenaciously hangs on to her long distant youth, decrying direct light and its "merciless glare." Carly only feels alive when she believes she is an object of adoration, whether it is from her husband, other people's husbands, or her children. Alan prides himself on the fact that he is the movie star stud whose aim and purpose is to perform that role, thereby fulfilling the fantasies of his hordes of adoring female fans. The Histrionic often resorts to role playing by assuming the guise of helpless, delectable little girl (or little lost boy), which provokes the patronizing, controlling father/master in others. "You're a big girl now," Hank says to Carly after she has exhausted one of her rants.

Their appearance (one of their main assets, or so they believe) is of vital importance to them. Histrionics will customarily keep attention focused on the external and attempt to draw attention to their bodies to stave off intrusion into their troubled souls. If things are kept stirred up with drama, who has time to ponder things deeper than the skin? Blanche Dubois "can't stand a naked light bulb." Far too much will be seen. Carly realizes that "a woman's charm is mostly illusion, after all." She is terrified of the aging woman in the mirror that is reaching out to take her place. They keep arousal high, they parade their vanity, and they may be exhibitionists. *Rocky Horror's* Frank-N-Furter never walks through a room, he struts—and he usually struts in high heels and fishnets. In *Blue Sky*, when she notices a helicopter flying overhead, Carly takes this as a cue to gambol in the surf, doing the Dance of the One Veil.

Histrionic Personalities may see themselves as childlike—as little girls or little boys—helpless and in dire need of rescue by their daddies. To this end, they gravitate toward older men. These caretakers, men with greater power, are idealized members of the opposite sex. Through them they gain vicarious self-esteem. Blanche is forever seeking—and unfortunately finding, in the series of young men under her charge—that fey, fragile first love of her life, which unfortunately she mocked into suicide. Carly finds herself attracted—perhaps detrimentally so—to military men (surely the supreme icon of masculinity). Aurora Greenway, trying to cope with the *Terms of Endearment*, falls for nothing less than a famous astronaut. *Victor/Victoria's* Norma dances up to a Chicago gangster. *Kiss of the Spider*

Woman's fey hairdresser, Luis, finds solace with an imprisoned revolutionary. *La Cage aux Folles'* Albin has his resilient Renato. Arthur (*Arthur*) has his manservant, Hobson, and Brick (*Cat on a Hot Tin Roof*) his love/hate for Big Daddy.

Seeing themselves as small, fearful, sensitive children, they often believe they are handling difficult situations as well as they are able in a world dominated by powerful and alien people. They see themselves as not responsible for what happens to them. Characters such as Peter O'Toole's Alan Swann and Dudley Moore's Arthur delight at the possibility that they might be under the care of handlers. They prefer to have all responsibility taken away from them. For Swann, he prefers it so much that he eschews the wearing of timepieces on the grounds that he mistrusts them because one hand is shorter than the other. In a childlike way, he is very happy. He can drink himself comatose. There will always be someone to strap him into a luggage dolly and get him to where he needs to be. Alan needs a safety net—he will not allow himself to be responsible for his own actions. So much so that he can't trust himself to do live television. He needs the security of multiple takes and the editor's skill. "I'm not an actor," he rants hysterically. "I'm a movie star!" For Arthur, the death of his manservant (a glorious turn by Sir John Gielgud) and his dependency on him will prove a major plot point.

Histrionics regularly assume passivity; they give up easily, and often cannot plan or think with complexity. They may see themselves (and promote others to see them) as insubstantial, irresponsible, and incompetent: "Sometimes I think I could just disappear and no one would ever know I'd been here," Carly says; *La Cage aux Folles'* Albin and his noble but failed attempt to "walk like John Wayne" and save the day of his adopted son. They see problems as insoluble, and make themselves unable to handle difficult situations. This lets them off the hook. This way they do not have to face threatening decisions. They let other, more powerful, people take care of things.

THE FACADE

This exuded shallowness is generally a result of their difficulties in being authentic with their feelings. Authenticity can bring a greater understanding of themselves and of their pasts. Authenticity also brings pain. Instead, they have a tendency to delete information that may be troublesome or uncomfortable. They blur or completely block out thought processes that may reawaken awareness of matters better left buried: the helpless Brick of *Cat On a Hot Tin Roof* stumbles his way through an evening, literally on crutches, drinking away memories, hiding from the great tragedy of his life; the irresponsible, childlike behavior of the lost little boy inside Dudley Moore's *Arthur*, unable to face what money cannot buy. They usually prefer to go for the greater drama and hysterical reaction to avoid the self-analytical probing that deeper thought entails. Anything to prevent forcing a resolution. Most likely, emotional problems will seem too difficult to solve. This contributes to the Histrionics' belief that they are incompetent, insubstantial. Faced with a situation in which hysterics will not do the trick, they may resort to altering their states of consciousness through alcohol or drugs or risk physical safety. Blanche Dubois certainly enjoys a good tipple, usually under the guise of misplaced gentility and Southern charm. Alan Swann is certainly no stranger to the bottom of a bottle of hooch. When Swann is first introduced, he is plastered. He does, nevertheless, manage to do an inebriated somersault onto the boardroom table and promptly go unconscious. Later he explains it to Benjy: "You know what they say about me, you can always depend on Alan Swann. He'll always let you down." Suicidal attempts are possible, but these attempts are usually just that—attempts, not successes. They usually serve as another avenue for acting out and drawing others into the melodrama.

Their reactions are often seen as strictly emotional (and thus volatile) as opposed to cerebral. They react to what they see (or feel) and not to how they think. Their judgments seem rash, harsh, and based on the visual, as opposed to a more deeply thoughtful consideration. Quite commonly there is an absence of factual and reality-based discrimination. They react solely based on the veneer, on the surface. They also react quickly, especially when threatened by the reactions of others. Blanche pathetically plies her charms on Stanley when he wants to talk finances. She becomes the inappropriately winsome waif in the face of a necessity for rationality. Alan Swann, in the middle of charming a table full of Benjy's relatives during dinner, finds himself confronted with the fact that he has abandoned his daughter. His first action is to get very drunk and start playing the movie star full force, engaging in life threatening daring-do and scaling the side of a skyscraper. "It worked in the movies," he tells Benjy. "That was the movies, this is real life," Benjy responds. "What's the difference?" Alan shoots back.

LOOSE CANNONS

The Histrionic world (similar to that of the Borderline Personality) is a world of stagy over-stimulation. A world in which they are quick to act out their emotions. They react violently to the external and avoid completion of thought processes at all costs. Carly moves from lovely Hawaii to a dingy rathole of an army base in Alabama. She walks into her new home and, instead of resigning herself to her fate and making the best of it, she proceeds to go on a rampage. She destroys what there is of the tattered furnishings and then, for good measure, smashes the car. In the cellar of their Southern home, Brick explodes in front of Big Daddy. He literally tears up and destroys the remnants of his past. This emotional reactivity of the Histrionic serves to coerce the environment into taking responsibility for them and their perpetual dependency. Hank Marshall does just that. He waits out the storm, calmly talks Carly down from the edge of her emotions, and then cradles her in his arms.

Persistent and intense intellectual concentration will seem to have very little place in the world of the Histrionic. They more often than not become distracted or despondent when the necessity of careful thought and consideration would serve them well. A nice dramatic scene never fails to sidestep the issues at hand. Blanche, when going over the ruined finances of Belle Reve, would rather not think about it. She would rather blow away any serious concern with the flutter of an eyelash. When Stanley pushes her, she claims it's too much for a girl educated only in the school of charm to handle. When Hank discusses the vitally important topic of the safe disposal of nuclear waste, Carly slyly manages to bring the conversation down to the topic of her breasts. These outbursts typically get others involved in the ongoing melodrama that provides a continual distraction.

CENTER STAGE

Similar to the Narcissist, the Histrionic is uncomfortable when not the center of attention. They are ill at ease when not expressing their emotions and they never miss an opportunity for theatrics. It's their cue to enter the spotlight. Silence or withdrawn behavior, such as that of Brick in *A Cat on a Hot Tin Roof*, frequently achieves the same results as an overblown dramatic scene. Brick's refusal to come downstairs to Big Daddy's birthday party has made him the center of attention. In Denton (the "Home of

Happiness"), Dr. Frank-N-Furter (an illegal immigrant from the planet Transsexual) runs rampant in his over-wrought castle. He seduces men and women alike, indulging in everything from incest and cannibalism to production numbers. He captivates followers to witness the unveiling of his experiment to create the perfect sex slave—hung, blond, and mute (fulfilling the Histrionics' greatest fantasy: creating a world the way they see it). He will stop at nothing to be the center of attention, from donning women's underwear in public to dry-humping gym equipment in front of guests: anything he can do to win the hearts of the crowd through the audacity of a performance. Throughout *Blue Sky*, Carly manages to find herself in the spotlight. She entertains naked on the beach, disrupts a parade, and rides horseback into a nuclear test sight. When Alan Swann passes out, he does not do so quietly but only after attempting gymnastics and then only after he has dis-tracted everybody in the room. He does not care about the kind of impression he makes, as long as he makes an impression. "They always love big entrances," he believes.

The Histrionic oftentimes attracts crises, and if there is no spotlight, no grand emotional moment for the taking and exploiting, the Histrionic commonly has no compunc-tion with creating one, no matter how inappropriate. Sally Bowles (*Cabaret*) loudly announces her pregnancy in the hush of a crowded library. Carly knows not only a sure way to stop a nuclear test, but also where the news cameras will be. She rides a horse into the middle of the test site in a lovely top that accentuates her handsome shoulders. When the test is aborted, she seems unsatisfied. She may have prevented the contamination of the Nevada desert, but it holds little interest compared to the flashbulbs aimed at her as she dismounts the horse. The egomaniacal sexpot and Hollywood silent film star, Lina Lamont rides through her scenes in *Singin' in the Rain* like a tornado, an ear numb-ing, screeching tornado. Jean Hagen's much honored performance as Lina (a movie star with a voice to make dogs howl and obviously not suited for the approaching talkies) is on a Histrionic rampage. She takes no prisoners in her soon-to-be lost quest to remain the center of attention. Courageous Albin in *La Cage aux Folles* (Albert in *The Birdcage*) is not content to quietly sit and simply offer up an everyday, run-of-the-mill "mother" for a scheme designed to deceive his conservative in-laws to be. No, he finds himself compelled to pull out all the stops and present the ultimate mother of all good mothers: head of the definitive moral family. The Histrionic rarely does anything small and results are rarely what they imagined. The secret to great comedy.

ONCE AND AGAIN

There tends to be a high degree of repetitive behavior with Histrionics. This further aggravates the perceived lack of authenticity of their actions as those around them see the same patterns (perhaps with the same life scripts and scenarios) repeated over and over again. After Carly has lost her husband yet another post, she promises to be good the next time. "That's what you said the last time," Hank responds. Carly's behavior is no surprise to anyone who has known her long. Alan Swann's hedonistic ways are not news to anyone. In truth, Swann's behavior is so much of a public concern that he is anything but hirable. When Benjy admits to being a little worried, Alan expresses shock. "A little worried?" Swann asks. "I'd have thought my reputation would have warranted major concern." As for poor Blanche Dubois, it is discovered that she is not nearly as genteel as she would believe. Instead, she is fleeing in disgrace after another scandal involving the seduction of another young boy.

DISASSOCIATIVE EPISODES

Histrionic Personalities often suffer from **Disassociative Episodes** and these episodes almost always show up in a pivotal scene. A disassociative episode occurs when stress becomes too high to manage with more adaptive defenses. In a disassociative moment, they separate thoughts, feelings, and actions. They react in an unconscious manner. They may reflexively act provocatively, but are unaware of any sexual thought or feeling. Carly bumps and grinds and all but uses her tongue when dancing with Hank's boss, Colonel Johnson. To make matters worse, she does this not only in front of her own husband, but in front of Mrs. Johnson as well. "It didn't mean anything, you know that," Carly tells Hank after she has taken her provocation to its logical extreme and bedded the Colonel. Blanche Dubois plays her flirting sexuality to not only gloss over the unpleasantness of her past but to attract Stanley and win a dominant place in her sister's household.

A displacement of feelings and thoughts often occurs when Histrionics are present in a setting in which they do not belong. Carly blows up when she sees that her new home is a hovel. Compared with the paradise that she has been forced to leave, things appear to be quickly going downhill. Carly runs off, with Hank in hot pursuit. When he corners her, she venomously berates him. She tells him to keep his "filthy contaminated hands" off her. Clearly she is reacting to something perhaps deeper and more incestuously traumatic than the current relocation of her household. Blanche, about to betaken away to an asylum, graciously offers her hand to the committing doctor and tells him that she has "always depended on the kindness of strangers." Misplaced grace, certainly, in such squalid circumstances.

Other common defenses in the Histrionic pantheon are defined (for purposes here) in five basic defenses. These defenses are:

- Regression

- Reaction Formation

- Denial

- Acting Out

- Conversion

Regression occurs when the Histrionic Personality finds himself faced with fear-inducing situations and insecurity. As a result, he is likely to become helpless and childlike. When Carly makes a mess out of an evening at the (appropriately enough) "mess" hall, Hank upbraids her. She counters this by slapping him. Hank is not playing. When Carly realizes that she is being faced with an actual adult confrontation, she melts and leaps into his arms, crying, "Take me, Daddy." When Alan Swann finds himself in a situation that he cannot flirt himself out of (such as being scolded by Benjy's mother for his irresponsible treatment of his only daughter), he further retreats from responsibility. His response is to get even more drunk, swashbuckling his way into society parties where he has not been invited.

Reaction Formation. In order to circumvent an unacceptable idea or impulse, Histrionics adopt behavior that is diametrically opposed to what they fear. They behave seductively when unconsciously they dread sex. They behave as an exhibitionist when they are in reality ashamed of their bodies. Examples: the righteously zealot politician or clergyman who privately is morally corrupt.

Denial. A direct rejection of overwhelming stimuli that is usually coming from the external world—as with Blanche's fabled stories about her past and her unwillingness to face its tragic truth. Acting Out is the need to take action against internal stimuli that is anxiety provoking as is seen in the case of the as-handsome-as-he-is-aimless Brick (*Cat on a Hot Tin Roof*) and his eternal alcoholic search for "the click." This click is the avoidance of Brick's true reason for not having sex with his wife, Maggie. (It should be noted here that in referencing the film *Cat on a Hot Tin Roof*, it is done with a nod more toward the intentions of the playwright Tennessee Williams and his original stage play than what actually ended up on screen. The moral code existing in 1958 did not allow the filmmakers to address the issue of homosexuality the way Williams had intended. To its credit, and noteworthy of Richard Brooks and James Poe's screenplay, is that rather than change the point being made by author Williams, their script did the best it could to avoid what, so many years later, seems only too obvious.)

Conversion. The symbolic representation of an internal conflict in physical terms. Perhaps best glorified time and again in any number of Woody Allen's characters. The constant whining about ailments in order to avoid doing the inevitable.

RELATIONSHIPS

Within relationships there is frequently a high propensity for role-playing: Albin plays wife to Renato (*La Cage Aux Folles, The Birdcage*); Arthur's incorrigible, spoiled little boy to Hobson (*Arthur*); Leon's desire and devotion to be all the woman Sonny will ever need (*Dog Day Afternoon*). Their relationships can be highly sexualized. They often see themselves mainly as objects of sexual desire. Sometimes it is the only way they know how to relate to the world around them. All three primary film characters (Carly, Blanche, and Alan Swann) can barely utter a sentence without it being laden with innuendo. Carly thrives in her role as vixen. The only way she relates to her daughters is as a fellow girl concerned about boys. Blanche lures a completely bewildered delivery boy in a flutter of powder and musty gentility, insisting that he is her long anticipated gentleman caller. Alan reflexively finds the prettiest girl in any given room. He immediately proceeds to seduce her as all other concerns fall to the wayside.

The opposite sex—or the sex with which they seek to be intimate—is consciously important. Unconsciously they are the targets of hostility. The Histrionic habitually over-values the importance of the opposite sex. Their relation-ships are customarily marked by a repetitive or game-like quality. Carly repeatedly misbehaves to such a degree that the family must frequently relocate. She doesn't see herself as responsible for this, though it is perfectly clear to her adolescent daughters and husband. She has gotten away with it as long as she has by pouting and seducing Hank before he raises any serious issues. She promises to be a good girl the next time. Blanche finds herself forced to relocate regularly, plagued by scandals of her own making. Alan's drinking and carousing and his inability to distin-guish real life from his period movies has given him a deservedly notorious infamy that his actions do little to dispel. It is a pattern familiar with Histrionics: sexual seduction followed by either submission or by rage or forceful rejection.

Histrionics (similar to the Borderline Personality) may also exhibit a split between those prospective sexual part-ners who excite and stimulate sexual arousal and those who instead stimulate heartfelt affection. They have two very different sets of needs that must be met, and the nature of these two demands dictates that a single person rarely meets them. If they could have sincere affection and their sexual agenda satisfied, it would leave the Histrionic feeling vulnerable . . .and being vulnerable is too close to the scenario of their initial injury.

When the Histrionic finds a partner, they oftentimes become dependent on the other person and view their part-ner's needs as being more important than their own. "Are you going to be happy?" Hank asks Carly. "Only if you still want me," she replies. Dependent on and drawn to power-ful individuals, they find themselves repelled by weak ones. They see the with righteous indignation at their very existence. How dare they be so weak as to not be able to tame the libidinal and emotional excesses that they (Histrionics) foster?

With members of the same sex—or members of the sex in competition—the Histrionic Personality is often less than charitable. They view these individuals as a threat, as rivals. Since the Histrionic Personality sexualizes relationships, those with the same talents—if not (as in Dr. Frank-N-Furter's case) the same sex organs—have little purpose for them except to get in the way. Blanche is very dismissive of Stella—sending her out on errands for "lemon cokes with plenty of chipped ice." She treats her not unlike she would a servant. She expects to be waited on by her sister. By degrading her, Blanche undermines Stella's position in the household and makes it easier to vie for the available males. Alan Swann, a walking encyclopedia of suave matinee idol clichés, uses all his rehearsed and weary charms to take any and all females from whomever. One of the most attractive qualities a girl can have for Alan Swann is a husband or boyfriend. He seems to choose his conquests solely on their potential for alienation of their men. The more dangerous the spouse, the more desirable the woman.

Following this course of action, the Histrionic character tends to drift toward triangles—triangles either as the other woman, or with two men with whom she can play alternate roles. The resultant turmoil serves a defensive function. It keeps things at a high boil so as to avoid any soul searching. Blanche becomes the other woman in her sister's marriage. Carly beds Colonel Johnson, pitting him against Hank. Alan Swann alternately tries to weasel his way into K.C.'s affections and then (with almost disastrous results) those of a gangster's moll.

Histrionics customarily long for an exciting but safe male to protect them. Seldom do "exciting" and "safe" occur in the same partner. They are therefore infamous for cultivating alternating relationships. In the first instance, they may play the coquette: naive, sweet, kittenish. In another setting they may play the vixen de luxe: the evil, man-eating seductress.

As with the Borderline, Histrionics may split and involve themselves with caring, older, but non-arousing men. Then suddenly they switch. They find themselves a cruel, mean, yet very stimulating man. For men, this tendency oftentimes indicates the "Madonna/Whore" syndrome. They block these inconsistencies and keep the cycle going, keeping the revolving themes of *blackguard/victim* and *nurturing parent/helpless child* going. These rapid shifts safely fulfill their desire for an idealized parent and the treatment of these parents as sex objects. This frequently indicates the actual scenario of their childhood. Sexual abuse is not uncommon.

The Histrionic can also prove to be empathic to the weak, the suffering, and the abandoned. Their nurturing reflects the absence of nurturing they themselves received as children. Carly, despite her fits of destruction and striptease floorshows, is a very attentive, caring, and available mother. She appreciates her daughters' distinct personalities and fosters their growth as strong, independent individuals. Blanche Dubois states it ever so succinctly: "Sick people have such deep sincere attachments." Histrionics can relate to the weak and the put-upon and are only too willing to take on the role of nurturer. Margo (*All About Eve*) Channing's downfall is letting Eve Harrington into her life. By the time she decides to fight back, it's too late. By the end she gives up. What is significant is that she gives up for an important difference between the Histrionic and the Narcissist. She gives up for the sake of love.

BACKSTORY

The childhood of the Histrionic Personality is vital to understanding them, because much of their behavior will be repeated in the present. The disorder customarily stems from a damaging relationship experienced with their parents. Fathers (and sometimes mothers) are central players in the stories of the Histrionics that constitute *Arthur, Blue Sky, Cabaret, Cat on a Hot Tin Roof, My Favorite Year, Postcards from the Edge, Terms of Endearment, The Turning Point,* and *A Torch Song Trilogy.*

In the early home life, the father figure (or mother figure) may have been seductive, emotionally infantile, and incestuous. This may have happened either covertly or overtly, the distinction here being the difference between innuendo or ambiguous physical attention and outright sex acts. This type of behavior repeatedly continues into adulthood. The father (or mother) does not desist with the advances. They continue sharing the intimate details of their sex life, off color jokes, or symbols of special affection more appropriate to lovers than to children.

More often than not, the home life is one of isolation, either geographically (the insular world of Belle Reve) or socially, as seen in the fact that Carly's father was in the diplomatic corps. As a member of the Armed Services they moved frequently, preventing the family members from establishing close ties outside their nuclear unit. This means that the immediate family circle usually satisfied the child's entire needs. It also established the father's position of dominance. In *Blue Sky,* this behavior is repeated with Carly's own family: the Histrionic pattern of repeating history.

The exploitation of the child is highly damaging, but it also bestows on the child a special place in the abusive parent's eyes. This special attention, which gives them a primacy of place with the parent, may be highly over stimulating to the child and unable to be productively integrated into their burgeoning psyche. The nascent Histrionic commonly resorts to hysteria to deal with family corruption. Corruption (by its very nature) demands that the most powerful prey on the least powerful. In this instance, the child will be left to shoulder the lion's share of the blame.

The male Histrionic may have also suffered from maternal depravity due to a hysterical or rigid mother and may look to his father to satisfy his emotional needs. If the father (who may as well be suffering from severe deprivation) accepts the male child's longings, the male child may become "Daddy's Little Boy." The male Histrionic can then suffer from the same neurotic tendencies as his female counterpart. Brick (*A Cat on a Hot Tin Roof*), despite all the hopes and dreams he has managed *not* to live up to, is Big Daddy's favorite and always will be.

In males, Daddy's Little Boy may become highly competitive with his father in order to gain his love and approval. The male child may reject the father and discontinue his pursuit when he realizes he is powerless to compete with his father, or he may become frightened by his longings for his father. As a result, he may pursue celibate pursuits (such as the priesthood) to unconsciously maintain unwavering loyalty to his mother. In such a manner, he may look for other male avenues of approval through hyper-masculine, male bonding activities (such as bodybuilding or contact sports). Sadly, the direction such a male takes is often the relentless and abusive pursuit of women. All this may be done to ward off feelings of inferiority and femininity caused by the interdynamics with the father. His heterosexual relationships maybe centered on his desire to prove himself as superior to his father and ward off his hysterical homosexual panic.

When these powerful and confusing feelings emerge (especially in a world that is highly polarized and does not encourage diluted boundaries), repression or projection as acting out becomes necessary. This occurs in order to relegate these feelings back into the unconscious. If stress and pressure from everyday life begin to build up and a mastery of life comes into question, feminine feelings may emerge. When this occurs, feelings may surface in the form of a need for closeness with those of the same sex (again, the excessive male bonding or hyper-masculine activity). This is led by a strong desire to find from other men a form of security, love, and empathy. As these needs manifest, they are often interpreted as homosexual feelings and a man's own self-identity may be threatened. As the fragile self is internally attacked, this threat can rise to such an extent that self-hatred and revulsion may manifest in the form of a hysterical projection of intense rage or paranoid terror. When Brick explodes with anger in the basement, he rages at Big Daddy and the "mendacity" of their lives. What Brick actually wants to express is his love to both his father and his fallen friend.

THE ARC OF A
HISTRIONIC FILM CHARACTER

The character arc of Carly Marshall in *Blue Sky* accurately follows the arc of a Histrionic Personality. Few films do it as well as this small, wonderful gem. *Blue Sky* is that rarity in which the Histrionic character is the journey.

When we first see Carly, she is securely defined with an establishing shot of her personality and the attendant conflict. She gambols nude in the surf, hyper-aware of the helicopter flying overhead and the servicemen inside. The conflict escalates when Hank returns home from a reprimand that his job is threatened (again) by his wife's behavior. He finds her in the backyard. Carly is dressed in a fashion that would be the envy of any courtesan, performing seductively for a visiting battalion of Frenchmen. Carly, we quickly learn, is in denial that she is responsible for all the upheaval in her family. The goal of maturing, of claiming that responsibility, is set up for her.

The first major plot point is at the end of the First Act. Carly has a psychotic break and smashes up the family's new barracks. It is a home that appears to be nothing short of an ascent into hell. Hank manages to placate her and she resigns herself to her new surroundings. All the conflict that will arise in the film is set in motion. We are given a glimpse of Carly's destructive behavior as well as the regressive issues of possible abuse by her father (abuse inferred in that she calls her husband "daddy" before telling him not to touch her).

The obstacles in the Second Act are sown. Her tendencies to act rashly (with its usual destructive results) and her attraction to powerful men (preferably in uniform, who serve as father figures) all serve to trip her up along the way. She is not helped either by her unconscious belief that she is nonexistent except in the regard of men or by her immature and avoiding behavior. She alienates her family and new friends. She flirts injudiciously with Hank's superior officer. Not heeding the disastrous results that will inevitably ensue, she places her husband in deep trouble with the army on yet another count. This time a mere transfer to another base will not suffice. Hank is committed to a mental hospital.

The significant second plot point occurs when Carly is forced to look beyond herself. She is forced to give up play-acting or risk forever losing everything that she has. The end of Act Two leaves Carly with her husband incarcerated and no one to rely on. She is forced into the role of responsibility that she has her whole life managed to avoid. She must finally act with a clear head and maturity or her family will be destroyed.

In Act Three, she realizes what her responsibilities are and must find the strength and self-reliance to take on the challenges. She learns to act instead of being acted upon. She realizes that it is she who is solely responsible for her family's upheavals. She learns to use her rage in productive ways—ways that will serve to not only get Hank released from the hospital, but also to serve his cause of drawing attention to the harmful testing of nuclear weapons.

The last glimpse we catch of her shows her with her newest look: the glamorous hair-do of Elizabeth Taylor. We see that she has become a grown up woman. Carly has matured (as did American culture at this point) from the blond, ineffectual, male-defined pinup of her Marilyn Monroe into the dark-haired, self-sustained, and independent woman. Though she is still Histrionic, she has made some progress. This is an important, realistic touch to the film and one that serves the story well. It would take a lot more to undo all the entrenched damage she still harbors. Though still Histrionic, she has at least taken on as a role a more independent, active model—one that shows some desire for responsible behavior.

THE HISTRIONIC PERSONALITY SUMMARY

Examples of the qualities and qualifications that define a person with a Histrionic Personality:

- A pervasive pattern of excessive emotionality and attention seeking
- Their personality frequently seems inauthentic and melodramatic
- Histrionic Personalities are usually unhappy or uncomfortable in situations in which they are not the center of attention
- Their behavior is customarily categorized by flagrantly sexual, seductive, or provocative actions, no matter what the setting or specific interaction
- Histrionics consistently use their physical appearance (in particular, their sexual allure) to draw attention to themselves
- They regularly view themselves as sex objects
- They tend to rely on their appearance for social acceptance
- The expression of emotions in the Histrionic is generally shallow and equally often tends to shift rapidly
- They repeatedly become distracted or despondent where careful thought and consideration are required
- Histrionics are intensely theatrical and are prone to exaggerated, stagy expressions of emotion and self-dramatization
- Judgments are recurrently rash, harsh, and based on the visual
- They are easily swayed by the influence of others and by circumstance. They are highly suggestible

- They commonly consider (and treat) relationships as much more intimate than they actually are
- Personal relationships are frequently arranged in triangles
- They often do not view themselves as responsible for what happens to them
- They very likely suffer from disassociative episodes
- Common defenses are regression, denial, acting out There is a high propensity for role playing

NOTEWORTHY CHARACTERISTICS OF THE HISTRIONIC PERSONALITY

SPEECH

> Prone to florid exclamations, dramatics, and excessiveness. What it will generally lack is details and specifics.

PROFESSIONS

> Oftentimes found in entertainment, fashion, beauty, teaching, and sales. It would be extremely rare to find this type of personality as a surgeon, scientist, or CEO.

DRESS

> A tendency to be flamboyant, flashy, loud, abrasive, and seductive. Jewelry, colors, and design that bring attention are customarily worn. Notable examples are found in the characters of Blanche, Carly, Helen Sinclair, Aurora, Albin, Tina, Sally Bowles, Auntie Mame, and Dr. Frank-N-Furter. There is not a costume amongst them that does not feature a couture that captures the consistently fluctuating, almost ethereal nature of their personalities.

HEALTH

> Consistently vocalize. Pains and woes are regularly mantras. Histrionics complain a great deal about bodily problems, women's problems, "the vapors," fainting. Persistent concerns about weight, aging, and appearance.

POPULAR CLICHÉS
ASSOCIATED WITH HISTRIONICS

- A woman's intuition
- A woman's right to change her mind
- Life of the party
- Bed hopping
- Daddy's Little Girl
- The Diva
- The Drama Queen
- The Tough Guy (the Macho Man)
- The Femme
- The Stud
- Theatrical
- Melodramatic
- Artificial
- Overdone
- Fake
- Overwrought

SIMILAR PERSONALITY TYPES
TO THE HISTRIONIC

- THE NARCISSISTIC PERSONALITY
- THE BORDERLINE PERSONALITY

VIEWING SUGGESTIONS FOR
THE HISTRIONIC PERSONALITY

All About Eve (1950)—Drama, 138, No rating.
A great opportunity to see a Histrionic (Davis) go head to head with a Narcissist (Baxter). Both Davis and Baxter were nominated for Best Actress Academy Awards. The film was nominated in nearly every category. Fourteen nominations, it won six Oscars, including for the wickedly brilliant script.

Arthur (1981)—Comedy, 97, Rated PG.
For Dudley Moore's Academy Award nominated performance as Arthur Bach. Also Oscar nominated for the deft writing.

Auntie Mame (1958)—Comedy, 143, No rating.
For banquet philosopher, Mame (Rosalind Russell).

Beaches (1988)—Drama, 123, Rated PG-13.
Bette Midler as C.C. Bloom. A good example of the damage wrought by histrionic behavior.

Birdcage, The (1996)—Comedy, 119, Rated R.
Nathan Lane as Albert. One of the better (and more successful) American adaptations of a French film. See *La Cage aux Folles*.

Blue Sky (1994)—Drama, 101, Rated PG-13.
For Jessica Lange's Academy Award winning turn, Carly Marshal. A brilliant creation.

Bullets Over Broadway (1994)—Comedy, 99, Rated R.
The Histrionic actress, Helen Sinclair. Woody Allen was Oscar nominated for some of his most free-spirited writing.

Cabaret (1972)—Musical/Drama/Dance, 128, Rated PG.
Sally Bowles, a Histrionic doing her best in the most Narcissistic of all worlds: Hitler's Germany. Perhaps the best adaptation of a stage musical to the screen. Pure gold. Nominated for ten Academy Awards, it received eight. The two it lost, Screenplay (based on material from another medium) and Best Picture, went to the film that lost everything else to *Cabaret*—Francis Ford Coppola's *The Godfather*.

Cat on a Hot Tin Roof (1958)—Drama, 108, No rating.
For Oscar nominated Paul Newman as Brick. One of the few films offering the "quiet male" version of the Histrionic Personality. Though the movie does not have the mettle to live up to Williams' full intentions, it is much better than might be expected from a homophobic Hollywood at the time. Nominated as well for the writing.

Dog Day Afternoon (1975)—Crime, 130, Rated R.
For Chris Sarandon's Academy Award nominated performance as Leo. Frank Pierson's writing, a devastating character study, won the Oscar for the Best Screenplay.

Funny Girl (1968)—Musical/Biography, 155, Rated G.
Histrionics are nothing new for Streisand—here, perhaps more so than others, because it was her first portrayal.

Kiss of the Spider Woman (1985)—Drama, 119, Rated R.
For William Hurt's award winning perform-
ance as the fey Molina. Oscar nominated for
Leonard Schrader's screen adaptation.

La Cage aux Folles (1978)—Comedy, 91, Rated R.
For Michael Serrault's priceless perform-
ance as Albin ("Zaza"). See *The Birdcage*.
Oscar nominated for the screen adaptation.

My Favorite Year (1982)—Comedy, 92, Rated PG.
Peter O'Toole in an Academy Award nominated performance as Alan Swann.

Nashville (1975)—Drama, 159, Rated R.
For Ronee Blakely's award nominated performance as Barbara Jean.

Postcards from the Edge (1990)—Drama/Comedy, 101,
Rated R.
Two rich and shaded performances from
mother and daughter displaying Histrionic
traits.

Rocky Horror Picture Show, The (1975)—Musical/Horror
Dance/Comedy, 95, Rated R.
The four-part genre description possibly
says it the best. A bit of everything. Offers
remarkably clear (if cartooned) examples.

Royal Family of Broadway, The (1930)—Drama/Comedy,
82, No rating.
Life in the theater.

Singin' in the Rain (1952)—Musical/Dance, 102, No rating.
A movie that pays homage to the Histrionic
in many disguises. Pay attention to Jean

Hagen as Lina Lamont, the bombshell leading lady. Not surprisingly, an Academy
Award went home with her.

Stardust Memories (1980)—Comedy, 91, Rated PG.
The concept here is celebrities-in-residence
weekend resort. The famous and their fans.

Streetcar Named Desire, A (1951)—Drama, 122, No rating.
Oscar winner Vivian Leigh as Blanche
Dubois and Williams' nominated screenplay.

Terms of Endearment (1983)—Drama/Comedy, 132,
Rated PG.
For Shirley MacLaine in her Academy
Award performance as Aurora Greenway.
Director James L. Brooks also took home an
Oscar for his direction and screen adapta-
tion.

To Be Or Not To Be (1942)—Comedy, 99, No Rating.
Wonderful classic offering backstage life
during the war. A priceless performance
from Jack Benny.

Torch Song Trilogy (1988)—Drama, 177, Rated R.
Solid adaptation by Harvey Fierstein, from
his stage play. Concerning the life and times
of a New York drag queen.

Turning Point, The (1977)—Dance, 119, Rated PG.
Classic theater characters annoying other
people's lives. Nominated for some wonderful writing. Interesting Oscar worthy
film—nominated for eleven Academy
Awards, it received none.

Victor/Victoria (1982)—Musical/Comedy, 133, Rated PG. For Leslie Ann Warren's spirited (and nominated) performance as Norma. The performance and the character have both wisely taken their cue from *Singin' in the Rain*'s Lina Lamont.

PRIOR TO READING THE NEXT CHAPTER
IT IS RECOMMENDED THAT THE FOLLOWING
FILMS BE VIEWED:

SILENCE OF THE LAMBS
WALL STREET
SERIAL MOM

A LIST OF FILMS PERTAINING TO THE
ANTISOCIAL PERSONALITY CAN BE FOUND
AT THE END OF THIS CHAPTER.

2

THE ANTISOCIAL PERSONALITY

Whenever we needed money, we'd rob the airport.
To us it was better than Citibank.
—Henry Hill/Nicholas Pileggi, Martin Scorsese

CLARICE STARLING IS a tyro FBI agent eager to find *The Silence of the Lambs*, the quieting of the voices of innocent creatures being slaughtered that have haunted her since youth. In order to do this, in order to stop the rampage of mutilation being carried out by a killer named Buffalo Bill, Clarice must enlist the help of Dr. Hannibal Lecter—"Hannibal the Cannibal." Dr. Lecter (he is a psychiatrist) is incarcerated in what can only be described as the deepest, darkest dungeon that our judicial system has to offer such criminals as his epithet aptly signifies. (He eats the internal organs of those who annoy him.) He is so insidiously dangerous that he doesn't even need to make physical contact with you to get so thoroughly inside your head that he can kill you. Dr. Lecter is a man of exquisite intelligence and a near complete absence of emotion and conscience. Though sealed off completely from any human contact and the recipient of the harshest and strictest penal conditions, he somehow always manages to establish the rules. And Clarice, in order to save the life of a young girl (an "innocent creature"), readily follows those orders.

Millionaire monster of *Wall Street*, Gordon Gekko (aptly named after a lizard that can shed its skin to avoid capture), spends his days raiding companies and stealing them away from their stockholders. So rich is Gekko he hardly seems concerned with money earned or lost—the prize in his eyes is the pleasure taken from vanquishing his opponent—upper-class men Gekko despises for their blue blood breeding. Into Gekko's oak-paneled lair strolls working-class kid, Bud Fox, trying to break out of the second-class lot in life. He works as a broker well aware that he is on the fast track to the minor leagues. Gekko, for the price of Bud's soul, offers to make his wildest dreams come true.

Meanwhile, in Baltimore, Beverly Sutphin (*Serial Mom*) proudly steers her model suburban family through a life of stringent domestic bliss. She joyfully recycles. She nurtures her children with a kind but firm hand. She can whip up a meatloaf that inspires awe. Yet when the kids are off to school, when her dentist husband is off to tend to his patients, Beverly delights in making obscene phone calls to her neighbor, using language that would make a longshoreman blush. She also runs over her son's math teacher with the family station wagon when a PTA meeting doesn't go her way.

FAVORED SONS

The Antisocial Personality (once referred to as the Psychopathic Personality) has been a staple of films—specifically horror and crime—from the first days of Hollywood. The appeal of these films appears to be as universal and hideously attractive today as it was with Fritz Lang's 1931 film, *M* (notable for Peter Lorrie's shocking performance of raw nerve).Our fascination continued through early Hollywood classics such as *Double Indemnity* and *Strangers on a Train*, finding its way to such recent works as *Pulp Fiction* and *Natural Born Killers*. The objects of all the interest and allure are (to name but a few of their more stellar characteristics) morally corrupt, ruthless, soulless, evil, and murderous—the proverbial worst nightmare. By many accounts, they are also the favored sons for those in the movie business.

The term "psychopath" comes from the roots "psycho" (meaning *mind*) and "pathic" (meaning *sick*). *Mindsick*: a fusion of words that says it all and tells you nothing. And though the term "psycho" is evocative, it is hardly descriptive. Nowadays, the more broadly based clinical term "Antisocial" is favored by the psychological community. (For our purposes, the term Antisocial will be used, whereas "psychopath" or "psycho" is the term most widely used in the films referenced.)

Audiences are fascinated by the Antisocial Personality for the simple reason that they find it appalling. An audience reacts this way because the Antisocial is the closest thing we have to a human monster—and monsters (especially the human kind) are the bread and butter of generation upon generation of storytelling that reaches far beyond the history of film. Relevant writings and admonitions extend back to Sophocles and Euripides. Shakespeare, too, put into verse a few things he needed to get off his chest. The bottom line is that in the big business of motion pictures, the Antisocial Personality has an essence so pure—so accessible—that it plays as well in Kansas as it does in Katmandu. The Antisocial is easy to identify because the characteristics are often highly black and white. Being that these characteristics are easy to identify, they are easily assimilated and installed under an audience's skin.

Their influence in the film market can be categorized into four subgenera. Far from scientific and hardly academic, the four categories do cut to the chase:

- The Scary Antisocial

- The Clever Antisocial

- The Uptown/Downtown Antisocial

- The Comic Antisocial (an illustrious and short list)

The Scary Antisocial entails the actual mother lode. These films range from slasher films (the successions of *Nightmare*'s, *Halloween*'s, *Friday the 13th*'s, the *Scream*'s) to more character-driven psychodramas (*Single White Female, Blue Velvet, Kiss of Death, The Stepfather*). They include characters we hate because they are so methodically demonic (*Cape Fear, In Cold Blood, Reservoir Dogs*) and characters we love because their self-absorption into evil is . . . well, just so damned interesting (*Pulp Fiction, Psycho, Taxi Driver*).

The Clever Antisocial encompasses the more sophisticated personality such as the femme fatale. It is a category in which smart women and evil deeds get to shine (*Black Widow, Body Heat, Double Indemnity, Basic Instinct, La Femme Nikita*). Although sometimes inhabited by an occasional male character, it is rare to find them here. For some curious reason audiences prefer their male Antisocials plain and mean, while at the same time favoring women with an IQ as sharp as their aim.

The Uptown/Downtown Antisocial is where we find organized (and disorganized) mayhem: Mafia and gangsters (*Bugsy, The Godfather, GoodFellas, Miller's Crossing, Scarface*) and outlaws on the lam (*Bonnie and Clyde, The Grifters, High Sierra, Sugarland Express, A Perfect World*). A few blocks north and a bit more tidied up you'll find corporate goons, lawless lawyers, and political hoodlums (*Wall Street, Disclosure, The Firm, Winter Kills*).

In the final category is found the **Comic Antisocial**. Given the nature of the beast, it is not a fashion often attempted by authors. In all cases, the comedy is black. This monstrous personality is ripe for lampoons and the results can offer substantial rewards (*To Die For, Serial Mom, Repo Man, Swimming with Sharks, The Opposite of Sex*). Worth noting about the Antisocial is that although characters such as Sharon Stone's cold blooded and sexy Catherine Tramell (*Basic Instinct*) are usually Antisocial, not all Antisocials are murderers. Some Antisocials are soundly functional within society. Keep in mind that the Antisocial Personality occurs (as do all personalities) on a continuum and that there is such a thing as the "Good Antisocial." The Good Antisocial channels his demons toward the forces of justice. You will, however, be hard pressed to find one without a dark side. It is a category overrun with spies, superheroes, no-name cowboys, and cops with a chip on their shoulder (James Bond films; *Day of the Jackal; The Ipcress File; Dick Tracy; Batman; The Good, The Bad, and the Ugly; Dirty Harry; Unforgiven*).

With the exception of the slice-n-dice variety (a la *Halloween*), all of these subgenera have one important quality in common: although not always the scariest, they are by far the most disturbing of films produced. The Antisocial character with a significant, full-bodied presence in a story (such as a main character) usually means we the audiences are going to experience a certain degree of empathy for their plight: the plight of a soulless creature given some modicum of soul. Not an easy trick to pull off. When an Antisocial character allows us to stand in his shoes and to see through his eyes, the effect can be as unnerving as it is unforgettable. Barry Levinson/James Toback's spectacularly realized *Bugsy* is a standout—the film aggressively challenges the audience to try and not be charmed by the ruthless gangster Ben Siegel. Warren Beatty found his way on several occasions to the Antisocial (*McCabe and Mrs. Miller, Dick Tracy, Bugsy*).

Evoking compassion and/or understanding for an individual so removed from anything we might experience is perhaps the greatest magic the spell of film can weave. Growing up, we find certain movies for which we will always have fond memories; perhaps it's a movie like *It's A Wonderful Life* or *The Black Stallion*. For each of us there are well-remembered images through which we fell in love with the movies. But rarely were these the stories that struck a chord so deep we found ourselves inexplicably drawn to check under the bed or turn on lights before entering a dark hall. The movies I am referring to here are something altogether different. They left memories, all right. They simply were not the ones considered fond. Some of us still check under the bed. Whether we hate the Antisocial or love him, our knee-jerk response to him stays in our blood and nerves and psyche. The reason being that this particular genre does something none of the others can: it takes the old adage of "it's only a movie" and makes the audience regret ever having thought or said those words.

THE DESIRE FOR POWER

The Antisocial Personality has a pervasive pattern of disregard for and violation of the rights of others. Most significant is the substantial lack of remorse for the crimes they commit. Antisocials also often exhibit an inability to control their violent impulses. They erupt without warning. Another benchmark of the Antisocial Personality is a tendency to act out the literal, because they have great difficulty with abstract thought. The Antisocial Personality might opt to kill and eat a loved one instead of keeping the loved one with them by the more symbolic act of reliving memories through family snap-shots or lockets (more on this Epicurean concept in a moment).

The most prominent aspect—a pattern of disregard for the rights of others—is the result of an unmitigated quest for absolute power and control. The Antisocial Personality so fears a lack of power in himself that he can only assuage that fear through the despotic manipulation of his environment. In Chicago, an itinerant ex-con, Henry (*Henry: Portrait of a Serial Killer*), moves from job to job and lives with his old prison pal, Otis. He has been recently paroled from prison after stabbing—or shooting, or bludgeoning—his mother. He can't quite remember the details, except that it happened on his fourteenth birthday. Working at temporary gigs as, ironically enough, an exterminator, he moves through the world dispassionately. He leaves behind a string of murdered women, some violently mutilated, some cleanly dispatched with a simple, single bullet. The murders, while creating hysteria and chaos in the world, bring a sense of order to Henry's world. Beverly Sutphin (*Serial Mom*) must keep the world orderly and neat, separating plastic from glass, and will kill those who violate her sense of the world's order. When her son Chip's math teacher suggests that Chip might benefit from therapy and that the Sutphin family may not be as ideal as their carefully maintained veneer would have outsiders believe, Beverly's ordered world is threatened. She has no choice but to kill the instructor.

This fear of powerlessness prompts the Antisocial Personality to construct elaborate defense mechanisms to keep him safe. Beverly Sutphin (*Serial Mom*) uses the ultra-sterile facade of suburban respectability. Gordon Gekko (*Wall Street*) hides behind a fortress of glass towers built with the emotion-proof mortar of stock commodities and the endless surplus of cold hard cash. Hannibal Lecter (*Silence of the Lambs*) uses his extreme intelligence and circuitous logic as an aegis to keep others from getting a glimpse inside—to gain access to his inner, insecure, wounded self. Lecter takes control early in the game, manipulating his opponent's fear and revulsion, creating an intellectual maze. Since he creates the game, he holds the power. He is smart enough to know how repellent his actions are to the normal person, and he uses this knowledge to put them on the defense. His opponents fearful, he thereby maintains the upper hand.

Having the upper hand plays significantly in the 1990 Curtis Hanson/David Koepp thriller, *Bad Influence*. Rob Lowe gives an arresting performance as a stranger known only as Alex. In the course of the story he takes control over the life of a timid financial analyst, Michael Boll (James Spader). When it is discovered Alex has beaten up a colleague of Boll's, Boll orders the manipulative Alex out of his life. Reacting as a jilted lover, Alex steals everything inside Boll's apartment—literally, down to the last picture nail. Alex does this—he later tells Boll—for no other reason than to show Boll he can. Alex uses this demonstration to horrify, control, and dominate his new friend. As did Hannibal Lecter, Alex creates the game and the rules, letting his repellent behavior put his opponents on the defense.

Bad Influence's screenwriter, Koepp, explored similar terrain (also with considerable results) two years earlier in the 1988 underrated edgy thriller, *Apartment Zero*. Director Hanson, for his part, would come back to re-explore this terrain two more times. In 1994, Hanson would deliver a wild ride with the criminals-on-the-loose adventure, *The River Wild*. Four years later, Hanson would helm with spectacular success, *L.A. Confidential*. With this accomplished film he offers an extraordinary array of examples superbly envisioned.

As earlier indicated this desire for power is not always lurking in the dark with big kitchen knives. Sometimes we find it in broad daylight and wearing a police badge. In addition to the required Antisocial bad guys, *L.A. Confidential* offers up the character of Officer Bud White.

Russell Crowe delivers a riveting and hooded performance that affords us the opportunity to witness an Antisocial Personality that functions within the constraints of society. Albeit, his police badge gives him more license to legally vent his compulsions where most people would not be allowed. Officer Bud White is a character reacting to much of the film's story, guided by the voices and images of his own dark and disturbed past. The same holds true for the tough detectives made famous by authors such as Mickey Spillane and Raymond Chandler and idolized in films such as *The Big Sleep, The Long Good-bye, Key Largo,* and in more recent years with films such as *Chinatown, Lethal Weapon,* and *L.A. Confidential.* They all feature fractured men as heroes: men haunted by a dark past and living at the edges of society, the fine line between good and evil blurred at best. Clint Eastwood created an industry and reinvented his career with the man-with-no-name spaghetti westerns (*A Fistful of Dollars, For a Few Dollars More*). No fool he or Hollywood, these films were followed by the enormously successful *Dirty Harry* series. Finally, he perfected the Antisocial beyond cash at the box office to Oscar gold with *Unforgiven.*

The quest for omnipotent control takes precedence overall other considerations—human life, for example, or the laws of God and man. The Antisocial is nothing if they are not driven. Driven to what is another matter. Ben Siegel (*Bugsy*) wants to invent Las Vegas as well as assassinate the Italian dictator Mussolini. Despite being one of the most ruthless killers in the country and the head of organized crime in Hollywood, Siegel is obsessed with being the hero that must kill the dreaded Mussolini and save the free world. Near the end of Lawrence Kasdan's steamy homage to film noir, *Body Heat,* the poor chump, Ned Racine (William Hurt), tries to explain the woman who suckered him into committing murder and left him to take the fall: "That was her special gift. She was relentless. Maggie was the kind of person who could do what was necessary. Whatever was necessary." Crime fighters from Mike Hammer to Dick Tracy are obsessed with getting their men to the point that their lives are isolated and lonely—abandoned by wives, girlfriends, and family. Gordon Gekko (*Wall Street*) will walk over the bodies of as many corporate raid victims as is necessary in his desire to satiate the thirst of his obsession. He will bust unions and devastate the lives of factory workers if it will quell the pain he feels for his working stiff background. In Gus Van Sant/Buck Henry's 1995 black comedy, *To Die For*, Nicole Kidman plays to perfection Suzanne Stone, a woman who will stop at nothing to achieve stardom in a television career. That includes the murder of her husband. Early on, it becomes clear that she is a force to be reckoned with. Suzanne chooses for her honeymoon a resort hotel that is hosting a television news media convention. It is Suzanne's hope to use the ceremonial occasion of holy matrimony to do some all important industry networking.

This instinct for self-determination is the fuel the Antisocial needs to achieve his power and control. Control is the key to power. *Pacific Heights* tenant from hell, Carter Hayes (Michael Keaton), sets about methodically destroying the lives of his young landlords. *Cape Fear*'s Max Cady plays the Bowden family the way a cat would a terrified mouse—landing swats now and then, terrifying it into submission. Control. Bond and Batman use their gadgets to attain the upper hand. The Jake Gittes' and the Mike Hammer's capitalize on their ability to sink into the underworld. Hannibal Lecter, his smarts. Beverly Sutphin has her fanatic Martha Stewart-like domestic fervor. It is all about control.

Just as the Antisocial is not always the villain, his overpowering need to call the shots can also manifest itself in a humorous outlet. The 1967 cornerstone film, *Bonnie and Clyde*, includes a wonderful interlude halfway through the story in which, in order to feel as though they have friends, the two gangsters kidnap the mousy Eugene Grizzard (a smart performance by Gene Wilder) and his timid fiancée. They don't appear to be hostages or in much physical danger. They've been taken for what seems to be a rueful desire for plain old neighborly conversation—some ordinary civility missing from the Barrow's Gang life—something to hide the ugly truth that they are on the lam as bank robbers and savage murderers. That idyllic world is shattered the moment the Gene Wilder character mentions he is an undertaker. The real world comes crashing down on Bonnie and Clyde and in a heartbeat the young couple find themselves standing on a deserted country road.

Nothing will be permitted to come between the Antisocial and the control he seeks. When someone or something (usually someone) comes between the Antisocial and his control, we have the all important *plot point*. Suzanne Stone (*To Die For*) decides to kill her husband when he suggests she give up her dream of becoming a television news personality and go to work for his father, videotaping special events at the family restaurant. When he tells Suzanne that her dreams are only dreams and that she will never go anywhere, it proves too much for her to accept. In a marvelous effect that captures the tone of this Antisocial character, the director (Gus Van Sant) literally chooses to shutter down the view on the husband as he stupidly makes his pronouncements about Suzanne's fate and, in the process, seals his own. The P.O.V. is Suzanne's, and as the husband (Matt Dillon) babbles on ,the room around him vanishes into black. The view telescopes down to merely him. All Suzanne can see is the horrible obstacle to her goals. All she can perceive is one man, one problem, and one solution.

IT'S ALL ABOUT ME

Narcissistic qualities are quite common in the Antisocial Personality. The Narcissistic Personality is char-

ةoning

acterized by exalted, self-centered behavior and a grandiosity about themselves, their achievements, and their place in life. There is also a discernible lack of empathy and a sense of entitlement that blinds them to all needs except their own. Suzanne Stone (*To Die For*) interviews for her first job as a gopher at a local cable station. She proudly announces that the reason she must be hired is that through television and the news she sees herself as a voice to the people. She considers herself—in the most pious sense—a messenger. Ben Siegel (*Bugsy*) impulsively buys homes and luxury cars on the spot and out from under people who had no intention to sell. Later, he proves himself more worried about how his photograph looks in the morning newspaper than the fact he is sitting in jail on murder charges. Virginia Hill, Siegel's love interest in Hollywood, would put it succinctly: "We both want whatever we want, whenever we want it, and we both want everything."

To feed their narcissism, it is not surprising to see the Antisocial brag about his exploits. Hannibal Lecter (*Silence of the Lambs*) is only too happy to recount the gruesome details of his crimes to anyone who will listen, going so far as to name the side dishes and wine he had when consuming a victim's liver. When the Baltimore police come to the Sutphin (*Serial Mom*) household investigating the death of Chip's math teacher, Beverly is quick to correct them that it was a murder and not merely an accident. Bonnie Parker of Bonnie and Clyde fame writes poems for the newspapers about their exploits and legendary status. *Bad Influence*'s Alex murders a young woman in Michael Boll's apartment, capturing it on videotape. While at a party in his home, Gordon Gekko tells his young protégé to "stick around for the fun" as he invites a competitor over for the purpose of making him squirm. Gekko's hatred for his competitor is palpable and decidedly more apparent than any excitement he has about the money he stands to gain from the business deal.

This high level of narcissism has an enormous effect in the area of employment and work and can lead to remarkably contrasting end results. It can lead to big success or to tragic failure. At one end of the spectrum, the Antisocial Personality has a tendency toward inconsistent work habits and failing to honor financial obligations. They follow no rules but their own. To acknowledge rules would strike the Antisocial as a sign of weakness—it would allow others to control them. Drifters are at the center of the core characters in *High Sierra, The Grifters, Miami Blues, La Femme Nikita,* and *Bonnie and Clyde.* Clint Eastwood's man-with-no-name cowboy is conceivably the ultimate drifter (even named so in *The High Plains Drifter*). At the other end of the spectrum, the "drifting" nature can be anything but aimless and can bring great success. For all intents and purposes, millionaire Gordon Gekko of *Wall Street* lives in a drifting world of stocks and bonds—never sure what the next turn in the road may hold—never so tied to anything that he would not gamble it all to appease his personal obsession. Gekko is not wealthy and successful because it was a smart thing to do and his impulses motivated him to do well with money. Gekko got to where he is by way of his obsession with his past—a common trait of the Antisocial. Gekko battles with his feelings of inferiority growing up as a second class citizen. His lot in life afforded him only the opportunity to go to a less than stellar college—the type of school that situates you in the right places, playing in the best game. He was told he could never compete with the Ivy League rich kids. It is the silver spoon kids that Gekko is out to destroy. The money seems a by-product, an accessory. In much the same way, Henry (*Portrait of a Serial Killer*) is little concerned about how temporary his temporary job has become. How could he be? His thoughts are with his actions—which happen to be that he tends to kill any woman that comes within throttling distance. Gekko takes out the competition that reminds him of all the Ivy

Leaguers. In the women Henry kills, he is looking to kill his mother. The past lives in the present.

When there is financial acclaim and success, it is not too surprising, nor does it come as much of a shock, to discover that the business at hand is the business of crime. The business (both big and small) of crime is well suited to the Antisocial. They tend to gravitate toward illegal operations—occupations above the law—since laws are made to dictate and control behavior. They do not subscribe to others' notions of good and evil, right and wrong. They make their own laws, the primary dictate being that any behavior on their part is acceptable. They are ideally suited to illegality because there is no ceiling to their quest for power; there is no place for remorse or guilt. There is also a surfeit of opportunity for the Antisocials' propensity for damaging things, including people. They may work within the crime structure in grandiose fashion such as in the *Godfather* films, or they may work against the crime structure. The cop, the gumshoe, the secret agent, the superhero—righteous as they may be, they adhere to many of the basic tenants and standards as your Hannibal Lecters and Beverly Sutphins:

- Illegal operations
- Occupations above the law
- Not subscribing to others' notions of good and evil, right and wrong
- Making their own laws
- Any behavior on his part is acceptable

It is a philosophy that incorporates every do-gooder from Bond to Zorro.

They are also ideally suited to elicit vocations because the Antisocial Personality has little or no regard for the truth. They lie often and hard—a handy trait to have if one is going in for the kill . . . vocationally speaking. They lie for a variety of reasons and without qualms (again, the only rules that they are required to follow are their own). Beverly Sutphin, though she lies profusely, never denies murdering her victims, of which she is very proud. Instead, she cleverly manipulates the testimonies of the witnesses and, in so doing manipulates the jury. They may lie for self-preservation, as is the case for the devious-as-she-is-smoldering Matty Walker (*Body Heat*), her sights set on being rich and living on a tropical island; or the is-he-or-isn't-he cold-blooded killer Jack Forrester (*Jagged Edge*), looking to inherit his murdered wife's fortune. They may lie to avoid responsibility or adherence to the rules of others. They may lie for the pleasure of it, pure and simple—to con others or throw them into confusion or in harm's way. In *Silence of the Lambs*, Hannibal Lecter relishes playing with Clarice by stubbornly refusing to be forthcoming. He will not tell her the truth directly, but instead, when it suits his needs, he communicates with cryptic hints so that he can watch her scramble to find his meaning.

It is a knee-jerk response to their experience of a high degree of paranoia. Those issues of power and control show themselves central to their makeup. Key to their obsession with power (and their fear of losing it) is an obsession with the lack of power. They are constantly on guard and paranoid that their power is being eroded or taken away from them. Anthony Perkins in *Psycho* personifies this quality (Norman believes his mother wants to control his life). They feel they must continually fight to keep whatever control they have over others. They also fight to get more. When he is away on business, if only for a day, Bugsy Siegel is obsessively calling back to Hollywood and having his men (the older ones, preferably) check up on the activities of his girlfriend, Virginia Hill. Not that it did much good. While he was concerned about her sleeping with other men, Hill manages to steal two million dollars from under his nose.

The need for power in the more traditional Antisocial may be sated in more socially accepted ways. Buddy Ackerman in *Swimming with Sharks* is a prime example. He is a movie studio executive who has clawed his way to the top, leaving behind a trail of casualties who stood in his way. He has assumed a position where he can (as methodically as a stalker) emotionally pulverize his underlings. Buddy takes a morbid joy in his harassment and terrorization of others. Gordon Gekko is respected and emulated for his blatant greed and manipulation. But poverty and issues of class haunt Gekko. Despite his eloquent (and now legendary) "greed is good" speech, Gekko is motivated not by greed alone, but by a wanton wish to reek havoc and seek revenge on the upper-class. He wants the blood of the privileged peers he detests. Bud White—the tough, aggressive cop playing by his rules in *L.A. Confidential*—has the central dynamics of his character spelled out in the first few scenes. He helps a woman being abused by her husband. He is compelled to save women, even if they are not particularly looking to be saved. Yet we know from his short-fused anger and the aggressiveness of his response he is clearly motivated by much darker reasons.

A DANCE OF DOMINANCE AND SUBMISSION

The manipulation of others is an extended exercise in control and often gives the Antisocial sexual pleasure. Dispatching her first victim gives Beverly Sutphin an aphrodisiac rush. She turns into a wildcat in bed that night. *Body Heat, Double Indemnity, Blue Velvet, Basic Instinct, Badlands, Psycho, The Grifters, Dead Calm*—all use the acts of their crimes as a form of sexual intensity. Their ability to manipulate—dominance for submission's sake— is nothing short of a turn-on. In *Bonnie and Clyde* the sexual high is turned on its ear—while the acts of lawlessness infuses their attraction to one another, Clyde is impotent.

The more crimes they commit, the greater the desire for sex (if not the ability) overshadows their lives. His impotence—the writers seem to suggest—is directly related to Clyde's criminal problems. Consumed by self, he can't feel others. It is a brilliant take on the character. Interestingly, near the end of the story, when Clyde sees Bonnie's poem in the newspaper and realizes they have become famous—that he would be remembered—he gets an erection for what we are led to believe is the first time in their relationship. In the 1991 version of *Cape Fear*, Max Cady (Robert De Niro) plays a game of psychological rape over young Danielle Bowden (a fearless Juliet Lewis). Control, manipulation, and seduction. Playing better than the bloodbath of Act Three, this moment ends up being the most memorable moment in the movie.

Since the Antisocial story is a male-dominated arena, quite often this dance of dominance and submission is played out man against man. Homoerotic tension is inevitable. Director Curtis Hanson's smooth stab, *Bad Influence*, and the dynamically realized *L.A. Confidential* (as do author Koepp's *Bad Influence* and *Apartment Zero*) both present men inexplicably drawn to one another and fighting for dominance, the sexual tension lying barely concealed beneath the skin. This sexual element is prevalent in movies as diverse as the goofy vampire and teenage-objects-of-his-affection horror flick, *FrightNight*, to the brutal *In Cold Blood* (in which Dick Hickock and Perry Smith depend upon each other in a way we might expect from lovers). In *L.A. Confidential*, two cops, Bud White and Officer Ed Exley (Guy Pearce), working for the same good are pitted against each other. Exley works by the book whereas Officer White prefers the gray areas between right and wrong, between just and abusive. The turning point in their relationship occurs over a woman (and a classic femme fatale at that). She (a wondrous Kim Bassinger) is a Veronica Lake look-a-like whore. Knowing that she has been having sex with Bud, Ed Exley barges in on her to accuse and threaten. Before Exley leaves, he plans to have his own way with her. Whether Exley wants sex because he is obsessed with her or the other police officer is a point not lost on the well-paid call girl. Her cold and telling response: "Fucking me and fucking Bud aren't the same thing!" Desperate to concentrate, Exley's anxiously responds: "Stop talking about Bud!"

In Henry's case (*Portrait of a Serial Killer*), the culmination of his arousal is not ejaculation, but murdering his prospective mate. The actual manipulation can also take the form of torture or sexual perversion. Buffalo Bill (the killer in *Silence of the Lambs*) keeps his victims in a pit—taunting them as he prances around, using their screams as a background as he dolls himself up in preparation for trying on their skin.

THE GEOGRAPHY OF EMOTIONS

Steady relationships are a big problem. Successful relationships involve compromise, a give and take, a respect for the wishes and desires of others, a sharing of emotions. This is something with which an Antisocial has intense difficulty. Janice Maretto, the suspicious sister-in-law in *To Die For*, lets her feelings be known about her doomed brother's wife: "She's like a China doll. You ever kiss a doll? They don't kiss back." Bugsy Siegel, although married and the father of two young girls, seduces women in elevators and trains—flatly pronouncing that, "it will be one time only." The grief for Bruce (*Batman*) Wayne over the loss of his parents and his inability to save them leaves his heart with little room to properly love anyone. Bond (until the P.C. of the 90s) preferred to love em and leave em . . . sometimes love em and leave em and kill em. There are also the Sam Spades of the world who seem to pick their women for the steamer trunks of trouble they drag along behind them. For heroes such as these, their obsessions—saving a dame or saving the world—are their first and only love. But, oddly, it is not the girl or the world they serve. They are not on the scene to rescue the girl for the sake of the girl; nor are they saving the world to make the world a safer place for all. They are there to bring about an order to things that they feel is missing. It is immediate and it is personal. It is always about something in their life they need to put straight. And when this happens—from super spies to super heroes to serial killers—wives and girlfriends fair rather poorly. In truth, *poor* would be a good prognosis. Most wind up dead, either directly at the hands of their loved one or because of actions caused by them.

Where relationships are concerned, the Antisocial will usually go it alone (*Psycho, Cape Fear, Bad Influence, La Femme Nikita, Pacific Heights, A Perfect World, Shadow of a Doubt, Taxi Driver*). When the Antisocial does cohabit, it is usually with someone of his or her own ilk. The results are nearly always disastrous, if not fatal (*Badlands, Sugarland Express, Bonnie and Clyde, The Grifters, High Sierra*). Be it husband and wife, boyfriend and girlfriend—or a skewered version of male bonding such as in *Apartment Zero, Bad Influence,* and *In Cold Blood*—they all end in bloodshed and body counts. Sometimes the relationships are for their own nefarious reasons. They use sex to make them rich—*Body Heat*'s Matty Walker knocks off her husband for the insurance money. They use sex to get them acquitted—*Jagged Edge*'s Jack Forrester seduces his defense lawyer. They use sex to get places—*To Die For*'s Suzanne Stone manipulates sex with a young student—a boy willing to kill for the privilege of a sleepover.

The bottom line always seems to come down to the fact that the Antisocial tends to have an inability to feel emotion. Dr. Chilton describes to Clarice that when Hannibal Lecter was chewing the face off of an attending nurse, "his pulse never got above 85, even when he ate her tongue." *To*

Die For's Suzanne Stone (after killing her husband), instead of grieving, fixes her hair and makeup and goes out to meet the cameras and press. In the cold-blooded killers of such films as *Day of the Jackal* or *Scarface* we have come to expect (not to mention pay to see) this behavior. Where it plays more effectively is with the Antisocial that errs on the side of good—the Philip Marlowes, the Sam Spades, and the Bud Whites of the world. The good heart that seems buried and lost in an unhappy past, a heart that may or may not be within reach of saving.

Because of the absence of emotion, Antisocials have great difficulty in articulating their feelings. They are not given over to thoughtful reflection. Push the button and they act. Henry explains why he kills to his friend Otis: "It's you or them." Suzanne Stone explains her determination to succeed in broadcasting: "You're not anybody in America, unless you're on television." For Suzanne it's that simple. If she doesn't have the *T.V.Q.*, she doesn't exist. ("Television Quota" is a term used to indicate how well a celebrity is recognized.)

Perhaps the most inhuman aspect of Antisocials is their lack of demonstrative behavior. They seldom show how they are feeling because they have difficulty feeling anything. They display minimal empathy. Because of this lack of empathy, the Antisocial's actions must be drastic, their pleasure often violent. They must create sharp experiences that will give them stimulation. They have difficulty feeling at all unless they are in a manic state or a blind rage. They need intensity; subtlety is lost on them. They often complain of boredom and depression. Only ultimate moments are real—thus the need for high levels of aggression. They often self-mutilate their lives in order to feel themselves. Bonnie (*Bonnie and Clyde*) goes off on a life of crime because she would just as soon die as stay in the uneventful, suffocating life she is living. The "high" of the crimes and the notoriety it brings becomes the all-important fresh air she requires. Not surprisingly,the first major plot point in the story occurs when Clyde's brother Buck (Gene Hackman) starts talking to Clyde about pursuing some form of a domestic life. The prospect of an idyllic life—living as neighbors with the in-laws—makes Bonnie anxious. A family dispute erupts and the seeds of a continuing discord in the Barrow Gang are planted.

The Antisocial has a distinct pattern of irresponsibility that starts in childhood and will continue (with the marked polish of years of practice) into adulthood. As kids, they lie, steal, vandalize, pick fights, and commit cruel acts. They feel no remorse. Whether they are a Mafia hitman, a tough-jaw private eye, or Superman cleaning up Metropolis, they need to be cold blooded about their job or there is a good chance they will fail. When married or parents, Antisocials also tend to be spousal and child abusers. Abuse breeds fear, fear breeds control. In *The Grifters*, the legacy of mother and son plays out to tragic conclusions. Bud White (*L.A. Confidential*) finds himself raising a fist in anger to a woman he loves, and the ensuing self-realization that he is nothing less than his father's son terrifies him. Films such as *Henry: Portrait of a Serial Killer, In Cold Blood, Badlands, Bonnie and Clyde*, and *Blue Velvet* all make allusions to childhood traumas that precipitated current affairs.

Antisocials have great difficulty and little interest in articulating feelings. Feelings are abstract. Communication (language) is a series of symbols: abstract thought versus literal thought. Empathy (understanding the feelings of others) is also abstract thought. Bugsy Siegel kills people at the drop of a hat. Yet, for fear of hurting her feelings, he cannot ask for a divorce from a wife he rarely sees or speaks to. In one of the more deadly hilarious moments of *To Die For*, Suzanne Stone attends the funeral of her husband and puts a boom box on a tombstone and plays a tape of the song, "All By Myself." Instead of communication, the Antisocial would rather use manipulation to get what he wants. The control one has is much more literal.

A WORLD IN BLACK AND WHITE

The Antisocial Personality may be very literal in his thinking. Little gray area exists. The Antisocial may not say, "You remind me of my mother" (an abstract thought), but rather, "You are my mother" (a concrete thought). An Antisocial may not keep a fading bouquet to remember a lover; he will keep the actual heart. They need something tangible, concrete. When Hannibal Lecter points out to Clarice that he never kept souvenirs, Clarice points out, "No, you ate them." As a child, Bud White (*L.A. Confidential*) was tied up and left helpless as his father beat his mother to death. Three days passed before anyone found him or his mother's body. As an adult and as a cop, he sees his mother in all women (*you are a woman in trouble/you are my mother being murdered*). Unable to do anything as a child to change the gruesome fate of his mother, Bud relives the painful guilt and loss. Fanatically, he devotes his life to saving his mother in all women, be it from actual physical harm or from themselves and the more lurid prospects the dreams of Hollywood stardom might offer.

Because of this literal thinking, Antisocials live very much in the present and are unable to relive the past or fully conceive of a future. As might a healthy person, Norman Bates (*Psycho*) cannot keep his mother alive in his memory. Instead, he must actually keep her mummified corpse in a chair in his house. Take as another example of this literal thinking the thriller, *Single White Female*, which offers us the roommate from hell in Hedra Carlson (Jennifer Jason Leigh). She is one half of a surviving twin who is willing to kill to be a twin again (*you are my roommate/you are my dead sister*).

This form of literal thinking can manifest itself in various emblematic ways. **Disassociation** is common with Antisocials. This occurs when they separate themselves from their actions ("The devil made me do it") by using various defense mechanisms, allowing them to distance themselves from the pain of the traumatic incident. Christopher Gill (the serial killer in *No Way to Treat a Lady*) actually adopts different costumes and behaviors. In a sense he becomes different people with each dowdy matron that he kills. Bugsy Siegel, after a hard dose of killing, recites a tongue twister he has memorized to help him feel confident about fitting in better with the well bred. Blood on his hands, he recites the mantra to ease the harsh reality of his crimes. Bonnie (of B*onnie and Clyde*) writes poems in the third person to purify and elevate her crimes. Her lover, Clyde, doesn't see things much clearer. He cannot understand why the police are on a manhunt for them. As Clyde sees it, "[they] should be out protecting poor folk, instead of chasing us."

Dissociative Amnesia is often present. Henry (*Portrait of a Serial Killer*) is unsure of how he actually killed his mother. Norman Bates holds his mother accountable for his present mess. Likewise, Antisocials often cannot remember evasions of responsibility. Clyde shoots and kills a bank employee: "Why'd he try to kill me? I didn't want to hurt him! I ain't against him." Not only does Clyde delineate between banks and people to rationalize his behavior, but he also clearly refers to the victim in the present tense (shot through the head, he is most certainly dead). Suzanne Stone (*To Die For*) sees her murder dilemma in a very matter of fact way. She is willing to believe (if only others will) that she had nothing to do with convincing a love-lost student to commit the murder of her husband. Period. Life is as they say it is.

Another prevalent Antisocial device is **Projection**. They project their internal pain onto others. Henry (*Portrait of a Serial Killer*) must kill every woman he meets because all women are whores and all whores are his mother (his mother brutalized and humiliated him as a child). Bud White (*L.A. Confidential*) saves all women because he could not save the one he loved the most (his mother). Bruce

Wayne (*Batman*) wipes out crime and scum because he was helpless to do so as a child and his parents paid the ultimate price. Batman—perchance the Pure Antisocial—the greatest of all dark heroes, lives in the haunted shadows of his parent's murder.

Another key to Antisocial behavior is **Acting Out**. The Antisocial Personality has very limited (if any) impulse control. This is the inability to harness or communicate their feelings. They are geared toward action (preferably immediate) to do something before the rage dissipates. They act out as the impulse hits them and they act out in the most literal way—the only way available to them. Harsh, irrevocable blows. The Antisocial has little capacity for caution. There is little ability to plumb an emotion and examine its roots, to weigh the pros and cons. There is little ability to project the future consequences of their actions in the present. The Antisocial is unable to deal with a levelheaded sense of tension. There is no analysis, only the immediate fit of destructive rage to serve as a release. Bugsy Siegel flies off the handle (even toward those he admires) when referred to as "Bugsy." It is a name he detests. Henry, when confronted with the amorous advances of Otis' sister, Becky, must go out and look for an anonymous victim in order to prevent himself from killing her. Beverly Sutphin, unable to foresee the consequences of her actions, decides against trying to reason with Mrs. Jensen about inconsiderately not rewinding her videotapes. Instead she opts to cold cock her with a leg of lamb. There is no slow boil. The heated response is intense and sudden.

Antisocials often employ **Primitive Envy**—a wish to destroy that which one most desires. "Each man kills the thing he loves," as Oscar Wilde so eloquently put it. Being human, they are not beyond wanting a little love and affection. Unfortunately, this object of affection then becomes a target precisely because of this affection. The Antisocial, not unlike the rest of us, can't help succumbing to tender passions, but they are driven to devalue, to deprecate, to destroy all that reminds them of tenderness. Perry Smith and Dick Hickock (*In Cold Blood*) annihilate a happy family merely because they are so—a family. In fact as in fiction, the Antisocial may also eat those that he is attracted to as a way of keeping them with him. His literal mind is often unable to otherwise understand his emotional need (as with real life killer, Jeffrey Dahlmer). If the one they truly love is their own being, this can at times lead to a desire to be killed. Their actions and the path of destruction then become focused on this desire. Unable to commit the act themselves, they will search for and put themselves in positions where their deepest wish might come true. *Bad Influence, Blue Steel, Jagged Edge, A Perfect World, Psycho, Taxi Driver*—all portray characters in varying degrees reaching out for this apocalypse. Many of these films incorporate a scene in which the character either challenges or flat out asks another character to kill them.

If the environment of the Antisocial changes, the threat of loss of control causes the Antisocial to aggress, to channel their hostility into actions against others. If you want to reveal the psychopathia of your character, you should put the character into a stressful situation. If you corner a cobra, the wait is brief before you are seeing its true nature.

A sure situation that would cause stress would be to present the Antisocial with a situation where insightful, reflective thought is required. This occurs in *Silence of the Lambs* when Clarice challenges Hannibal Lecter by asking him if he is "strong enough to point that high-powered perception at (himself)." Such self-reflection and questioning of motives and methodology would be nothing short of unthinkable. He becomes enraged and tells Clarice that the last person who tried to test him was a census taker and that he "ate his liver with some fava beans and a nice Chianti." He will become enraged because he is confronted with a situation in which he has no control. Antisocials build self-esteem through aggression, and when challenged they need to replenish. This sudden, inappropriate rage, if placed early in a script, may provide clues to the other characters that all is not right. Early on in *Body Heat*, Matty Walker sits with Ned Racine in a bar that she frequents while her husband is out of town. In an instant, she turns and slaps Racine on the side of the face. She then storms out, leaving him with a smarting cheek. Though she is planning on having sex with him later that night, she wants to keep up the image with the local bar patrons that nothing will come of the two of them. Her degree of cleverness—her manipulation of the scene—should have been a fair warning to poor Racine.

BACKSTORY

You may not choose to explore much of a character's past, but it is essential to your knowledge of the character in the present that his behavior is well entrenched and second nature by the time he is an adult. Knowing the irresponsible pattern of your character's early years will dictate his behavior as an adult. It can also offer insight into other possible behavior that can only enrich your characterization. This behavior is not new behavior. Antisocials are very comfortable with their crimes.

How do Antisocials become Antisocials?

The formation of the Antisocial Personality is almost always a product of the damage they sustained during their formative years. This backstory may or may not be revealed, but a template to understand how the character authentically behaves is useful. Hannibal Lecter's childhood is never discussed; we meet him as a fully blown monster. But there is an undeniable sense of past. A good deal of credit can go to a brilliant performance, but there is astonishing writing as well.

Often the childhood trauma is explored. In the case of Henry (*Portrait of a Serial Killer*), it happens when he describes his mother's abuse to Otis' sister, Becky. They bond as a result of this baring of the soul. Structurally for writers, the early trauma is often used as a third act plot point. In *Psycho*, Norman's abusive, controlling mother is revealed to be a dusty corpse preserved in a rocking chair. The murderous creature is Norman himself, projecting the damage that was planted within him at a very young age. Trauma can be conveyed in many textures—depression, a flat affect, developmental delays, fixations, fits of rage, disassociation.

The childhood of an Antisocial is often filled with insecurity and chaos. Harsh discipline and lack of empathy is a predominant feature. Mrs. Bates was certainly hard on poor Norman, accusing him of motives that he did not have and punishing him for crimes that existed only in her imagination. She accused him of the dirty crime of sexual intercourse. There was a transference of her guilt at having incestuous unclean thoughts and jealousy that her son would take another lover—even if the sexual relationship was never consummated. The result of this damaged Norman so deeply that the only way he could penetrate a woman was with a butcher knife.

The early life of the Antisocial is colored with family discord, fracturing, and a generous exchange of abuse. Divorce, dissolution of the family, and general instability are prevalent. The crooks of *Sugarland Express*, *Cape Fear*, *GoodFellas*, *In Cold Blood*, *La Femme Nikita*, *Miami Blues*, *Pulp Fiction*, *A Perfect World*, and *Thieves Like Us* all have juvenile delinquent histories. In many of these cases the stories pick up as they are being released from prison, either by the government or via their own creative arrangements—they fly the coop. Once back in the real world, it doesn't take long for things to start to go haywire. This is a very important characteristic. It is very difficult for the Antisocial to function in society without getting into some form of trouble. Of all the personalities, this is one of the most difficult to treat. The prognosis for change or recovery is very slim and hope is fleeting. Therapy works about as well as incarceration, meaning poor at best. Unless it is court ordered, most therapists will say that they rarely see an Antisocial Personality. They are as uncommitted as they are unresponsive to the psychoanalytical process.

Mothers of Antisocials often tend to be exploitative, masochistic, and depressed. The fathers are inconsistent, alcohol and substance abusers, and lean toward the sadistic. These descriptions are statistical, the parental figures interchangeable. It was Henry's mother who was sadistic, whereas Mrs. Bates remained true to form and exploitative. What is always evident is an absence of loving or an adequately protective family. There is no sense of power or control during their formative years. They internalize the chaos of their environment. This leads them to create relationships in their adult lives in which their control is omnipotent. Bud White (*L.A. Confidential*) falls for the Veronica Lake look-a-like not for her beauty or the woman behind that beauty, but for what he perceives as her lost-and-in-need-of-salvation standing.

As with their behavior, the emotional response patterns of Antisocials also begin in childhood and are carried with them into adulthood. As children they experience weakness and vulnerability. They cannot control themselves. In order to overcome these helpless feelings they seek to dominate and control their environment. This is particularly true of children who lose one or both of their parents or an influential sibling at a young age. Often they feel guilty and responsible that they could not change the tide of events. They turn their sense of hostility at their own vulnerability into a sense of power (their feelings of weakness in themselves into victimizing others). This behavior leaves them in control.

Ultimately, when you take away the big knives, the big guns, the body count, and the brutal rough exterior, there is a profound sadness to the Antisocial. In real life as in films, they are lost souls, creatures in need of salvation with no hope of where to look and, more importantly, how to accept. Treatment against the deep scars and damage done to their psyche is a very fragile and fleeting thing. Bugsy Siegel was a smart, clever man—some might say genius—who by some accounts single-handedly invented Las Vegas. It was an act, a dream—an impassioned desire to save himself and to bring a kind of honor to his life. But it was far too late. The outlaw Bonnie Parker reflects at the height of their drama: "I thought we were going somewhere. Instead we were just going."

THE ARC OF AN
ANTISOCIAL FILM CHARACTER

Character arcs for the Antisocial may seem a moot point, because they are generally (in movies) one-dimensional killing machines who follow no rules or logic but their own. Character arcs are generally reserved for the hero, the one who vanquishes the Antisocial. The character of Dr. Hannibal Lecter is a glorious exception.

When we first meet the doctor he is standing rigidly and exactly in the center of his well-ordered cell. He is in absolute control of his own little environment. He is well into middle age—the appropriate time for Antisocials to burn out, either through self-destruction or by apprehension. Though he is seemingly at the nadir of his controlling powers, he still uses his extreme intelligence to find the right chink in a personality to gain access and then manipulate that person for his own means. He toys with his fellow inmates: he is able to cause his neighbor, Multiple Migs, to commit suicide simply by talking him into it. One would think that, being in the superlative maximum security facility that contains him, his bargaining power with the authorities would be somewhat stymied. But Dr. Lecter is too good at what he does. He manipulates Clarice ("quid pro quo") into giving tidbits of information about her in exchange for information on the identity of Buffalo Bill. Throughout the game it is never in doubt that Dr. Lecter has the upper hand. The first plot point occurs after Multiple Migs hurls his ejaculation at Clarice. Dr. Lecter cannot tolerate rudeness and agrees to look at the police reports in order to make up for such a breach in etiquette. The parameters of what constitutes rudeness (hurling semen at a woman) and what doesn't (killing and eating his patients) are definitely of his own devising. He decides to join forces with Clarice.

In Act Two, the stakes are raised when Clarice offers Hannibal a deal. In return for his full cooperation in the investigation, he will be transferred to a new cell that has a view and will be granted one week's swimming privileges (under the surveillance of SWAT team). The deal is non-negotiable and it would certainly appear that Lecter has very little leverage. But he does manage to seize control. Though he cannot bargain for the terms of his internment, he can bargain for glimpses into Clarice's own life and troubled past, placing the onus of accepting the bargain on her for the sake of the life of the abducted daughter of a senator. At his seemingly most powerless, Hannibal is able to gain the upper hand and take complete control. He does this again when bargaining with the senator herself. He is in a straight jacket, bound securely to a furniture dolly, and wearing a muzzle. He is immobile and would seem to be harmless. But with a sadistic instinct as sharp as a scalpel, he is able, with a few words, to get into the senator's most sacred maternal place and emotionally annihilate her.

His second plot point occurs when he is presented with the obstacle, while being transferred, of how to escape. He overcomes it through the inadvertent help of his nemesis, Dr. Chilton, who carelessly leaves a pen within Hannibal's reach. Through the use of the pen to pick open the handcuffs and his facility with removing the flesh from the head of one of his guards and wearing it himself, he is able to escape. Before he does, he gives Clarice the clue that is needed to find the identity of Buffalo Bill.

In Act Three he is free, and we do not see him again until the very end when he contacts Clarice and a bond of respect has formed. He is an Antisocial and he will continue to be an Antisocial, but the rules set up in Act One that govern his psychopathology allow for this relationship to develop. This is a nice arc because it gives the inhuman "Hannibal the Cannibal" a hint of the human. Though he maintains a respect for Clarice, even helps her, and resists any impulse to mutilate her, this is no therapeutic arc. The rules of his pathology were set up early. He neither respects nor helps Clarice because he likes her, or because he has become a better person, but because of his own strict belief system. He cannot tolerate rudeness. He only takes the side of Clarice and thus is allowed to form a respectful relationship, because first Multiple Migs and then Dr. Chilton treat her disrespectfully. He takes her side because he takes the side against his enemies. His arc allows Clarice and us an opportunity to know Lecter. Such knowledge leads to our humanization of him, and with that humanization comes a frightening experience at the movies.

THE ANTISOCIAL PERSONALITY SUMMARY

Examples of the qualities and qualifications that define a person with an Antisocial Personality:

- They are often drawn to illegal professions
- They tend to be loners. They don't like to be associated with others
- They display a pervasive disregard for and violation of the rights of others
- They have a pattern for performing acts that are grounds for arrest
- They detest rules and regulations
- They proudly show a blatant disregard for societal norms, customs, and laws
- They are natural con men and deceive others constantly for both profit and pleasure
- They tend to lie and use aliases
- They tend to be heedless and impulsive
- They are very irritable and aggressive. They are prone to physical altercations
- They have a pronounced disregard for their own safety and also for that of others
- They are irresponsible. They do not honor their word
- They have difficulty in holding down a job
- They ignore financial obligations
- They are very unemotional. They have blunted affects
- They show a startling lack of remorse
- They tend to rationalize their hurtful treatment of others
- They rely on primitive defenses

- They fail to establish human attachments
- They show increased sensation-seeking behavior
- They require sharper experiences of life to feel anything
- They have an inability to articulate emotion
- They act instead of talk
- When they do feel, it is either blind rage or manic exhilaration
- They have a need for omnipotent power and control
- They have an absence of conscience
- They tend to brag about their crimes, but often feel ashamed of their misdemeanors
- They tend to burn out by middle age
- They act out. They don't think. They are slaves to impulse
- They equate normal emotions with weakness
- They have difficulty with abstract thought

NOTEWORTHY CHARACTERISTICS
OF THE ANTISOCIAL PERSONALITY

SPEECH

Charming. Articulate. Persuasive. Manipulative.

PROFESSIONS

Places of power. Politicians, crooks, financiers, gangsters, superheroes, detectives, cops.

DRESS

Flashy. Designer clothes. Dress for success. The opposite can also hold true. They can be disheveled, unkempt, natty, soiled, and thoughtless in choice.

HEALTH

Premature death due to violence is typical. Wounds. Gunshots. Facial and head injuries. Drug and alcohol abuse. Sexual addictions. Sexual abuse as children is very common.

POPULAR CLICHÉS
ASSOCIATED WITH ANTISOCIALS

- Psycho
- Dimestore Detective
- Serial Killer
- Mass Murderer
- Gumshoe
- Man With No Name
- Gunslinger
- Gun for hire
- Mercenary
- Iconoclast
- Con man
- Avaricious
- Parsimonious
- Greedy
- Self-seeking
- Predatory

SIMILAR PERSONALITY TYPES
TO THE ANTISOCIAL

- THE PARANOID PERSONALITY
- THE NARCISSISTIC PERSONALITY
- THE BORDERLINE PERSONALITY

VIEWING SUGGESTIONS FOR
THE ANTISOCIAL PERSONALITY

Apartment Zero (1988)—Thriller, 124, Rated R.
Hart Bochner as Jack Carney, a spooky boarder in Buenos Aries.

Bad Influence (1990)—Thriller/Mystery, 99, Rated R.
L.A. Confidential director Curtis Hanson's earlier film shows signs of the enormous talent to come. This is a top notch variation on Hitchcock's *Strangers on a Train*. Offers both solid performances and solid examples of antisocial behavior.

Badlands (1973)—Drama/Crime, 95, Rated PG.
On the run, Martin Sheen is the soulless killer, Kit. Sissy Spacek is his delinquent girlfriend.

Basic Instinct (1992)—Thriller/Drama, 127, Rated R.
Sharon Stone as suspected ice-pick murderer, Catherine Tramell. A great ride. Solid interpretations of behavior (in spite of an overblown sense of itself). Stone's career-making performance aside, the film is not quite up to par with writer Joe Eszterhas' early film that explored much of the same terrain, *Jagged Edge*.

Batman (1989)—Drama/Action, 126, Rated PG-13.
For the Dark Knight himself. Wonderful psychological overtones. Way over.

Big Sleep, The (1946)—Mystery/Crime, 114, No rating.
Perhaps the best of all the antisocial good

guys, Philip Marlowe. With the best of all
actors, Humphrey Bogart.

Black Widow (1986)—Mystery / Crime, 103, Rated R.
Smart women and crime has always been a
seller. Theresa Russell (Catherine) dispatch-
es her husbands to their graves.

Blue Velvet (1986)—Mystery, 120, Rated R.
For Dennis Hopper as Frank Booth. A terrific portrayal.

Body Heat (1981)—Crime, 113, Rated R.
In her film debut, Kathleen Turner as femme
fatale Matty Walker. Despite owing much to
Billy Wilder and *Double Indemnity*, Lawrence Kasdan's script stands well on its
own. First rate acting and directing.

Bonnie and Clyde (1967)—Crime, 111, No rating.
Nominated for an Academy Award for the
writing. The antisocial as outlaw. One of the
best representations in this form.

Bugsy (1991)—Romance / Drama / Crime, 135, Rated R.
Returning many years after *Bonnie and
Clyde*, Warren Beatty has honed the antisocial monster into something that is nothing
short of mesmerizing. James Toback's script
was nominated for an Academy Award.

Cape Fear (1962)—Thriller, 105, No rating.
Robert Mitchum as lethal ex-con Max Cady.
Big, bold strokes.

Cape Fear (1991)—Thriller, 128, Rated R.
Robert De Niro replaces Mitchum. This time
in color and a lot more blood to soak it up.

Casino (1995)—Drama/Crime, 182, Rated R.
Vegas. The mob. Scorsese. De Niro.

Clockwork Orange, A (1971)—Science Fiction, 137, Rated R.
Stanley Kubrick directed and wrote (and was nominated for both efforts). Worth viewing for futuristic gang member, Alex (Malcom McDowell).

Day of the Jackal, The (1973)—Thriller, 141, Rated PG.
A chilling performance by Edward Fox as The Jackal.

Dead Calm (1989)—Thriller/Horror, 96, Rated R.
Billy Zane as the misunderstood Hughie Warriner.

Diabolique (1955)—Thriller, 114, No Rating.
French film offering terrific performance from Vera Clouzot and Simone Signoret as the wife and mistress plotting the demise of the man in both their lives. American remake in 1997 (under the same title) offers an equally clever script. The original, as with most originals, is tough to beat.

Dirty Harry (1971)—Crime, 102, Rated R.
Clint Eastwood in a series (notably the best) of films involving the antisocial San Francisco renegade cop, Harry Callahan.

Double Indemnity (1944)—Crime, 106, No rating.
Barbara Stanwyck as Phyllis Dietrichson. The strange pairing of Billy Wilder and Raymond Chandler resulted in a nomination for writing. Too bad no one ever made a film of this unique and odd collaboration.

Fistful of Dollars, A (1964)—Western, 96, No rating. Forever noted for giving us the spaghetti western, as well as The Man With No Name, and delivering Clint Eastwood into stardom.

Fright Night (1985)—Horror, 105, Rated R. Glorious fun. Delightful performances from Chris Sarandon (as Jerry the Vampire) and Roddy McDowall (as Peter Vincent).

Godfather, The (1972)—Drama/Crime, 175, Rated R. The Mafia and Antisocials. Academy Award winner for Screenplay Adaptation.

GoodFellas (1990)—Drama/Crime, 146, Rated R. The Mafia and Antisocials. Academy Award nominated for the writing.

Grifters, The (1990)—Crime, 113, Rated R. Wonderfully realized characters and performances from all three Antisocials: John Cusak (Roy Dillon), Angelica Huston (Lily Dillon), and Annette Bening (Myra Langtry). Huston and Bening took Oscar nominations, as did Donald E. Westlake for the writing.

Henry: Portrait of a Serial Killer (1990)—Horror/Crime, 90, Rated X. Brutal and often tough to take. Extremely accurate. Not for the faint of heart.

High Sierra (1941)—Crime, 100, No rating. Bogart back doing an Antisocial with a heart of gold—something he perfected over the years.

In Cold Blood (1967)—Crime/Biography, 134, No rating. Nominated for an Oscar for the writing (Richard Brooks). Disturbing interpretation about real-life killers Perry Smith (Robert Blake) and Dick Hickock (Scott Wilson).

Ipcress File, The (1965)—Spy, 108, No rating. Michael Cain as Harry Palmer. Crook turned secret agent.

Jagged Edge (1985)—Thriller/Mystery, 108, Rated R. A terrific Jeff Bridges as Jack Forrester. A secure and stylish thriller. Writer Joe Eszterhas at his best.

Key Largo (1948)—Crime, 101, No rating. Edward G. Robinson as gangster Johnny Rocco. Holding people hostage during a Florida storm. Film features one of the great performances of all time: Claire Trevor as moll Gaye Dawn (she's anything but). No surprise, Ms. Trevor carried home the Oscar.

Kiss of Death (1947)—Crime, 98, No rating. Richard Widmark in an amazing film debut as a psychotic killer. Nominated for Academy Awards for both Widmark's frightful portrayal and for the writing. Both hold up remarkably well today.

L.A. Confidential (1997)—Crime/Drama, 1997, 136, Rated R. Brilliant portrayal of the antisocial locked inside the good man. Exceptional writing, direction, and performances. Top notch opportunities for Antisocial examples in something other than a killer mode.

La Femme Nikita (1990)—Drama/Action, 117, Rated R.
Wonderful telling of an Antisocial turned into an assassin. Anne Parillaud as Nikita. Remade in the USA, *Point of No Return.*

Lethal Weapon (1987)—Crime/Action, 110, Rated R.
Mel Gibson for his now infamous loner cop, Martin Riggs.

Long Goodbye, The (1973)—Crime, 112, Rated R.
Elliott Gould taking on Philip Marlowe. Robert Altman's updating of Raymond Chandler.

M (1931)—Horror/Drama/Crime, 99, No rating.
Peter Lorre in a performance as unnerving today as it was then. A remarkable gamble by an actor.

The Mask of Zorro (1997)—Adventure, 136, Rated PG.
Rousing adaptation of a legendary hero that does not shy away from the darker side of the character.

Miami Blues (1990)—Crime, 99, Rated R.
Alec Baldwin turns in a smooth performance as the Antisocial, Fred Frenger.

Miller's Crossing (1990)—Crime, 115, Rated R.
Irish mobsters.

Night of the Hunter, The (1955)—Thriller, 93, No rating.
Very scary performance by Robert Mitchum as psychotic preacher Harry Powell.

No Way to Treat a Lady (1968)—Mystery/Comedy, 108, No rating.
Rod Steiger as lady-killer Christopher Gill. For those who prefer their humor very dark.

Pacific Heights (1990)—Thriller, 102, Rated R.
Michael Keaton as Carter Hayes, the tenant
from hell.

Pelican Brief, The (1993)—Thriller, 141, Rated PG-13.
Criminal lawyers. The kind you don't get a
degree for in school.

Perfect World, A (1993)—Drama/Crime, 137, Rated PG-13.
Fugitive Kevin Costner (Butch Hayes)
chased through Texas by cop Clint
Eastwood.

Psycho (1960)—Thriller/Horror, 109, No rating.
Anthony Perkins as Norman Bates. Oscar
nominations to Hitchcock and shower victim Janet Leigh. Regardless, it is Perkins'
show.

Pulp Fiction (1994)—Drama/Crime/Comedy, 154, Rated R.
Insanely great portrayals, all of which are
over the top. Took home the Oscar for the
writing effort. Nominated for six others.

Repo Man (1984)—Science Fiction/Comedy, 92, Rated R.
Two wonderful, loony characters: Bud
(Harry Dean Stanton) and Otto (Emilio
Estevez).

Reservoir Dogs (1992)—Crime/Drama, 99, Rated R.
More group insaneness from writer
Tarantino. Be forewarned, contains an
extremely violent torture scene.

River Wild, The (1994)—Thriller/Drama/Crime, 108,
Rated PG-13.
Kevin Bacon as Wade.

Scarface (1932)—Crime/Biography, 90, No rating.
Paul Muni as mobster Tony Camonte.

Scarface (1983)—Crime, 170, Rated R.
Updated remake. Highly refashioned with
Al Pacino as Tony Montana.

Serial Mom (1994)—Crime/Comedy, 93, Rated R.
Terrific turn by Kathleen Turner as Beverly
Sutphin.

Shadow of a Doubt (1943)—Thriller, 108, No rating.
Joseph Cotton as possible psycho Uncle
Charlie. Nominated for an Oscar for the
writing.

Silence of the Lambs, The (1991)—Thriller/Mystery, 118,
Rated R.
Anthony Hopkins as Dr. Hannibal Lecter.
Academy awards for Hopkins as well as
writer Ted Talley.

Single White Female (1992)—Thriller/Drama, 107, Rated R.
Jennifer Jason Leigh as the roommate from
hell, Hedra Carlson.

Something Wild (1986)—Drama/Comedy, 113, Rated R.
For Ray Liotta's startling performance as
Ray Sinclair.

Spy Who Came In from the Cold, The (1965)—Spy, 112,
No rating.
Richard Burton as dispirited agent Alec
Leamas.

Stepfather, The (1987)—Thriller/Horror, 98, Rated R.
Terry O'Quinn as psycho stepfather.

Strangers on a Train (1951)-Thriller, 101, No rating.
Guy and Bruno (Farley Granger and Robert
Walker) set the tone for so many to come.

Sugarland Express, The (1974)—Adventure, 109, Rated
PG.
Terrific early Spielberg. With Goldie Hawn
and William Atherton as husband and wife
on the run.

Swimming with Sharks (1995)—Drama/Comedy, 101,
Rated R.
Great performance by Kevin Spacey as
movie studio executive, Buddy Ackerman.
One of the best love-to-hate performances
ever created. Frank Whaley as his assistant,
Guy, pushed over the edge.

Taxi Driver (1976)—Drama, 113, Rated R.
Robert De Niro as Travis Bickle.

Thieves Like Us (1974)—Crime, 123, Rated R.
Three fugitives on a crime spree.
Overlooked at the time, this is one of Robert
Altman's best.

To Die For (1995)—Black Comedy, 103, Rated R.
Nicole Kidman's not to be missed performance as Suzanne Stone.

True Romance (1993)—Thriller/Romance/Crime, 116,
Rated R.
Tarantino back again doing what he has
proven he does best.

Unforgiven (1992)—Western, 127, Rated R.
Eight Oscar nominations, including writer

David Webb Peoples. He delivered one of the best scripts in Clint Eastwood's career.

Wall Street (1987)—Drama, 124, Rated R.
Michael Douglas in his Academy Award winning performance: the "greed is good" monster, Gordon Gekko.

PRIOR TO READING THE NEXT CHAPTER
IT IS RECOMMENDED THAT THE FOLLOWING
FILMS BE VIEWED:

DR. STRANGELOVE . . .
ZERO EFFECT
AMERICAN HISTORY X

A LIST OF FILMS PERTAINING TO THE
PARANOID PERSONALITY CAN BE FOUND
AT THE END OF THIS CHAPTER.

3

THE PARANOID PERSONALITY

I can no longer sit back and allow Communist infiltration,Communist indoctrination, Communist subversion, and the international Communist conspiracy to sap and impurify all of our precious bodily fluids.
—Gen. Jack D. Ripper/Stanley Kubrick, Terry Southern, Peter George

G ENERAL RIPPER, in *Dr. Strangelove, or How I Learned to Stop Worrying and Love the Bomb*, seals off his high security defense bunker, overrides the authority of congress and the president, and opens fire on his own troops. He does this so that he can initiate a "Code Red," which, in effect, means he has authorized the annihilation of the planet Earth. No one can be trusted, including men that are wearing the same uniform and saluting the same flag as he, who believes the Russians are responsible for fluoridation, an insidious Commie plot to contaminate the red-blooded American water supply. General Ripper cannot allow this conspiracy to sap all of our precious bodily fluids. This is the reason he will only drink grain alcohol and rain water and why he must eschew the culmination of the sexual act with women so as not to be drained of his essence.

Darryl Zero, in *Zero Effect*, is a modern example of the cinematic gumshoe. He is inarguably the "world's most private detective." He is so private, in fact, that he cannot bring himself to meet his clients; instead he sends his surrogate, Steve Arlo, to make deals and to collect payments. He spends his time blockaded in his apartment, surrounded by state of the art surveillance equipment, unwilling to leave even for food—he can subsist for untold days on nothing but Tab, bulk pretzels, and amphetamines. Darryl Zero has no social life and he has no social skills. But Darryl Zero is very good at his job. His paranoia is in no small way responsible for allowing him to be able to make such a claim as the world's most private detective. He is so distrusting that he feels compelled to employ a myriad of disguises: "[You] can meet him five times without knowing it's the same guy." He is also (typical for the Paranoid) suspicious of everyone and everything. Not a bad attribute for someone in his line.

Venice, California is the breeding ground for a lesson in *American History X*. Here, a young, muscled out, tattooed neo-Nazi skinhead named Derek (Academy Award nominee Edward Norton in a chilling performance), lives in a world of ultra-violence and White supremacy mongering. When he murders two Black kids who get too close for comfort, he is sent to prison. Three years later he returns a newfound man. Unfortunately, while Derek has been gone, his younger brother, Danny, has been carrying the racist torch in his brother's name (Derek having now reached the level of something akin to a fascist folk hero). Anxious to save his younger brother from the futile life of hatred that he once embraced, Derek discovers that the sins of the past (including his father's) are upon him. The struggle for the young boy's soul will be nothing less than a fight to the death.

ALL IN THE MIND

The Paranoid Personality centers on a pervasive distrust and suspiciousness of others such that their motives are interpreted as malevolent. This distrust is as imagined and unwarranted as it is unrelenting. They often spend an inordinate amount of energy (physical and psychological) scanning the environment for danger, certain the world is filled with hidden meanings. They rarely feel safe. There is an utter certainty that the world is inhabited with suspicious and menacing people, that the world is out to get them. Consumed by ill thoughts, they send them outward, onto others, attributing blame where none is warranted. Their personality is rigid, unable to relax, singularly preoccupied and resolved, and their demeanor is resolved, inflexible, pointless to argue with. Anger is often unprovoked and seen in sudden fits—a product of retaliation to their suspicions. These suspicions, however, stopshort of being delusional, and this is a very important point: if the individual is hallucinating (sight and/or sound)—such as Carol Ledoux in Roman Polanski's paranoia thriller, *Repulsion*—the diagnosis becomes much more serious and is classified outside the realm of the Paranoid Personality Disorder. In the case of *Repulsion*, the character suffers from Paranoid Schizophrenia. Paranoids tend to be rash and explosively reactive. They pride themselves on being unemotional and objective; in reality they appear as hostile, uncompromising, and defensive.

The essential concept of paranoia covers a vast and sweeping terrain. It can nonetheless be separated into two categories:

- Real Paranoia

- Imagined Paranoia

It is in this second category (the imagined) that the Paranoid Personality Disorder exists. To better understand imagined paranoia, it is worth first exploring the overall canvas of paranoia.

REAL VS. IMAGINED PARANOIA

In this urban 21st Century, paranoia has become such a catchphrase in lay society that it is a staple in political speeches, product marketing, coffee mug logos, bumper stickers, and (to little surprise) the movies. The 1950s gave rise to a slew of science fiction movies such as *Invasion of the Body Snatchers, War of the Worlds, The Thing, The Blob, The Crawling Eye,* and the movie that simply called them what they were . . . *Them!* These films flooded the market and popularized the idea of "paranoid films." Yet despite the moniker, these films do not explore the Paranoid Personality style of individual characters—the movies themselves are paranoid, products of the end of World War II and the mass hysteria of the ensuing Red Scare.

Also maturing from this hybrid are the films of spy paranoia and political paranoia (*Torn Curtain, Three Days of the Condor, No Way Out, The Hunt for Red October, Patriot Games, The Manchurian Candidate, Seven Days in May*). Distinct in both the earlier and later inventions, the plot lines of these movies involved people/aliens or governments/other worlds doing unspeakable evil on a national or international scale. They usually involved real paranoia (someone is trying to do evil) as opposed to imagined paranoia (it feels like someone is trying to do evil). They featured a story line involving a character recently shrouded in paranoia because of events thrust upon them. The paranoia, up until the issuing plot point, has not been an ingrained part of their everyday psyche.

In these instances their fears and their paranoia are all too real and immediate but they are not the result of a Paranoid Personality.

SECULAR AND INDIVIDUAL PARANOIA

Within this second category of imagined paranoia, there are two concepts to be considered:

- Secular Paranoia

- Individual Paranoia

First, **secular paranoia**. Paranoia as a social event. *Dr. Strangelove* illustrated how paranoia can be infectious, affecting entire nations. During the Cold War, the enemy is faceless, devious. They represent undiluted evil and will stop at nothing to obtain their goals. They have no value for human life, not even their own. Stopping them is the righteous crusade of General Ripper, who, he himself believes, represents undiluted, God-fearing good. His crusade is not unlike that of other paranoid men—men such as Adolf Hitler (or cinematically, Adenoid Hynkel in Charlie Chaplin's *The Great Dictator*)—who fomented an entire nation into committing unspeakable atrocities. These are individuals who choose an enemy as a convenient receptacle for all the ills of the world. As the cultural climate changes, so does the face of the enemy—from the dreaded infidel of the Crusades, to the Holocaust and the Red Scare of the Cold War. Whether this issue is segregated America or brewing homophobia, the Paranoid Personality is able to set himself up as the righteous oppressor. They see themselves as having God on their side—the chosen enemy taking on the role as the obstacle to the triumph of good. Marker examples include the Bible-thumping fundamentalist, William Jennings Bryan (*Inherit the Wind*), Otto Preminger's Washington insider soap opera, *Advise and Consent*, and 17th century Salem's McCarthyistic witch hunts (*The Crucible*).

A key issue to secular paranoia is the abject terror of outside forces that may trigger emotional responses of inferiority and humiliation. Given this bent, it is not surprising that paranoia surfaces as the unmitigated hatred or fear of whole, distinct groups. As such, film genres were created specific to themselves from the phobias that underlie racism (*Mississippi Burning, To Kill A Mockingbird*), anti-Semitism (*Chariots of Fire, Sophie's Choice*), urban nightmares (*Death Wish, Dirty Harry*), and homophobia (*Philadelphia, Torch Song Trilogy*).

Although the majority of films involving paranoia may only explore the personality in a symbolic sense, most films present the culmination of paranoia in at least one character, **individual paranoia**. It is usually a character who embodies the abject terror toward the group in question. Quite dramatically, this is seen with the hardened suspicions and dislike that Chief of Police Bill Gillespie (Rod Steiger, *In the Heat of the Night*) has for the cop from Philadelphia, Virgil Tibbs (Sidney Poitier). We see it as well in the rabid racist, Deputy Pell (Brad Dourif in Alan Parker's moody *Mississippi Burning*). It is also crystallized in Denzel Washington's homophobic lawyer, Joe Miller, facing off with his HIV client, Andrew Becket (Academy Award winner Tom Hanks in *Philadelphia*).

There are also many films in which the paranoia is not directed toward an outside group but is portrayed as an internal plight. Such characters cannot accept themselves and are, in effect, self-hating. It might not seem as though there is much in common with *Boys in the Band* and *Boyz N the Hood*, but remarkably there is. Gay films such as *Jeffrey* and *Parting Glances* and the Black America of Spike Lee's *Do The Right Thing* and *Jungle Fever* have, at their center, a study of the effects of an internalized paranoia. In these situations you have a self-hate that does not allow for self. For the boys of *Boys in the Band*, their own ingrained self-hate releases itself in angry, vindictive, jealous attacks on one another. Michael, the worst of the lot, breaks down at the end and weeps: "If we could just not hate ourselves." For the boys of *Boyz N the Hood*, their self-hate takes it a little further than vicious bitch attacks at a birthday party. These "boyz" kill one another. The fights your character chooses to fight—the accusations that he levels at others—are therefore very revealing. It is precisely what they notice (and fear) about their own lives that will influence the roads they travel.

CHARACTERS, NOT COUCHES

It is vital to note that although it might be imagined paranoia, this secular paranoia is (as with real paranoia) not truly considered a diagnosis for Paranoid Personality Disorder. Within the psychological community, the true Paranoid Personality Disorder is considered to be independent of cultural factors and is not a transient state growing out of group dynamics. Racial and sexual phobias would not fall into this category. Whereas that may be well and good for the therapist's office, what is of importance here are characters not couches.

Whether dealing with real paranoia (*Enemy of the State, North by Northwest*), an extreme case of Paranoid Schizophrenia (hallucinations such as John Carpenter's *In the Mouth of Madness*, Polanski's *Repulsion*), or internalized paranoia (*The Boys in the Band*), the noted films are worthy of study, their value insightful, even if they do not meet the criteria of what is clinically deemed a Paranoid Personality. Although such films may not be at the heart of the disorder, they may well be at the heart of this chapter. Truth is, there are few films that specifically address the issues and lifestyle of the true Paranoid Personality. The reason being they can be extremely difficult to root for when portrayed as a major character or entrusted with carrying a significant story line. Most films portraying a paranoid character tend to fall into these fringe categories, as opposed to the rigid diagnosis. The bottom line is that the fundamentals for all of these types of paranoia are rooted in similarities that can be found and applied no matter which direction a character may be headed. Therefore, a wide array of film examples will be offered from which to grasp a better understanding.

BASIC TRAITS

Paranoid Personalities suspect (without sufficient basis) that others are exploiting, harming, or deceiving them, and these cases usually involve inflexible patterns of perceiving, relating, and thinking. The skinhead, Derek (*American History X*), has an inflexible, unjustified, and irrational fear of all non-Anglo races. He suspects the motives of all other races as being malevolent in nature—and this leads him toward a kill-or-be-killed mentality. Darryl Zero's (*Zero Effect*) inflexibility is apparent in his absolute distrust of everyone around him. The common link among the various modes of the Paranoid Personality is fear—fear of losing control, fear of being controlled, fear of violence, fear of love. Fear of those trying to get close, because secretly the other person is trying to take over. Fear of their own low self-esteem that leads them to foster issues of station and dominance. Fear over concern that persons of authority will humiliate them or expect them to be submissive. They struggle righteously against fear. General Ripper (*Dr. Strangelove*) reacts to the perceived threat of his homeland being laid to waste by the commies. The fear and paranoia is so real, Ripper will shoot his own officers to be on the safe side: "Fire on anyone within 200 feet! Shoot first, ask questions later!" Derek (*American History X*) uses guns and brute muscle to combat the wild male animal he imagines in his head. Darryl Zero (*Zero Effect*) will go to extraordinary and complicated lengths to outsmart the least smart.

The Paranoid Personality is also preoccupied with unjustified doubts concerning the loyalty and trustworthiness of friends and associates. Although Darryl Zero would be socially crippled without Arlo (and reluctantly trusts him with a good-sized portion of his life), he still can never take him completely into his confidence. He keeps him in the dark about the very errands he is running. In Nicholas Hytner's film adaptation of Arthur Miller's Broadway play, *The Crucible*, this distrust is the heartbeat of an entire community. Pointedly, the theme of paranoia is fermented throughout the story in many characters and on many levels other than the prime concern of witch hunting. Near the end of the Third Act, Elizabeth Proctor (a seamless performance by Joan Allen) speaks for the final time with her condemned husband: "I counted myself so plain, so poorly made, no honest love could come to me. Suspicion kissed you when I did." Her self-hate has participated in their downfall and it speaks volumes about those that flame the firestorm of the Salem witch trials.

For the Paranoid Personality, no one is beyond unrelenting suspicion. They dread any kind of defeat and view all around them (either specifically or in general) as persecutory. They must constantly ward off humiliation and threats to their safety by staying one step ahead and taking the offensive: in Derek's case, with fascist, ultra-violence; in General Ripper's case, with nuclear warheads; in Darryl Zero's case, with a multitude of slippery identities.

Interesting here is the dichotomy between the self-representation as omnipotent, vindicated, and triumphant over the world and the deep-seated image they harbor of themselves as impotent and completely humiliated—a vision of their life as despised by the world as well as by themselves. It is the tension between these two images and the experience of them in a subjective world that creates a sense of paranoia.

The Paranoid reads hidden, demeaning, or threatening meanings into benign remarks or events. The major manifestation of the Paranoid's fear is hyper-vigilance. They put every word and every gesture to extreme scrutiny. They monitor the slightest movement for threat of danger. Derek explodes at his widowed mother for bringing her date (a Jewish man) into their home and to their dinner table, infecting their lives. The Paranoids' consuming distrust and suspicion is what leads them to interpret the motives of all they come in contact with as malicious, which causes them to be anxiously sensitive and always on guard. Michael, the gay leader of the pack in *The Boys in the Band*, verbally batters his old college roommate and longtime friend. Convinced his straight act is just that (an act), Michael scrutinizes every word, every glance, and every move of the man. He interprets his behavior with such vile suspicion their friendship comes apart at the seams.

The Paranoid Personality suspects without reason that others are exploiting or deceiving them. They always look for the real, evil intent behind the actions of others and they will go to great lengths to take the offensive against threats against their well being. Zero barricades his front door. General Ripper cavalierly fires off rounds from his machine gun through the shutters of his office window.

The Paranoid Personality often has little sense of humor—every joke is taken as a veiled insult. They perceive attacks on their character or reputation that are not apparent to others. They tend to be taciturn, overly cautious, yet they are prone to fits of intense anger. This leap to anger or counterattack is sudden and without warning. These attacks (acts of defense in the Paranoid's mind) are nearly always portrayed in films as cold hearted, matter of fact, devoid of personal motivation. The all too justified cold stare in Byron Beckwith's eyes (the racist murderer in *Ghost of Mississippi*) is not that different a stare from that of Paul Kersey (the vengeance seeking widowed husband of *Death Wish*).

Shame is difficult for the Paranoid Personality to acknowledge or handle. This is because much of their denying of any faults, weaknesses, or blame is done at another individual's feet. They see and interpret their own failings as belonging to others. General Ripper lays the blame and responsibility on the president. Derek blames non-Anglos in general, and Zero, on a world too stupid to save itself. An important feature of the Paranoid Personality is that they rarely seek treatment. If they do seek treatment, they are usually brought in by a spouse or a family member tired of the accusations and exhausted by the obsessive behavior. Equally important is that they usually remain unconvinced that they are psychologically disturbed. In their view, their problems revolve around how other people have mistreated and betrayed them: the skinheads call to arms against the Blacks and Hispanics who have moved into their community (*American History X*); the gay party boys (*Boys in the Band*) who feel hated and despised by the straight world that they must live. Instead of focusing on themselves in a healthful way, they spend undue amounts of time and energy stopping (or offensively harming in preemptive retaliation) others who might cause them shame or humiliation. In *American History X*, Derek organizes a vigilante group of neo-Nazis to raid and vandalize a neighborhood store that has been lost to them by an encroaching ethnic mixed bag. On the surface, his rhetoric and anger is about the loss of jobs in their community to the "aliens" and that the time had come to take back what is theirs. Underneath this pro-violence rabble rousing is a much deeper and darker motivation. As Derek's community is overtaken by what he and his friends see as second class citizens, they are faced with an overwhelming sense of humiliation and abandonment. They believe that "White America" has left them behind. They believe they have been forsaken and lumped together with the "aliens." They see themselves as the chosen people (the most powerful), yet they are powerless, impotent. It appears to them that the America they know and believe in has given up on their community (in this case Venice, California). It has cut its losses and moved on to more desirable locations. This act by a "greater America" to leave them on the side of the road (to essentially de-class them) is central to igniting the fire and forcing to the surface their issues of self-hate.

The Paranoid Personality is reluctant to confide in others because of unwarranted fear that the information will be used maliciously against them. They fear that if people got to know them, they would use the knowledge of the Paranoid's failings against them. The maligned loners of urban dramas, renegade cops and cowboys, the secret midnight meetings of vigilantism, the solitude of a spy—all show a great fear of any level of intimacy. Sometimes at stake is merely an issue of feeling vulnerable, other times it's an issue of life and death.

The Paranoid Personality persistently bears grudges. They are unforgiving of insults, injuries, and slights. They can also be extremely jealous and devious and can locate disloyalty wherever they choose to look for it. They are always on the lookout for slights or threats, and will create one if necessary. These threats they perceive against themselves may be physical (as in General Ripper's concern over the infiltration of his precious fluids), but underlying this is the fear of losing face, of being exposed as grandiose: all-powerful, but ineffectual. This is certainly the case of the race inspired hatred of *American History X*, *Rosewood*, and *Ghost of Mississippi*. Paul Kersey (*Death Wish*) can clean up the scum of the streets and make New York a safer place to live, but he could not save the life of his wife. The anxiety of his failure and loss of power vents itself every time he goes out into the streets. Darryl Zero has a morbid fear of being outsmarted and will go to any lengths to prevent this, even if it means hiding his identity from everyone save one person. Paranoids' sense of self-esteem is attained only when they feel that they have exerted power over authority. They want to feel triumphant, vindicated. This need makes them highly aggressive and irritable. They think they are on the righteous crusade, so this empowers them to act aggressively—they are irritable because of their hyper-vigilance.

RELATIONSHIPS

The Paranoid Personality has recurrent suspicions, without justification, regarding the fidelity of their spouse or sexual partner. An intimate relationship with a Paranoid can be a cruel one, a war, a true example of love-hate. They fear that the hate (suspicion) will overpower and destroy the relationship (as it does for Elizabeth Proctor, *The Crucible*). Paranoid Personalities experience others as discontinuous; no relationship is perceived as enduring. They are, from the beginning, waiting for it to fail. They live in the moment, unable to place any credence on the history of the relationship. In nearly all the films referenced, the Paranoid character is either void of a meaningful relationship or has experienced strained relationships at best.

Relationships for the Paranoid Personality are difficult because the issue of trust is quite problematic. This debilitating lack of trust and fierce vigilance of interpersonal borders naturally leads to a near absence of intimacy. You can't get too close to Paranoids because that is precisely what they fear the most. It is what sends them into complete terror. They lack warmth, choosing instead to keep a safe distance. They also tend to isolate themselves and see themselves as completely self-sufficient. General Ripper, Derek, and Darryl Zero physically barricade their lives—they shut down emotionally. Derek sports a barbed wire tattoo across his biceps—a symbolic image of no trespassing.

To handle these egocentric feelings, the Paranoid uses a high degree of the following:

- Projection
- Denial
- Reaction Formation

Projection is the ability to project one's own feelings (of such things as fear, inferiority, and pain) onto others. Paranoids substitute an external threat for an internal threat. The character tries to get rid of his feelings by projecting them onto others. He causes the other person to feel the feelings he cannot feel. An example of this process is seen when the Paranoid is jealous of another individual's accomplishment. They will say that the accomplished person is trying to undermine them out of envy. Thus Darryl Zero, highly suspicious and fearful, feels that everyone from car rental clerks to the woman he is sleeping with is likewise suspicious and must be lied to. He convinces himself of this because he is the best at what he does, and everyone else wishes that they could have his high degree of detachment.

Denial is defined as a direct rejection of overwhelming stimuli that usually arises from the external world. An example of denial would be when Darryl Zero tells Arlo that he is making a mistake by leaving him, that Arlo needs him, when in fact he is denying that he is the one who will be lost if Arlo leaves.

Because of the Paranoids' propinquity to become convinced that they hate what they actually love—**reaction formation**—they may experience and express the opposite of what might be expected. They may hate their partners for what they perceive is hatred from them. They may feel manipulated, and thus humiliated, and accuse their partners of treachery. The Paranoid Personality approaches every relationship (sexual or otherwise) with the belief that the other person will slip up and confirm their suspicions. Elizabeth Proctor (*The Crucible*) exemplifies this. She has such a low opinion of herself that she does not believe a man of true merit would fall in love with her. Therefore, when John Proctor marries her, she suspects from the very beginning that there must be something about him that is less than honest. *What's wrong with him for not seeing what's* *wrong with me?* A woman of self-hate, she cannot accept that someone might desire her for herself. Her suspicions lead her to be cold and aloof, if not downright frigid: "You could freeze beer, Elizabeth!" This pushes her husband away and leads him to an affair—thus proving what she suspected all along.

SHAPING THE CHARACTER

The challenge for an artist is to construct a Paranoid character and then find a way of getting that character to trust another person—this is the essence of *Zero Effect*. For a chance at love, the character must find a way to trust. Storylines involving the arc of a Paranoid Personality move in the same trajectory as that of a therapist working with a Paranoid Personality. The overall goal is to shift their perceptions of the origin of their problems from an external sense to an internal sense. This can take the form of a catastrophic event, a life and death situation to shock the character out of his personality style. For Derek in *American History X*, it is his arrest and incarceration in prison that finally opens his eyes.

(With *American History X*, it could be argued that the filmmakers are saying that the best way to cure a neo-Nazi is to send him to prison to be gang raped in the showers. This does occur and it is presented as the most blatant and brutal turning point. But there is also a much quieter series of moments building in the Second Act. This is seen in Derek's relationship with a Black inmate who not only befriends him but also saves his life when Derek turns his back on his Aryan brothers. This kindness from a stranger is perhaps the most crucial of the pivotal moments. The movie presents options—one savage, one sensitive—and leaves the door open to interpretation.)

BACKSTORY

The childhood of the Paranoid Personality can be one of a harsh home life. For the Paranoid individual, criticism and ridicule dominates the family dynamic. It is often focused on the budding Paranoid, who serves at the receiving end of such unwanted attention. They assume (or have it thrust upon them) the role of family target. They are generally in a position of familial weakness, and are consistently mocked. Such action will cause them to hate who they are. The ridicule generally takes the form of teasing and sarcasm, but the hostility toward them is clearly there; it simply comes out cloaked.

The primary caregiver in the formation of the Paranoid Personality is usually characterized by a distorted maternal experience. The Paranoid mother fosters the Paranoid offspring. When a child's primary source of knowledge is so confused, the child experiences a desperate sense of uncertainty and the need to feel safe. These mind-muddling transactions get replicated repeatedly in the adult relationships of the Paranoid.

The world of infancy is simplistic and the basic things we take for granted as adults take on, in the eyes of the child, paramount importance. For an infant, social, communicative, and complex needs have not yet advanced. The primary relations take on a consuming importance. They become central. They signify life and death. Life is viewed as either all good or all bad. If they are fed properly, their frustrations are satiated and life is good. If food is denied, life is harsh, confusing, and frustrating. Such imprinting during the most receptive stage of the human psyche is profound and lasting. When fixation or arrest occurs, the paranoid individual withdraws into emotional isolation, and this sets off a pattern of major aggression. There is the self-hate of the homosexual who is unable to express or experience love because of a history of attacks from family, church, and society that has him insisting he should hate himself. The self-hate of the brothers of *Boyz N the Hood* who kill one another because they are the product of a racism that sees little value in their lives.

THE ARC OF A
PARANOID FILM CHARACTER

When we are first introduced to Darryl Zero, his character arc is at a point at which his Paranoid Personality is firmly entrenched. We first meet him in absentia, as Steve Arlo is taking a meeting with a client: "He never meets clients, he doesn't negotiate his fee. He never even leaves the house," Arlo tells us. Later, Arlo describes him less charitably to a colleague in a bar: "He's a rude asshole."

The first time we see Darryl Zero, he is in his home and crime lab, a place possibly guarded as securely as the most severe of federal penitentiaries. He is raving, unkempt, and always on edge—no doubt due to the fact that he hasn't slept in three days because of all the amphetamines that he has been digesting. "They're good for my skin," he claims. He prides himself on his "objectivity and observation—the two obs." He mistrusts everybody, including Steve Arlo, who, after first lulling him into complacency with small talk, he snaps at accusingly: "Where the fuck have you been?" He does this knowing full well that Arlo has been briefing a client.

The first plot point occurs when Darryl decides to actually go and solve one of his cases at hand. He pursues great lengths to ensure that he eludes even the most benign glances by donning numerous disguises and assuming numerous false identities—three in the course of one plane trip from Los Angeles to Portland, Oregon. Distrusting and detached (two points of pride with him), he can't bring himself to speak face to face with Arlo in an airport. "Too fishy. Two guys in an airport," he believes. Instead they speak to each other from adjacent pay phones.

Act Two begins when Darryl arrives in Portland and begins the job of unraveling the blackmail scheme against his client, Mr. Stark. Mistrusting everyone (hallmarks of both a good detective and a Paranoid), Zero pursues Stark to his gym, never revealing his true identity as he runs on the treadmill next to him. At the gym, Darryl also meets Gloria, who he also immediately distrusts and likewise investigates. Act Two progresses with Darryl deploying his own particular brand of sleuthing. The hunt incorporates a methodology that is in no small part informed by his paranoia—the layers of the onion are slowly peeled away on the case of bribery against Mr. Stark. Darryl finds himself getting closer to Gloria, not only because she is the prime suspect as the briber, but also because he has become undeniably attracted to her.

Faced with his feelings for her, he must overcome his debilitating distrust and his abject fear of allowing anyone to become intimate with him on a sexual, social, or professional level. He also must face the dilemma that his entire relationship with Gloria is built on the deception resulting from his occupation—she believes he's a banker named Nick Carmine.

As Act Two approaches its crisis point, the stakes are raised for Darryl. Steve Arlo tells him that he is going to quit. Steve provides a vital function for Darryl in that he is the only one who Darryl trusts and thus serves as his only social conduit. Darryl flies into a rage at the news, tearing up his motel room and calling Steve an "ungrateful fuck": "What am I supposed to do?" he asks him. "Start taking meetings? Start talking to people?" He is being forced to call into question the seal of paranoia he has erected around his life.

In Act Three, Darryl's character arc takes a dramatic turn as he decides to let Gloria in. "Look at me in the eyes and talk to me," she tells him, and he opens up to her. They share painful memories of a similar traumatic childhood— something that Darryl has never before allowed himself to do. He feels safe with Gloria. How can you not trust somebody who is at least as wounded as you are? Hesitantly, he falls in love and they become intimate, something that was unthinkable to Darryl before he met Gloria. "I've never said the words before, to anyone," he tells her.

In the end he makes Gloria an offer to further their relationship, but she, guilty of bribery and rich from her crime, must leave the country. It doesn't matter. The important thing is that someone did breach Darryl's defenses. He is now at least able and willing to experience closeness and contact with others and still feel safe. All of this is due to what he dubs, "The Case of the Man Who Lost His Objectivity when He Lost it Over a Lady Blackmailer."

THE PARANOID PERSONALITY SUMMARY

Examples of the qualities and qualifications that define a person with a Paranoid Personality:

- A consuming distrust and pervasive suspiciousness of others
- They tend to interpret the motives of others as malevolent
- They reflexively react with suspicion (without any tangible basis) that others are exploiting or deceiving them
- They are consumed with unsubstantiated doubts concerning the loyalty and trustworthiness of not only people with whom they work but also of friends
- They are reluctant to confide in others
- They worry that any trust they give or confidence they share will be used maliciously against them
- They perceive demeaning or threatening nuances in the benign remarks of others or in neutral events
- They tenaciously hold onto grudges
- They do not forgive insults, injuries, or slights—even if they are the only ones who perceive them as such
- They are convinced that attacks and injurious slander are aimed at them and their reputations, though others may not see this
- They immediately react with anger and counterattacks to any slights (either covert or overt) that they perceive
- They are plagued with suspicions regarding the fidelity of their mates
- They have unwarranted and consistent feelings of being attacked

- They generally avoid intimacy
- They tend to isolate themselves
- They are ardently self-sufficient
- They tend to be very jealous
- They tend to be very fiercely argumentative
- They are hypervigilant of the words and deeds of others
- They tend to be very cold emotionally and seldom display warmth and tenderness
- They pride themselves in their rationality, objectivity, and the suppression of emotion, even if they are the only ones who think so
- They have difficulty with authority figures
- They often appear as uncompromising, stubborn, and defensive
- They are prone to being hostile
- They jealously guard their independence
- They seldom take responsibility for their own feelings, but instead assign it to others
- They are constantly expecting to be attacked and exploited
- They externalize emotions and attribute their own motives and impulses onto others
- They are impressed with power and rank
- They hold those with less power and those who are weak in disdain

NOTEWORTHY CHARACTERISTICS OF THE PARANOID PERSONALITY

SPEECH

Hyper-vigilant. Distrustful. Careful. Demonstrative. Can be soft spoken or loud and pushy to ward off feared attacks.

PROFESSIONS

Loners. Career military. Religious leaders. Hi-Tech. Engineers. Jobs not known for individualism. Jobs that are group affiliated. Jobs out of the public eye.

DRESS

Often subdued. Sometimes representing group affiliation. Oftentimes little emphasis on a desire to be individually recognized.

HEALTH

Issues concerning Hypochondriasis. Severe paranoia about health in general and specifics. Fatalistic view. Self-medication with substance abuse is common. Panic attacks with and without Agoraphobia. Phobias, sexual difficulties from stress-inducing situations. Ejaculatory problems. Sleep disorders. Sleep terrors and nightmares.

POPULAR CLICHÉS
ASSOCIATED WITH PARANOIDS

- Vigilante
- Loner
- Skinhead
- Bigot
- Racist
- Computer Nerd
- Righteously corrupt
- Morally indignant
- Misfit
- Outcast
- Pariah
- Puritan
- Partisan
- Zealot
- Monomaniac

SIMILAR PERSONALITY TYPES
TO THE PARANOID

- THE ANTISOCIAL PERSONALITY
- THE BORDERLINE PERSONALITY
- THE MASOCHISTIC PERSONALITY

VIEWING SUGGESTIONS FOR
THE PARANOID PERSONALITY

Alien (1979)—Science Fiction/Horror, 117, Rated R.
For Sci-Fi paranoia.

American History X (1998)—Drama, 117, Rated R.
For racial paranoia. Edward Norton's chilling and well deserved Academy Award nominated performance as the skinhead, Derek.

Blob, The (1958)—Science Fiction, 86, No rating.
For Sci-Fi paranoia. A product of the Red Scare and the end of World War II.

Blow Out (1981)—Mystery, 107, Rated R.
For political paranoia.

Boys in the Band, The (1970)—Drama, 119, Rated R.
For homophobic paranoia. Interesting study of an internalized, self-inflicted paranoia. In this case, sexuality. A great deal of theatrics that all comes down to: "If we could only not hate ourselves."

Boyz N The Hood (1991)—Drama, 107, Rated R.
For racial paranoia. An interesting study of an internalized, self-inflicted paranoia. In this case, color and race. Nominated for an Oscar for the writing.

Chariots of Fire (1981)—Sports/Biography, 123, Rated PG.
A study in anti-Semitic paranoia. Won the Oscar for writing.

Crucible, The (1996)—Historical/Drama, 123, Rated PG-13.

> For political paranoia. Arthur Miller's look back on the phenomena of the communist red scare in America. A brilliant look at the nature of paranoia.

Day the Earth Stood Still, The (1951)—Science Fiction, 92, No rating.

> For Sci-Fi paranoia. Unquestionably the best of the paranoid films from this particular era.

Death Wish (1974)—Crime, 93, Rated R.

> For urban paranoia.

Do the Right Thing (1989)—Drama/Comedy, 120, Rated R.

> For racial paranoia. Interesting study of an internalized, self-inflicted paranoia. In this case, race. Spike Lee was nominated for his screenplay.

Don't Look Now (1973)—Mystery, 110, Rated R.

> A mix of Paranoid Personality and Paranoid Schizophrenia.

Dr. Strangelove or: How I Learned to Stop Worrying and Love the Bomb (1964)—Black Comedy, 93, No rating.

> For General Ripper (Sterling Hayden) as a Paranoid Personality. Satirical and over the top, but the points are made. Nominated for an Oscar for the writing.

Ghost of Mississippi (1996)—Historical Drama, 130, Rated PG-13.

> For racial paranoia. James Woods' Academy Award nominated performance as real-life racist and murderer Byron Beckwith.

Great Dictator, The (1940)—War/Comedy, 128, No rating.
> For political paranoia. Nominated for the
> writing.

Hidden Agenda (1990)—Political/Thriller, 108, Rated R.
> For political paranoia.

In the Heat of the Night (1967)—Crime, 109.
> For racial paranoia. Took home the Oscar for
> the writing.

In the Mouth of Madness (1995)—Thriller/Horror, 95,
Rated R.
> An example of Paranoid Schizophrenia.

Inherit the Wind (1960)—Drama, 127, No rating.
> For political paranoia. Oscar nominated for
> the writing.

Invasion of the Body Snatchers (1956)—Science Fiction,
80, No rating.
> For Sci-Fi paranoia. A product of the Red
> Scare and the end of World War II.

Invasion of the Body Snatchers (1978)—Science
Fiction,115, Rated PG.
> For Sci-Fi paranoia. One of the better film
> remakes.

Jacob's Ladder (1990)—Horror, 115, Rated R.
> For Paranoid Schizophrenia.

Jeffrey (1995)—Comedy/Romance, 92, Rated R.
> For homophobia.

Jungle Fever (1991)—Romance/Drama, 132, Rated R.
> For racial paranoia. Interesting study of an
> internalized, self-inflicted paranoia.

Longtime Companion (1990)—Drama, 96, Rated R.
For homophobia.

Love Field (1992)—Drama, 104, Rated PG-13.
For racial paranoia.

Malcolm X (1992)—Drama/Biography, 201, Rated PG-13.
For racial paranoia.

Man Who Knew Too Much, The (1934)—Mystery, 75, No rating.
For political paranoia.

Mississippi Burning (1988)—Historical/Drama, 125, Rated R.
For racial paranoia.

Naked Lunch (1991)—Science Fiction/Fantasy/Drama, 115, Rated R.
For examples of Paranoid Schizophrenia.

North by Northwest (1959)—Thriller/Spy, 136, No rating.
For spy and "wrong man" paranoia. Nominated for an Academy Award for writing.

Notorious (1946)—Thriller/Spy, 101, No rating.
For spy paranoia. Nominated for an Academy Award for writing.

One False Move (1992)—Drama/Crime, 105, Rated R.
For racial paranoia.

Parallax View, The (1974)—Thriller, 102, Rated R.
For political paranoia—and one of the better ones to do it.

Parting Glances (1986)—Drama, 90, No rating.
For homophobic paranoia.

Philadelphia (1993)—Drama, 119, Rated PG-13.
For homophobic paranoia. Nominated for an Academy Award for writing.

Repulsion (1965)—Horror, 105, No rating.
For examples of Paranoid Schizophrenia.

Seven Days in May (1964)—Political/Thriller/Drama, 118, No rating.
For political paranoia.

Shining, The (1980)—Horror, 142, Rated R.
For examples of Paranoid Schizophrenia.

Suspicion (1941)—Thriller, 99, No rating.
Joan Fontaine won an Academy Award for playing this wife who thinks her husband is trying to kill her.

Thing (From Another World), The (1951)—Science Fiction, 87, No rating.
For Sci-Fi paranoia. One of the better films from the 1950s' paranoid films period.

Three Days of the Condor (1975)—Thriller, 117, Rated R.
For political paranoia.

To Kill a Mockingbird (1962)—Drama, 129, No rating.
For racial paranoia. Won the Oscar for writing.

Torch Song Trilogy (1988)—Drama, 117, Rated R.
For homophobia. Interesting study of an internalized, self-inflicted paranoia. In this case, sexuality.

Wedding Banquet, The (1993)—Drama/Comedy, 111, Rated R.

> For homophobic paranoia.

White Dog (1982)—Drama, 89, No rating.

> For racial paranoia.

Winter Kills (1979)—Political/Mystery/Comedy, 97, Rated R.

> For political paranoia.

Z (1969)—Political/Thriller/Historical, 127, Rated PG.

> For political paranoia. Nominated for an Academy Award for writing.

PRIOR TO READING THE NEXT CHAPTER
IT IS RECOMMENDED THAT THE FOLLOWING
FILMS BE VIEWED:

SUNSET BLVD.
DOLORES CLAIBORNE
WHAT EVER HAPPENED TO BABY JANE?

A LIST OF FILMS PERTAINING TO THE
NARCISSISTIC PERSONALITY CAN BE FOUND
AT THE END OF THIS CHAPTER.

4

THE NARCISSISTIC PERSONALITY

And I love the audience. And the audience loves me for loving them. And I love the audience for loving me. And we just love each other. And that's because none of us got enough love in our childhood. And that's show-biz, kid!
—Roxie Hart/Bob Fosse, Fred Ebb

SPEEDING DOWN *Sunset Blvd.*, a destitute writer of B movies, Joe Gillis, escapes the Repo men by coasting into the garage of "a great big white elephant of a place, the kind crazy movie people built in the crazy 20s." Living inside is the tarnished Norma Desmond, the fallen goddess of silent films. She surrounds herself with her past glory—there are the faded publicity shots in gilt frames and an obsequious manservant, Max, who buoys and fluffs her ego with fresh batches of fan mail daily. Before he knows it, Joe Gillis is shanghaied into helping Norma make her return to her adoring public. She requires help in writing *Salome*, an ill-chosen vehicle she has created for the occasion of her return. Broke, Joe takes the job, but he soon finds that Norma's vanity and her need for unadulterated admiration is unquenchable. She wants him for an ornament—a fresh font of praise—and will not tolerate the slightest divergence of his attention. He must kowtow to her, enduring her private theatricals and endless screenings of her once great movies.

In Bangor, Maine there is another Joe: Joe St. George. He is the husband of *Dolores Claiborne* (David Strathairn in a performance as remorseless as it is brilliant). He is also the abusive father of their daughter, Selena. He will tolerate little from his long-suffering wife. Neither mockery nor affection is acceptable. When Dolores giggles at his split pants, he rewards her with a piece of timber across the back of her thighs. Joe mocks her attempts at reconciliation by berating her, telling her he never would have married her had he not been so drunk that he hadn't realized how ugly she was. For Selena, though, he has nothing but praise. He showers her with gifts and favors. The affection he bestows oversteps the parental and becomes sexual as well. He views his daughter as an object of his own gratification and diversion.

A little east of Norma Desmond's mansion lives another early film star who, comparatively speaking, has not fared quite as well as Norma. This is the former child star Baby Jane Hudson of the film that asks and answers the question, *What Ever Happened to Baby Jane?* As a little girl, Baby Jane was self-centered, demanding, and obnoxious. She not only got away with such behavior, she was rewarded for it. Baby Jane was "the Diminutive Dancing Duse from Duluth." In the sphere of her childhood, everyone— her parents, her handlers, her sister Blanche—catered to her selfish whims because, warts and all, she was the primary breadwinner. Times change, people grow and die, but Baby Jane tenaciously held onto the infantile world of which she was the center. Her appeal ended at puberty, when it began to take more than childish curls to sway the public. Her sister, Blanche, much to Jane's dismay, went on to greater and more enduring fame. Baby Jane's deteriorating world becomes more and more diffuse, clouded in gin fumes and nostalgia. She becomes enraged at the preeminence of Blanche and the erosion of her own inability to remain daddy's special girl.

MIRROR, MIRROR

Narcissistic personalities are characterized as having a pervasive self-centeredness, an all-encompassing grandiosity about themselves, their achievements, and their place in life. Along with this exalted self-centered behavior, there is also a discernible lack of empathy and a sense of entitlement that blinds them to all needs except their own. As Joe Gillis (*Sunset Blvd.*) remarks early on about the once famous silent screen star he has encountered: "She was still sleepwalking along the giddy heights of her lost career, playing craps when it came to that one subject, her celluloid self, the great Norma Desmond."

Poor Joe Gillis did not know how right he was when he referred to the builders of those Sunset Boulevard palaces as "crazy movie people." Most assuredly Billy Wilder, Charles Brackett, and D. M. Marshman Jr. (the writers of *Sunset Blvd.*) knew all too well and had little difficulty calling a spade a spade. The movie making business is overrun with Narcissistic Personalities. Some of them even managed to wind up on the screen. Smart writers, honoring the tenet "write what you know," found an arsenal of Narcissistic characters and stories in their own backyard. Not surprisingly, it is there, deep within the heart of the creature named show business,that some of the best examples can be found.

The most profound collection would appear to fall at the feet of the acting community. Bigger than life actors playing bigger than life actors is a tried and true formula. Inflicting havoc on the lives of others are, from the top: Anne Baxter in *All About Eve*, Olivier's *The Entertainer*, Albert Finney in *The Dresser*, Richard E. Grant as the self-absorbed Withnail of *Withnail & I*, the aggressive film debut of Kim Stanley in *The Goddess*. No need to stop there. Add to the list: *Gypsy, Noises Off, Purple Rose of Cairo, Stardust Memories, Day for Night, Sweet Bird of Youth, 8 1/2.* In all fairness, actors alone do not shoulder the burden of characters we love to hate. Within show business, storytellers have taken deadly aim at directors—*All That Jazz, The Stunt Man, Ed Wood, White Hunter, Black Heart*; producers—*On The Twentieth Century, The Producers, Barton Fink*; and news journalists—*Network, Broadcast News, Citizen Kane*. Sometimes the entire entertainment profession is held up, scrutinized, and taken to task—the Hollywood Hell of *Play It As It Lays, The Big Picture, Day of the Locust, S.O.B.* One of the best Narcissistic displays is seen in Robert Altman and Michael Tolkin's sharply clever black comedy, *The Player*. It offers the story of a studio executive more capable of murder than of making a movie. Tim Robbins as the cold-hearted Griffin Mill is threatened by a writer that he promised to call back and never did. They don't get much better.

The Narcissist is found everywhere—from great leaders (*Lawrence of Arabia*) to great killers (*Basic Instinct*). They are delightfully innocent (*Breakfast at Tiffany's*) and they are wonderfully corrupt (*The Manchurian Candidate*). We have them famous (*Becket*) and we have them impotent (*sex, lies, and videotape*). The pattern revealed shows a high concentration on dark dramas and thrillers. Comparatively, the canon of comedies is short and, at best, populated by black comedies.

The reason: Narcissism is not funny. With few exceptions, the story of the Narcissist is that of an arrogant, haughty, unsympathetic, and exploitative individual—not the most desirable type to bring home to mother (let alone find oneself trying to cheer for up on the silver screen). To make matters worse, rarely can Narcissists be counted on to redeem themselves by the Third Act. This is a less than desirable fate for a leading character. Villains, yes. Heroes, no. Not only is the Narcissistic Personality hard to stomach in a leading role, but there have been those occasions in which the actor in the role has found the character hard to live with. In 1960, Billy Wilder released *The Apartment*, a film in which he offered a few choice opinions about morality. Having had his way with Hollywood (*Sunset Blvd.*), he now had something to say about businessmen. Fred MacMurray plays the exploitative, self-centered boss, J. D. Sheldrake. Although the film was critically acclaimed, public response was extremely negative to seeing the much-adored MacMurray playing a disreputable, narcissistic white-collar thug. The mail he received so upset the actor that from that film on he would be very careful to accept roles in which the characters' moral credibility would never be questioned. MacMurray would become synonymous with Disney, as well as television's lovable widowed father of three sons.

The term "narcissism" is derived from Narcissus, a character from Greek mythology. As the myth has it, Narcissus saw his own reflection mirrored in a lake and fell in love with it. He was so enamored with the visage of himself and preoccupied with the contemplation of his own beauty that he eventually starved to death. As could only happen in the worlds of mythology or movies, Narcissus turned into a flower. His soul was sent to the underworld, where it still primps at its own image reflected in the river Styx.

Because the two share many of the same attributes, the Narcissistic Personality at times will approximate the Histrionic Personality. In both the Narcissist and the Histrionic, common traits to be found include excessive emotionality, excessive attention getting, egocentrism, and manipulation in relationships. An important difference is that Narcissists will usually exhibit a high level of arrogance as well as the inability to see fault in their actions.

This is something generally not found in Histrionics, who customarily not only see fault, but are quick to lay blame at their own feet. The Narcissist's emotional ups and downs tend not to be as wildly erratic as those of the Histrionic. The Histrionic Personality will most likely behave dramatically and seductively. Narcissists by comparison are often sternly grandiose and selfish—almost in a hostile way. A simple (though certainly not scientific) rule of thumb in distinguishing the Narcissistic from the Histrionic is the "Me Factor."

Consider the following:

- Is the character **consciously** arrogant or overtly caught up in orchestrating behavior and events to meet their own needs? (More likely Narcissistic)

- Do the character's emotions appear to run all over the map—do they appear more **emotionally** responsive in a situation, as opposed to a response that seems intended or designed? (More likely Histrionic)

Also apparent quite often is the tell-all factor of love. Histrionics commonly responds out of a desire to have love in their lives. The Narcissist, on the other hand, may harbor an idealized notion of being in love, but rarely actually knows how to love. Ultimately, the line separating the two psychological personalities is crossed and blurred. It may all come down to an issue of what is being created—a comedy or drama. When these characteristic traits are successfully displayed in a comedy, intent and forethought of character seem of marginal importance next to the demands of the high octane, plot-driven fuel required of comedies. Therefore, in comedy, characters tend to be

Histrionic. When this intermixing of personalities is involved in a drama, usually foul play is afoot, and the character becomes the love-to-hate Narcissistic.

THE OBSESSION

Like Narcissus, Narcissistic Personalities often are absorbed and consumed by their own perfection and harbor a tremendous need to keep their self-image full blown and intact. They will protect this self-image with all the means at their disposal. Typically, Narcissists are guided by their own self-importance. Norma Desmond promises to "return to the millions of people who've never forgiven me for deserting the screen." Baby Jane Hudson reprimands her parents: "I make the money so I can have what I want!" They crave attention and admiration: "Why do they still write me fan letters every day? Why do they beg me for photographs? Why? Because they want to see me! Me! Norma Desmond!" Their egos are bottomless pits. It is not unusual for them to exaggerate their achievements or talents. Eve Harrington, the devoted fan/aspiring actress/ruthless predator of the perfectly titled *All About Eve*, lies about her past so the star of Broadway, Margo Channing, will welcome her warmly and sympathetically. *Breakfast at Tiffany's* is (despite Hollywood's considerable and talented efforts to soft focus it otherwise) the story of a hooker and a hustler, albeit they are made handsome in the guise of heavenly Audrey Hepburn and hunky George Peppard. Fashionable to a fault, they dash about with urban madcap flare in their best Edith Head stitchery (in truth, Hepburn runs around in Givenchy, but that is another Hollywood story). Despite the dreamy, movie magazine looks, the fact remains they are prostitutes of a sort that recreate themselves in larger-than-life false self-images. Based on (but not nearly as wonderfully cruel as) Truman Capote's novella of the same name, *Breakfast at Tiffany's* tells the tale of an ambitious-if-innocent young woman, Holly Golightly (Hepburn), who, in glorious Eliza Doolittle fashion, remakes herself. At a party, Holly's agent (a modern day Professor Higgins) pulls aside her newfound friend and neighbor, the handsome-but-kept man, Paul Varjak. He asks him if he thinks Holly might be a phony. Before Paul can debate the question, he has his answer from the agent: "She's a real phony. She honestly believes all this phony junk she believes."

White Hunter, Black Heart is the thinly veiled true-life story of the on-location filming of John Huston's classic, *The African Queen*. Clint Eastwood portrays the Huston character (here John Wilson). Wilson is an obsessed, demanding, strong-willed, cold-hearted director whose exploitative nature demands his wishes before any others. The film retells an actual real life occurrence in which Huston placed the entire film shoot on hold in Africa while he went elephant hunting. Unmitigated grandiosity is a common key to the Narcissistic Personality. Granted, in the Huston/Wilson case, the self-importance was as true and palpable as the talent. More often than not, Narcissists routinely overestimate their abilities and accomplishments and often seem boastful and pretentious. Norma expects famous movie director DeMille to jump at the chance to make her movie: "I'm not just selling the script, I'm selling me." If their magnificence isn't apparent to others, they will not hesitate to make it clear. Baby Jane, ruminating on the life of being a big star, tells her accompanist, Edwin, "You can never lose your talent . . . you can lose everything else, but you can never lose your talent." Left-wing Broadway scribe, Barton Fink (of Ethan and Joel Coen's *Barton Fink*), makes a deal with the devil and attempts to sell out to Hollywood. He says he is interested in hearing and writing the stories of the common man, but when those stories are being offered to him, he is deaf to them because he is too busy postulating about being a poet.

Worse yet, at a USO canteen, this same Barton Fink goes off on a young sailor who, shipping out the next day, wants to cut in on his dance. As though armed with special rights in the world granted to him by his supposed talent, he screams at the innocent Yank, "I am a writer!" His lack of humility and presumption of status lands a hard fist on his chin soon thereafter. The point here: Narcissists' primary belief is that they are superior (or, at the very least, unique) and primary beliefs should be universal. On the surface the Narcissist may seem bold, self-assured, directed. Repeatedly they are. They are intensely focused on their own advancement and standing and, as such, they can be very successful professionally and personally.

Narcissists often will be seen seeking to excel in their work in order to receive the praise and admiration of others. They achieve their goals because their goals are their own self-aggrandizement—something in which they single-mindedly invest their time and energy. For the Narcissist, there is no room in the spotlight for others. Norma lives in a multi-room mansion full of pictures, and there isn't a picture of anyone else except her. In the Hudson household, Blanche finds photos of herself, but Baby Jane has mutilated all the faces. The Narcissistic Personality does an excellent job establishing the image of perfectionist, someone incapable of making a mistake. They are so driven by the obsession for admiration that they seem restless, eager, overachieving—classic workaholics. Hard work does not frighten them and they are fiercely ambitious. If the payoff means attaining a sense of perfection or stardom, nothing can stop them . . . nothing perhaps, but themselves, which often for storytellers provides their all important, pivotal Third Act. Favorite Narcissists undone by themselves: *The Grifters, Becket, The Goddess,* and *Dangerous Liaisons.*

ENTITLEMENT AND ENVY

Narcissists may foster unwarranted feelings of entitlement. Often they have unreasonable expectations of especially favorable treatment or automatic compliance with their expectations—a sense that the world owes them and they are not going to forfeit the debt. Rarely would they believe it their lot to struggle or work for their achievements. The rest of the world should recognize (as they recognize) how wonderful and valuable they are simply because of their mere existence. Not only should the world bow down to their needs, they should also feel free to shower them with a constant stream of admiration . . . excessive admiration.

The film *Becket* tells the story of two friends: Thomas Becket, Archbishop of Canterbury, and Henry II, King of England. Becket is described by the Vatican as "obviously an abyss of ambition." His own Gwendolyn professes, "You've not found anything in the world to care for." This before she stabs herself to death rather than be handed off to the King's bed as proof of Becket's loyalty. Becket himself admits candidly, "Humility is a virtue I've never really mastered." King Henry II, meanwhile, refers to himself publicly: "I'm so subtle. I'm so profound." People of lesser standing are referred to as "it."

Ultimately, King Henry proves himself willing to give up the crown of England to a son he despises simply to get back at Becket: "You love God more than me." Quite a pair they are . . . and rather frightful that the fate of a nation was bundled up in their psychological baggage. Both characters are enveloped in a shroud of narcissistic tendencies. Although the story of Becket essentially is about the separation of church and state, it also is about the all too real affairs of narcissistic wrath when pitted against one of their own. The King wants the one thing he will never have: the love (read: submission) of Becket. Becket, awarded all the prominence and prestige the King can possibly bestow upon him in a vain attempt to win that love, finds himself indulging in the worst vice imaginable of all superstars: he believes his own press. The screenplay by Edward Anhalt (adapted from the play by Jean Anouilh and honored with an Oscar) would appear to make it all very clear that Becket is much more interested in being in the league of God, rather than being a servant to him.

This is a fascinating take on the Narcissist's desire to be in love while not possessing the ability to actually love. For King Henry II, Anhalt and Anouilh have less pity. This Henry is nothing less than a nasty, spoiled, infuriating child, throwing temper tantrums that shudder a nation. People kill themselves and institutions crumble, all in the name of his fitful desire to have what he wants from Becket.

Envy is high on Narcissists' experience list. They envy greatly the accomplishments of others (which frequently they feel should be theirs). They also feel that others envy them (as the Narcissist feels they rightly should). This sense of entitlement often manifests in supreme arrogance and haughtiness. They patronize those around them because all others are inferior. Sometimes it can prove to be much crueler. Baby Jane is driven to distraction by all the attention being focused on sister Blanche. It is attention that she feels was stolen away from her. "Miss Rotten Stinking Actress!" she rants. "Ring a bell and you think the whole damn world comes running!" She acts out on her rage by serving Blanche her pet bird on a bed of sliced tomatoes for lunch.

RELATIONSHIPS

Important in creating Narcissistic characters is remembering they have little or no capacity for empathy. They are unwilling to recognize or identify with the feelings of others. It is unlikely they will comprehend or recognize (let alone soothe) others' emotions. All the concerns of others—the accomplishments, desires, and needs of others—are totally dwarfed by the grandeur of their own experiences. Max, Norma Desmond's erstwhile servant, suffers pain and humiliation because Norma does not consider his feelings in passing. Despite the fact that he was her first husband, as well as the man who discovered her, she keeps him subservient. She treats him with less respect and affection than she does her dead monkey. Norma flaunts her pathetic infatuation for Joe Gillis right under Max's nose.

For Narcissists, their interpersonal relationships are largely marked by exploitation. They take advantage of others to achieve their own ends. John Huston gives a shivering performance as the incestuous land baron Noah Cross in the Robert Towne/Roman Polanski production, *Chinatown*. Cross is a narcissistic monster. He has raped the land and his daughter and triumphantly has his eyes set on using his granddaughter for his own foul needs—all this done with the utmost sense of righteousness. Simon Gray's film adaptation of his stage play, *Butley*, presents a man (an English scholar and authority on T. S. Eliot) who must face the greatest truth of his life, a truth he has no desire to look in the eye: the emotional reciprocity of others. Butley (Alan Bates, in a stellar recreation of his stage performance) has spent his life in the pursuit and retreat of those around him by attacking and exploiting their weaknesses. Spending his days in psychological warfare, he battles with sarcasm, wit, contempt, insults, and (to say the least) a fair amount of booze. Faced with the news that both his wife and his closest friend are leaving him (not together, but for different men), Butley is forced to confront the unsavory nature of his psyche.

When two Narcissistic Personalities are pitted against one another for the purposes of exploitation, the results can be as fun to watch as they are dangerous to encounter. Along with *Becket* there is also a pristine example in the extraordinary play-turned-film, *Dangerous Liaisons*. Glenn Close plays the Marquise de Merteuil in a brilliantly written (Academy Award winner Christopher Hampton) and beautifully rendered portrayal of sexual power, deceit, and vengeance. Merteuil, along with the Vicomte de Valmont (John Malkovich), is the chief architect of an amoral game of seduction and conquest. The two former lovers plot and exploit to the breaking point. Forced to turn on one another, they declare an all-out narcissistic war. All three (*Chinatown*, *Butley*, and *Dangerous Liaisons*) examine central characters exploiting and manipulating the world around them for their own ends. These pervasive feelings of entitlement, combined with their inherent lack of sensitivity toward others, is the basis for the rules by which Narcissists live:

- Anything is permissible—exploitation, manipulation, lying—for the greater admiration, by themselves and others, of their being.

All other considerations are waylaid. The Narcissist simply feels entitled.

Along with the lack of empathy, important to note in the writing and portrayal of Narcissistic characters and their use of exploitation is the complete lack of guilt or concern for over exploitative manner. What rings frightfully true about characters such as Joe St. George in *Dolores Claiborne* and Noah Cross in *Chinatown* is their remorseless behavior for the sexual abuse they hurl upon their own daughters. A character deep in the neurosis of narcissism would be unable to subjectively reason their behavior, because they see it as just and right. They experience no guilt.

The opposite end of the spectrum is much the same. If they bestow affection, it is merely because that is the most expedient method to manipulate others to provide for their needs. Baby Jane is a little cool on Edwin Flagg (her accompanist) until she realizes that she needs him for her comeback. Joe St. George gives Selena his mother's locket and takes her on boat rides. The goal of his generosity is to get Selena alone so that he might coerce her into some petting. Narcissists will commonly use sex to advance their careers and marry to enhance their social status. They have even been known to possibly adopt children for the invaluable photo op that they provide. The character called "Joan Crawford" in the movie *Mommie Dearest* parades around her newly adopted daughter as she might her newest gown by Adrian, using the child as a means to change her hardened image and revive her sagging career. Her intent: sway public opinion to see her not as tough and ruthless but as the embodiment of motherhood. She needs the good press and goodwill being a parent will generate.

Narcissistic characters rarely have the ability to love, though they are nearly always consumed by the idea of being loved. Though Narcissists' need of others is deep, their love for others is shallow or, more commonly, nonexistent. Eighteen years after *The Goddess*, author Paddy Chayefsky returned to the Narcissistic Personality with a vengeance. His effort was called *Network*, and it delivered to Faye Dunaway (Diana Cristenson) not only one of the great Narcissistic characters an actor could hope to play, but also one of the five Academy Awards deservedly handed the Sidney Lumet film. Diana desperately wants to be in love. The trouble is, she has not a clue of where to look in herself to find the source of those feelings. When her lover speaks to her of love, she looks as if he has just spoken in a foreign tongue. A high powered programming executive, Diana is cold and calculated, obsessed with making it big in corporate television. She not only admits her willingness to use sex to get where she wants to go, but when she has sex, instead of cries and moans of corporeal ecstasy, she shouts out market shares and strategies for the ratings war.

Blinded by her ambition, Diana is unable to accept the love offered by Max Schumacher (William Holden), a man who—for a chance at love with Diana—has walked out on his wife of thirty-some years. When she proves herself not up to the task of being in love, Max (with a few parting words) walks out on her: "You are television incarnate. Indifferent, suffering, insensitive to joy. All of life is reduced to the common ruble of banality. You're madness, Diana."

Not surprisingly, Narcissists experience tremendous difficulty in establishing or maintaining healthy intimate relationships. There is no reciprocation. Anyone in the Narcissist's sphere is there only to be exploited for the greater advantage of the Narcissist. Commitment is extremely difficult for Narcissists because doing so would symbolize vulnerability, and vulnerability would activate underlying fears of inadequacy. Commitment would also require a shift in attention from the self and steal from their life-preserving self-absorption.

WORLD OF THEIR MAKING

Narcissists often appear to be very creative and talented. In truth, creative talent is usually greatly underdeveloped in the Narcissist because so much time and energy is expended on feeding their impulses. Archie Rice (*The Entertainer*) is a financially and emotionally bankrupt song-and-dance man. Living in the shadow of his father's class and style, he rages in frustration over his own mediocrity, unable to rise above it because of his own vain musings. Baby Jane cannot surrender her self-image as the adorable moppet, despite it having grown stale a half a century before. She still practices the same puerile songs in front of the mirror. She still fills the living room with life-size Baby Jane dolls. Norma Desmond's world is a hermetically sealed cocoon of self-indulgence, a shrine to herself and her glory. "How could she breathe in that house," wonders Joe Gillis in the voice-over, "so crowded with Norma Desmonds? More Norma Desmonds and still more Norma Desmonds." The pool of ancient Greece is replaced by the silver screen. Norma could starve watching herself in her own movie theater. To ensure it, she surrounds herself with toadies who not only will adore her but also protect her from any harsh reality that may dwell in the outside world. Forever faithful, Max writes all of the fan mail and will kill before he sees his goddess unmasked. Her legend is to be preserved and he will go to any lengths to prevent its erosion.

Narcissists will surround themselves with the trappings that enhance them, and they will struggle to maintain that environment. Such an environment includes the "right" people—people who will not threaten the fragile narcissistic ego. This circle is important but has little value other than adornment. Narcissists also have a propensity for procuring the flashiest car, the latest fashions, the largest house. They will become obsessive about having the best and being the most successful. Or, they may do exactly the opposite. They may portray themselves as victims, always in turmoil, fighting money problems. They do this to maintain center stage; their victimization assures them of their spotlight. Narcissists behave in these contrasting modes in order to validate their self-importance to themselves and (in their eyes) garner the admiration and attention of others. Mining some of the same territory he would later reap the rewards for in *Network*, Paddy Chayefsky in *The Goddess* gives us a vitriolic sermon about the American dream of stardom and the unloved (and unlovable) caught in the glare of Hollywood's headlights. Emily Ann Faulkner (Kim Stanley) is the poor Southern girl, unwanted from birth by her mother and the dirty joke amongst the boys in high school. She marries one man to get out of her small town hell and into the fire of

Hollywood. Like her mother, she casts aside a baby girl she does not want because it will only get in her way. After climbing her way to the top through a succession of producers, directors, and a famous prizefighter second husband, Emily (now Rita) sustains herself in fancy houses, automobiles, designer clothes, child-like tantrums, and emotional breakdowns that delay films and cause them to run over budget. She behaves so because it is the only course she knows. Her reason for doing so illuminates the only true desire in her life: she yearns for the love of her mother. It is a commodity she never attains and ultimately is left to rail against in rupturing agony at her mother's open grave.

The perfectionist tendencies of the Narcissistic Personality means that they can be extremely demanding of others. Norma drives Joe Gillis well into the night with his rewriting of her screenplay for *Salome*. Norma, never flagging herself, sits alert and coiled like a watch spring, though Joe can barely retain consciousness. John Frankenheimer's 1962 masterpiece, *The Manchurian Candidate*, presents a jaw-dropping portrayal of narcissistic evil in Angela Landsbury's highly acclaimed performance as "Raymond Shaw's Mother"—a character so despicable she's not given a name. This domineering, self-absorbed, exploitative creature not only runs roughshod over her skittish war vet son, but is the puppet master of her second husband, a poor boob of a politician and candidate for the Oval Office who must be told exactly what to do and say. She is a Right Wing nightmare, orchestrating the campaign smears of her husband's opponents, plotting an assassination, and seducing her son to do her bidding with a full mouth kiss on the lips. Nice to know the two political parties have always felt the same about each other. Nothing, however, can prepare the viewer for the revelations of what she is actually up to in the Third Act.

THE IDOLIZED SELF

When in a position of authority, it is not uncommon for Narcissists to unmercifully demean or abuse their subordinates, particularly if they feel that their superiority is being threatened. Joe St. George will beat Dolores bloody if she so much as questions him. Baby Jane will feed her sister vermin when Blanche suggests that she get help or (the supposition that Baby Jane will never tolerate) that it was in fact Blanche's film career that paid for their house.

Likewise, the Narcissistic Personality will require martyr-like devotion from their employees. The Christ-like Eli Cross (Peter O'Toole) in *The Stunt Man* has his paranoid fugitive. John Wilson (read John Huston) of *White Hunter, Black Heart* had his famous stars and film crew standing about Africa trying to anticipate his every whim. Lawrence (*Lawrence of Arabia*) had his men follow him to the ends of the earth. To achieve such ends, praise is often used as bait with subordinates in the hope they will ensure their devotion through of sense of debt. Nevertheless, the workaholic Narcissist will seldom, if ever, take responsibility for personal shortcomings. Instead, they will blame their own imperfections on others. The Narcissistic is also more than eager to steal the credit from others.

Sadly, beneath the surface of Narcissists lies a psyche that is insecure, vulnerable, and self-doubting, and they deploy a wide variety of defense mechanisms to cope with deep-seated feelings of shame. "Shame" in its reference here, can be defined as a response to failure that Narcissists experience in their inability to attain their grandiose idealized self.

Defenses commonly used to cope with intense feelings of shame include:

- Fantasy

- Projection

- Hypochondriasis

- Displacement

- Acting out

- Idealization

Fantasy. Grandiose fantasies of power will many times become stronger and more fortified as Narcissists experience a greater sense of denial in their personality makeup (*The Goddess*).

Projection. The ability to project one's feelings onto others. This allows Narcissists to transfer their inner contempt to the external world (*Butley, Dangerous Liaisons*).

Hypochondriasis. The conversion of psychological symptoms into physical ailments. This enables Narcissists to mask their feelings of ineptitude (*The Ruling Class, Withnail & I*).

Displacement. An unconscious defense in which feelings that are attributed to one source are redirected to another. A transference of feelings for one person in the past are transferred to another person in the present; for example: a parental figure that once caused the child to feel inferior becomes replaced by the perfectionist boss (*The Rose*).

Acting out. Physically acting out one's anxiety. Usually expressed by acts of lashing out against the social norm through such avenues as drugs, alcohol, sex (*All That Jazz*).

Idealization. The Narcissistic character often deals with self-esteem needs by idealizing other individuals—putting others on pedestals as monuments to perfection. They believe they are special and unique and can only be understood by (or should associate with) other special or high status people. Joe St. George worships Selena, praising her, ogling her, giving her gifts. No criticism of her is tolerated. When Dolores brings up the topic of Selena's poor grades, that is grounds enough for Dolores to be beaten. This idealization maintains the Narcissist's fragile self-esteem through identification with that idealized person. Norma adores Cecil B. DeMille, a man whose taste and artistry she deems above question. He, being a discriminating man, would therefore be the only one worthy of orchestrating Norma's return to the screen.

DENIAL OF REALITY

Narcissists are able to maintain self-esteem by constantly maintaining a steady stream of admiration from external sources. This requires a preoccupation with and constant vigilance over how the Narcissist appears to the outside world. As Norma prepares to start production, "[an] army of beauty experts invaded the house on *Sunset Blvd.*, a merciless series of treatments." Holly Golightly (*Breakfast at Tiffany's*) not only goes to Tiffany's and stares in the windows because it makes her feel special, but also she happily poses for press photographers while being carted off to jail on drug trafficking charges. Becket (after the King of England makes him Archbishop of Canterbury) has one of his many conversations with God, who he also subjects to his egotistical pretense: "I wish there was something I really regretted parting with so that I might offer to you." Even to God, he finds himself unable to sacrifice.

The Narcissistic personality is preoccupied with fantasies of success, power, beauty, and ideal love. Others are never to see how fraudulent, how unloved and unlovable—how inferior—the Narcissist feels inside. The Narcissist's desperate need for grandiose mirroring reflects a denial of reality, a reality of self-destructive habits and an inability to admit the most insignificant of faults. Narcissists are wholly invested in the unquestionable belief in their perfection and are unable to face failure. They run away from mistakes and sabotage those who would uncover them. When Elvira finds Blanche trussed and gagged in her room, Baby Jane goes so far as to murder her. Becket, unwilling to see less than his way, consuls: "We can always come to an arrangement with God." Frustration, difficulties, and imperfections are immediately blamed on an inadequate world. Norma decries the deteriorated state of the movies: "We didn't need dialogue, we had faces! Those idiot producers, have they forgotten what a star looks like? I'll show them!" After Baby Jane kills their dutiful maid with a hammer she wonders "how Elvira could've made me do something like that?" Becket sees himself as "someone who isn't afraid of God." Personal responsibility for shortcomings are not—cannot be—acknowledged. Others, by necessity, must assume blame.

NARCISSISTIC RAGE

This is both an important and a fun characteristic for storytelling. A failure to procure the admiration of others (or to procure enough of it)—called **narcissistic injury** — can result in narcissistic rage. This is an explosive anger not unlike that of a child denied something he believes is rightfully his. The child sees the parent as the source of their shameful feelings of inferiority, so the child must destroy what threatens it. *Becket* (as does Shakespeare's *Othello*) engages an undercurrent of sexual tension between two friends that uses this narcissistic injury—or rage—to drive the main dramatic engine of the story. Becket and King Henry II, Othello and Iago—stories that deliver narcissistic, arrogant men filled with jealousy and rage at not being loved.

Narcissistic characters are prone to quick anger, not only as a result of narcissistic injury, but also because it reinforces their superiority. Baby Jane explodes in rage throughout the film at the slightest word, no matter how innocuous, from Blanche. She also establishes her control and superiority by mocking all of Blanche's attempts to wrest compassion. The alternative—owning up to one's faults and limits and therefore succumbing to depression—would deflate the self-image . . . and that is something that must be avoided at all costs. When Joe leaves Norma, abandonment becomes something she cannot endure: "Shout at me! Strike me! But don't hate me, Joe! Say you don't hate me!" She tries to make him rage because that is something she can understand . . . something that she has created and can control.

NO HAPPY ENDING

When creating a Narcissistic Personality, remember that change often only occurs in life threatening situations. Yet even in such dire conditions, real change rarely occurs. Conditions must be extreme before Narcissists will abandon their self-centered beliefs. Without change, rarely is the outcome good (in fact, it's a safe bet to place your money on "doomed"). Narcissus starved to death, after all, because he would rather admire himself than tend to his corporeal needs. Both Norma Desmond and Baby Jane Hudson go off their respective deep ends. Joe St. George goes down a deep hole. Joe Gideon (*All That Jazz*) kills himself with pills and booze and smoke. *Mishima* kills himself the old-fashioned way: a planned, public ritualistic suicide—being disemboweled while being beheaded. Noah Cross (*Chinatown*) brings about the police killing of his daughter (and the mother of his child). The Marquise de Merteuil (*Dangerous Liaisons*) is publicly humiliated and rendered a social pariah. Raymond's Mother (*The Manchurian Candidate*) is shot dead by her son. Othello (*Othello*) strangles his Desdemona. Becket (*Becket*) martyrs himself on assassins' swords. His own men do in Captain Bligh (*Mutiny on the Bounty*). Col. Kurtz (*Apocalypse Now*) goes stark raving mad. Roy Dillon, Myra Langtry, and Lily (*The Grifters*) viciously do one another in. It's never pretty.

BACKSTORY

In developing the Narcissistic Personality it is important to consider the parental history. A highly critical family environment dominated by extremely demanding parents generally marks the childhood of the Narcissistic character. In such a family the child's primary function is to enhance the mother's or father's self-esteem: the child as accessory (*Mommie Dearest, Gypsy*); the child as proof of the excellence of the parent for producing it. When the child in such a family fails to live up to such stringent parental expectations (which are inevitable), the child will be the target of criticism, either direct or indirect, and suffer rejection. The damage occurs during the child's formative years, a time when nurturing and the discovery and fostering of a functional personality are crucial. King Henry II (*Becket*) demeans, criticizes, and physically abuses his children in much the same way as he was by his father. The Narcissist begets the Narcissist. Sometimes you see a variation on this. Baby Jane's childhood is a textbook scenario. She is well aware of her role as the breadwinner in the family, and she never hesitates to remind everyone of this. The role reversal of parent and child is evident when she chastises her parents for not immediately succumbing to her whim for ice cream. She is a father's stage dream incarnate. She sings to him, about him, and with him. He, starry eyed, is more than happy to use her as an extension of his own ambitions, and he jumps at the chance to join her on stage as her dancing partner. Baby Jane's mother, in turn, is taciturn, withdrawn, a woman who does not speak, smile, or venture a hand in her child's upbringing. Baby Jane is denied nothing and, thus, she develops without forming any of the barriers that entail restraint.

The Narcissist's mother often is emotionally cold and exploitative and tends to disregard her child's need for individuality. Instead of providing the child a healthy role model, she instead wants to use the child as a mirror. She molds the child to meet her own needs instead of guiding the child through its own growth. The emotional relationship is in effect reversed, the child providing the nurturing for the needy parent. Unfortunately, this is confusing to identity and to the formation of the child's nascent psyche. The child grows up frustrated and unable to develop in a positive direction. They are likely to strive in vain for perfection in himself, seeking to be an adequate mirror for a rejecting mother/father in order to gain her/his approval—approval that was withheld during the most crucial period of his early life. Emily Ann Faulkner (*The Goddess*) is motivated throughout her life—from scholastic achievement as a young schoolgirl to Hollywood stardom—by sole end of winning her mother's approval and love, something that was lost to Emily at a very early age. Such children typically grow up with identity confusion as well as with ingrained feelings of shame, emptiness, and inferiority. As a defense against these unpleasant emotions, the child often will exhibit their opposites. They may act contemptuously of others, self-righteous, proud, vain, and superior.

Freud suggested that the parents' selfless adoration of their child creates distortions in the child's self-perception. As children they grow doing as they are told, believing that they are wonderful and brilliant. As these parental distortions continue over the years, the child internalizes them and will develop an exaggerated sense of self-worth. Such children will become grandiose and insufferable. In many cases, the parents are merely trying to resolve their own disappointments in life by centering all of their attention and adulation on their children. They want their child to have it all and not to be subjected to the harsh realities of the same cold, hard life that made them so miserable. The pampered "Baby Princess" (Baby Jane) grows up to be the despotic "Her Majesty" (geriatric Baby Jane). Such a Narcissistic adult is little more than a child—one who is totally astonished when he does not receive the adoration and entitlement he feels is his due. Never forget Norma Desmond's immortal words, insisting, when the subject of her fallen star is broached: "I'm still big! It's pictures that have gotten small!"

THE ARC OF A NARCISSISTIC FILM CHARACTER

The arc of Norma Desmond in *Sunset Blvd.* is not necessarily the arc of the onset of the personality style. "Yesterday's glamour queen" is well past her narcissistic prime when we meet her. Her development has been arrested, her narcissism crystallized. In order not to grow old, she arcs toward psychosis and delusion.

We first meet Norma when Joe Gillis meets her. Like Joe, we find an aging, wealthy crowned head of Hollywood's silent era hermetically sealed in a shrine of her own self-aggrandizement. Images of herself (to the exclusion of all others) fill gilt frames and cover canvasses and play endlessly on the movie screen that she has installed in her living room. She has no qualms about pronouncing herself as the greatest screen idol of all time. Her luster has never diminished; the outside world simply has grown more philistine. She initially wants to throw Joe out, but she is cognizant of the fact that she needs help in assembling the disparate strands of her magnum opus— she is writing the screenplay that she believes will provide her glorious return to adoring fans. The script she is writing for herself is based on the Old Testament story of Salome—a monumental task. Norma knows she needs help finishing it, she decides to hire Joe.

Act Two begins as Joe Gillis is moved into the mansion on *Sunset Blvd.* He soon becomes (as all satellites do when they enter into orbit around a Narcissist) merely another purveyor of praise for the glorification of Norma Desmond. This is also the case with Max, her long suffering, emasculated servant who caters to and anticipates her every whim and keeps her continually supplied with a fresh stream of fabricated fan mail.

Joe not only serves to try to make sense of the vain, meandering script, but he also becomes a nice ornament— a new piece of jewelry on her arm. As such, without regard for his male ego, or his free will, she dresses him up as she chooses, the way she would a new doll. What begins as opportunism on Joe's part—a chance to escape his creditors and perhaps have a bit of a lark—soon descends into something more suffocating from which it might not be as easy as he thought to extricate himself.

Making sense of her behemoth of a script is nigh impossible as she forbids him from cutting any scene that had her in it, and since they all do he is somewhat stymied in his function as editor. Coming up against the monolith of Norma's narcissism proves a more powerful and entangling force than Joe had anticipated. What starts out as merely humoring her rapidly mutates into Norma wielding despotic control over his life. She refuses to let him chew gum, dictates where he sleeps and what he eats, and takes his reassurances that he is not stepping out by asserting that, "No, I won't let you."

The crack in her sealed world that let in the breath of fresh air that is Joe Gillis also serves to fan the fires of her narcissism to greater heights, prompting her to send her script to Cecil B. DeMille. This act allows her to fall fully headlong into a delusion of glamour and adoration from the masses. As her descent into psychosis picks up speed, Joe attempts to disentangle himself. This elicits a narcissistic rage from Norma that culminates in slashed wrists and brandished pistols.

In Act Three, Norma, freed from the constraints of reality, goes on a rampage. Ferociously jealous of Betty Shaffer, who she (correctly, by the way) suspects of having special feelings for Joe, she surreptitiously calls her and insinuates that Joe is an opportunistic monster, thus vanquishing her competition. When Joe at last tries to leave, he is no match for the awesome force of a narcissistic ego that has been left to ferment for decades: "We're not helping her, feeding her lies and more lies." When her threats of yet another suicide attempt fail to elicit Joe's concern, her delusions take a homicidal bent. "No one leaves a star . . . that's what makes one a star," she says and then points the gun at Joe.

After the murder, she is completely lost: "What is this scene? Where am I?" She can only be coaxed down to the waiting police car by the lure of Max saying, "Lights! Camera! Action!" Even then there's trouble because she's too damned happy, having once again found the spotlight she needs to do the scene properly.

THE NARCISSISTIC PERSONALITY
SUMMARY

Examples of the qualities and qualifications that define a person with a Narcissistic Personality:

- They tend to have active fantasy lives that revolve around their own grandiosity
- Their grandiosity bleeds into their behavior as well. They carry themselves in a grandiose way
- They display an unquenchable need for admiration
- They show a notable absence of empathy
- They have an overly inflated sense of self-importance
- They are preoccupied with dreams and fantasies of unlimited and unequaled power, beauty, intelligence, success, and idealized love
- They believe that they are special, a notch above all others
- They believe that they can only be truly appreciated and understood by other special people
- They desire to associate only with other special people. All others are beneath them, and any association with such a person would tarnish their luster
- They have a continual and insatiable need for admiration and praise
- They have a belief that they are intrinsically entitled to more than they have earned or deserve
- They tend to exploit any relationship that comes their way. No one is too sacred not to be used for the optimal benefit and betterment of the Narcissist
- They are unwilling to acknowledge the feelings or needs of others
- They tend to be obsessively envious of others and usually believe that others are covetous of all their possessions and attributes

- They tend to be arrogant
- They tend to be haughty
- They tend to be dismissive of anyone they deem as being of lower rank
- They tend to focus on themselves to an inordinate degree during conversations
- They tend to have fantasies of omnipotence
- They relentlessly pursue self-perfection
- Internally, they may feel phony and unlovable
- They secretly harbor fears of being weak, unworthy, insufficient, or inferior
- They often hide feelings of shame
- They generally overestimate their own talents and attributes
- They tend to be highly judgmental
- They tend to be preoccupied with ranking
- They tend to hold themselves up to impossible standards and unrealistic ideals
- They may elevate chosen others to the rank of perfect and then identify with that idealized person and thereby inflate themselves through the association
- They direfully need others in their life, but their love for those others is shallow
- They expect special treatment
- They handle criticism poorly. They react with either rage or indifference. Narcissistic injury
- They are usually very ambitious
- They insist on having their own way
- Their relationships are tenuous
- They often refuse to obey conventional rules of behavior
- They are usually prone to depression
- They handle aging poorly

NOTEWORTHY CHARACTERISTICS
OF THE NARCISSISTIC PERSONALITY

SPEECH

Attention seeking. A grandiose style. Self-centered in tone. Manipulative. Sarcastic. Often a very technical and/or impressive use of words and phrases. For the sake of attention, it can also be the opposite—silent, clipped, wounded.

PROFESSIONS

Acting, politics, medicine, law. Center of attention. Top in field.

DRESS

Dress to impress. Dress to make a statement. Dress to rebel. For the sake of attention, they may dress down to be noticed.

HEALTH

Due to the inability to express feelings, they often convert into physical ailments. Polar reactions occur: self-obsessed about health or don't care. Substance abuse issues. Addictive difficulties. Unrealistic view of body leads to obsession with such things as plastic surgery, tension issues, migraines, gastrointestinal difficulties, and eating disorders.

POPULAR CLICHÉS
ASSOCIATED WITH NARCISSISTS

- S.O.B.
- Ice Princess
- Puppet Master
- Workaholic
- Snob
- Egotist
- Diva
- Self-centered
- Entitled
- Schemer
- Self-anointed
- Arrogant
- Smart aleck
- Wise guy
- Conceited
- Insolent
- Brazen

SIMILAR PERSONALITY TYPES
TO THE NARCISSISTIC

- THE ANTISOCIAL PERSONALITY
- THE HISTRIONIC PERSONALITY
- THE BORDERLINE PERSONALITY
- THE OBSESSIVE-COMPULSIVE PERSONALITY

VIEWING SUGGESTIONS FOR
THE NARCISSISTIC PERSONALITY

8 1/2 (1963)—Drama, 135, No rating.
> Great study of the business at hand. Winner of Best Foreign Film. Nominated for the writing.

All About Eve (1950)—Drama, 138, No rating.
> For Anne Baxter as Eve—the quintessential Narcissist. Won the Oscar for Best Screenplay (amongst many others).

All That Jazz (1979)—Musical/Dance, 123, Rated R.
> Dark and brutally honest confession of self-absorption in the entertainment business. Nominated for an Oscar for the writing.

Apartment, The (1960)—Drama/Comedy, 125, No rating.
> For Fred MacMurray as the ultimate heel, Sheldrake. One of the last times to see this star play an undesirable soul. Took home the Academy Award for Best Screenplay.

Barton Fink (1991)—Drama/Comedy, 117, Rated R.
> Satirical and stylish representation of narcissism embodied by Hollywood-as-industry.

Becket (1964)—Historical/Drama, 148, No rating.
> Interesting look at narcissism not only in a costume drama, but also for the fact the personality is on full display in two (Becket and Henry II) characters. Both O'Toole and Burton were nominated for Best Actor in the same film. Amongst its many Oscar nominations, it won for the writing. Flawless fun.

Breakfast at Tiffany's (1961)—Drama, 115, No rating.
Gloriously fun film based on a story by
Truman Capote.

Butley (1974)—Drama, 127, Rated R.
Alan Bates gives a layered performance as
Ben Butley. A solid adaptation of the stage
play that examines the real-life nature of
narcissism.

Chinatown (1974)—Mystery, 131, Rated R.
For John Huston's portrayal of Noah Cross.
Nominated for eleven Oscars. Robert Towne
won for Original Screenplay.

Citizen Kane (1941)—Drama, 119, No rating.
Great character study of the successful
Narcissist. Oscar winner of Best Original
Screenplay (one of nine it took home).

Dangerous Liaisons (1988)—Drama, 120, Rated R.
Wonderful example of narcissism—Glenn
Close as Marquise Merteuil.

Day of the Locust, The (1975)—Drama, 144, Rated R.
Dark telling of one writer's experience in
Hollywood.

Dolores Claiborne (1995)—Thriller/Mystery/Drama, 131,
Rated R.
Accurately written portrayal of father-as-
sexual-abuser. David Strathairn as Joe St.
George in a performance as remorseless as it
is brilliant.

Ed Wood (1994)—Drama/Comedy/Biography, 124, Rated R.
Off beat and wonderful telling of a true life
Hollywood oddity.

Entertainer, The (1960)—Drama, 97, No rating.
Theater egos on shining display, this time with the help of the formidable Laurence Olivier as Archie Rice, an egotistical vaudevillian set on making everyone's life miserable.

Goddess, The (1958)—Drama, 105, No rating.
Writer Paddy Chayefsky's take on narcissism and the superstars it creates. Oscar nominated for the writing.

Lawrence of Arabia (1962)—War/Biography/Adventure, 216, No rating.
Peter O'Toole' star-making performance as T. E. Lawrence. Robert Bolt was Oscar nominated for his writing.

Manchurian Candidate, The (1962)—Political/Thriller, 126, No rating.
Angela Landsbury's Academy Award nominated performance as the dominating mother of all mothers.

Mishima (1985)—Biography, 120, Rated R.
True life bio that is as visually stunning as it is clinically calculated.

Mutiny on the Bounty (1935)—Adventure, 132, No rating.
For Charles Laughton as Captain Bligh.

Network (1976)—Drama, 121, Rated R.
Several great examples of narcissism in show biz. Chayefsky won the deserved Oscar for writing. Keep an eye on Faye Dunaway.

Othello (1952)—Drama, 92, No rating.
> Iago: one of the finest examples of well-engineered narcissism.Versions also made in:
> 1965—Drama, 166, No rating.
> 1995—Drama, 123, Rated R.

Player, The (1992)—Comedy, 123, Rated R.
> Dark, funny take on what we have come to expect from life in Hollywood. Michael Tolkin's script was nominated for an Oscar.

Rose, The (1979)—Drama/Musical, 134, Rated R.
> A retelling of the Janis Joplin story. Bette Midler's screen debut as Rose.

sex, lies, and videotape (1989)—Drama, 100, Rated R.
> Narcissism as a theme. Nominated for an Academy Award for the writing.

Stunt Man, The (1980)—Drama/Comedy, 129, Rated R.
> Peter O'Toole as self-righteous Eli Cross. Oscar nominated performance and script.

Sunset Blvd. (1950)—Drama, 110, No rating.
> The greatest of them all.

Sweet Bird of Youth (1962)—Drama, 120, No rating.
> Geraldine Page as Alexandra Del Lago. Remade in 1989.

Twentieth Century (1934)—Comedy, 91, No rating.
> John Barrymore as Oscar Jaffe, an egocentric Broadway producer. A hilarious send-up of the personality.

What Ever Happened to Baby Jane? (1962)—Thriller/
Comedy, 132, No rating.
> For Bette Davis as Baby Jane. One of her
> wickedest and wildest.

White Hunter, Black Heart (1990)—Drama/Adventure,
112, Rated PG.
> Terrific behind the scenes bio of John
> Huston's infamous filming of *The African
> Queen.*

Withnail & I (1987)—Drama, 105, Rated R.
> For Richard E. Grant's dead-on portrayal of
> the self absorbed actor, Withnail.

PRIOR TO READING THE NEXT CHAPTER
IT IS RECOMMENDED THAT THE FOLLOWING
FILMS BE VIEWED:

WHO'S AFRAID OF VIRGINIA WOOLF?
MRS. PARKER AND THE VICIOUS CIRCLE
FATAL ATTRACTION

A LIST OF FILMS PERTAINING TO THE
BORDERLINE PERSONALITY CAN BE FOUND
AT THE END OF THIS CHAPTER.

5

THE BORDERLINE PERSONALITY

I swear, if you existed, I'd divorce you.
—Martha / Edward Albee, Ernest Lehman

GEORGE AND MARTHA (Elizabeth Taylor and Richard Burton, *Who's Afraid of Virginia Woolf?*) are denizens of a small college campus and locked in a marriage that is less a marriage than it is an ongoing bloodsport. They spar. They wound. Eventually, they annihilate. Their weapons of choice in their ongoing feud are their merciless tongues and their eloquence with insults; both fueled by their seething, decades old pain. There can only be destruction in the spectrum of Martha's emotions, which isn't so much a spectrum as it is merely two points between which she flies with startling and unpredictable speed.

When two unnamed guests arrive they act as catalysts, transforming George and Martha's taste for blood into an all-out hunger. Actually, the two guests do have names— Nick and Honey—but that is all but lost on George and Martha. They don't need names because all the people in George and Martha's sphere merely serve as pawns in their all-consuming black hole of a union from which no light can escape. The man is simply the newest biology professor and his mate is "a wifey little mouse." They serve as unwitting victims caught in the path of destruction as they are initiated into the academia of New Carthage College (which, after this particular evening, should be re-christened New Carnage College).

Dorothy Parker (Jennifer Jason Leigh), the Mrs. Parker in *Mrs. Parker and the Vicious Circle*, is known as a writer, a wit, and a charter member of the Edwardian New York City Theater world glitterati. She is a woman of fierce intelligence—and equally fierce self-destruction—with undeniable talent, even genius, not only for the bon mot and her acerbic humor, but also for choosing the wrong men. She stumbles through a society of literature and drama, drinking her way through good times and bad, alienating friends and foes alike, and falling in love with married or abusive men. Occasionally, she will even write.

She moves from hovel to hotel, yearning for recognition and love, yet scorning it when it is offered. She is as brutal in her criticism of herself as she is with the hands that feed her (her various employers and the other members of New York's literary elite). She is fired from jobs because of her obduracy and she is left broken and alone by a string of men whom she can only insult.

In New York, Dan Gallagher (Michael Douglas) meets Alex Forrest (Glenn Close) in *Fatal Attraction*. What starts off as a simple, recreational extramarital romp soon becomes something much more disturbing and unpredictable—and dangerous. Alex goes from amorous to suicidal in a heartbeat; from rational to raving at the faintest perceived slight. Dan tries to circumvent the damage to both Alex and his family, but his attempts at rationality fall on irrational ears. Things become very tense as Alex insinuates her life into Dan's family just as her behavior becomes increasingly more violent.

THE ROCKY ROAD

The Borderline Personality is one that is defined by consistent patterns of instability in relationships with others as well is in self-image. Borderlines have little if any impulse control and suffer a pervasive sense of loneliness and depression. They can exhibit emotions that appear excessive—larger than life—and these emotions can be highlighted by rapid mood swings. They worry about being engulfed and losing identity while at the same time maintaining fears of abandonment.They often place demands on relationships with an air of entitlement that overwhelms and alienates their partners or friends. There is an inability to plan and a marked incapacity to defend against primitive impulses. They are unable to stop these impulses (usually the negative kind), unable to let their conscious be their guide to their behavior. They experience alternating and contradicting views of themselves. This tendency leads them to apply the same polar-extreme outlook to others (good people vs. bad people; Heaven vs. Hell). Characteristics include loneliness, emptiness, suicidal gestures, conscious rage, demanding natures, hostile and dependent relationships mixed with a great concern for interpersonal loss.

The Borderline Personality is a bastard breed, a dumpsite for categorizing those individuals that "sort of are" and "sort of aren't." The term, Borderline, first came to prominence in the 1950s and early 1960s as a way to describe patients who were exhibiting signs that classified them most commonly as neurotic. The difference with these individuals was that time and again their behavior was "on the border" of psychosis. These Borderline individuals have a variety of symptoms such as anxiety, obsessive/compulsive behavior, multiple phobias, sexually compulsive behavior, and substance abuse. As an interesting side note, three quarters of those diagnosed are women.

Although not constantly lost in a world of psychosis, these Borderline individuals do have episodes—called **micropsychotic episodes**. These individuals are termed **Borderline Delusional**. Over the years, Martha (*Who's Afraid of Virginia Woolf?*) has progressively moved closer and closer to a complete break. "You've moved bag and baggage into your fantasy world," George tells Martha. Her micropsychotic episodes have, you could say, become less small. Martha responds: "You make excuses—maybe tomorrow he'll be dead, maybe you'll be dead—then something happens one night and it goes snap." Mrs. Parker is also shown to be getting progressively less healthy. After having been tossed aside yet again—or having pushed her man away—she falls into bed with nothing but a bottle. Her dog is starving, as is she. Dorothy tells the animal, "We don't want to have a breakdown—messes kill us." Straddling the borderline, Dorothy is neurotic enough to sense the impending psychosis. It is also becoming clearer to those around her that her grip on her life is slackening. Her friend Robert Benchley objectively observes later: "You were a mess, bloody and drooling. You were pathetic and disgusting."

Borderline characters have the uncanny ability to create and sustain an environment of unhappiness in their day to day lives. Yet with the Borderline, it is something more than a garden-variety ennui they have grown accustomed to living with. Borderline Personalities have the rare capability of being miserable on a much grander and much more incomprehensible scale. They are volatile, edgy, unpredictable characters and are a boon for investing a scene with tension, because a viewer never knows what the Borderline will do next or when he will next explode. This personality has been called the "as if" personality—as in, "it is as if they suddenly went crazy!" George describes Martha's unpredictable behavior and rationale when, after the visiting biology professor expresses a polite interest in their abstract expressionist painting, George replies, "It's a pictorial representation of the order of Martha's mind." Snide, maybe, but perhaps accurate. Martha herself is not unaware of the volatility that characterizes their household. She freely admits that "it gets pretty bouncy around here." Borderline Personalities will keep life bouncy, rocky, and fraught with anxiety. The stories of these characters will never be labeled smooth sailing. A friend of Mrs. Parker describes her erratic lifestyle: "You're an artist, Dorothy. Sometimes artists lose their balance."

Borderline characters in films are a mongrel batch. It is a melting pot universe with crossover personalities well on their way to (if not the real thing) their own personal hells. There are the lethal ones (*Fatal Attraction, Misery, Fear*); the mother-monsters (*The Grifters, Mommie Dearest*); a boatload of drunks and substance abusers (*Leaving Las Vegas, The Lost Weekend, Under The Volcano, The Man with the Golden Arm, Pulp Fiction, Drugstore Cowboy, Bad Lieutenant*). And then there are those who simply seem lost (*Blue Velvet, Mrs. Parker and the Vicious Circle, A Woman Under the Influence*).

The Borderline's self destruction is a repetitive self-destruction. Self-mutilation, suicide attempts, and monumental substance abuse are merely ways to garner attention and express anger, or sometimes are used to numb themselves from themselves. In *Fear* (a shameless but solid knock-off of *Fatal Attraction* for teens), David slugs himself until he is bruised and carves the name of his beloved into his chest. Both Mrs. Parker and Martha prove highly self-destructive—abusing alcohol to such a degree as to make a sailor blush. Alex's (*Fatal Attraction*) first recourse when she doesn't get her way is to slash her wrists . . . and it works— Dan stays the night. Borderline characters, although they attempt suicide, are rarely intent on truly killing themselves. Suicide threats usually turn out to be just that, or, at the most, truncated efforts. They signal not so much a wish to die as they do depression over what the Borderline character perceives as abandonment. Borderlines need to counteract the despair by forcing someone to care, forcing rescue. Alex is very successful in this. When Dan goes to leave, she feels abandoned, so she slashes her wrists—not, of course, waiting for him to leave—and he stays and looks after her, spending another night.

Mrs. Parker also takes to slashing her wrists, but only after calling up room service and ordering dinner sent to her rooms—thus ensuring she will be found before it's too late. It is not a desire to cease to live, but a clarion cry to draw attention to her life and the misery that defines it. Mrs. Parker, hardly born yesterday, is quick to exploit it. At F. Scott and Zelda Fitzgerald's apres-midi she is confronted with a request: "Do honor us with one of your darling poems." Dorothy swills some liquor and humorlessly recites *Resume*—a poem detailing the most popular avenues of killing oneself. The assemblage is left stunned as she leaves the bandstand and heads to the bushes for casual sex.

Martha, at least within the time confines of the film, has not tried overt suicide, but she certainly displays other multifold talents for obtaining attention. As George says: "there isn't an abomination award going that you haven't won." She does enjoy doing battle, after all, and she and George have their confrontation to the death. Both are left annihilated.

MISERY

Mrs. Parker counsels: "A dependable fact of life, is everything is always worse than you thought it would be."

Profound emptiness is one of the key components of the Borderline character. Alex is so desperately alone that she insists on carrying Dan's baby in the hopes that it will force him into building a life with her. This unsettling emptiness is chronic. Borderlines are stricken with boredom and lack of fulfillment; Martha is literally screaming to be set free. Their lives, they feel, have been disappointing to themselves and to others. Mrs. Parker feels that she is a failure as a wife, a friend, and a writer; Martha feels she has squandered the one advantage that she had (being the dean's daughter) by marrying a man who wasn't ambitious enough. Their lives (so they feel) are predestined toward misery.

This emptiness endemic to the Borderline is perhaps no more poignantly portrayed than with Martha and her son, a "blue-haired and blond-eyed" heir to the couple's misery. She is alone, trapped and strangled in her "vile sewer of a marriage." Having completely pushed away her husband and unable to bear children, she has (with George's complicity) created an imaginary child, "Sonny Jim." When George commits the coup de grace and decides that Sonny Jim has died in a car accident, Martha is so broken and wrenched she can no longer fight. Disconsolate, she laments, "Who said, 'yes, this will do?' Who made the mistake of loving me? I must be punished for it."

As with the Histrionic Personality, the thought pattern of the Borderline is global—they think in the general, the extreme, and they don't concern themselves with nuance. The Borderline is not wont to ponder—instead, they react. They weigh and consider issues; they flit impetuously from thought to unconnected thought. And as seen in the Histrionic, deep reflection is avoided, because it usually proves uncomfortable. The Borderline is only too aware of the constant state of misery in which they live. To dwell, to stop for a moment to consider it, would prove devastatingly painful. An initial look at Rob Reiner and Stephen King's *Misery* might indicate the title is being used to describe Paul's (James Caan) condition for most of the movie. On closer examination it is not only the misery of the snared novelist that is of King's concern, but also the internal misery of the isolated woman (Kathy Bates).

Splitting

The most apparent behavior of Borderline characters is, customarily, their absolute division of the world and all its contents into extremes—all good and all bad. There are no fuzzy boundary lines here, no subtle distinctions. Interesting, since the criterion that defines them is filled with fuzzy boundaries and few subtle distinctions. This is what psychologist's call **splitting**. These characters can seem to have different personalities with different people at different times or they can seem to run hot and cold with the same person within any given moment. Primitive impulses take over. One moment they are throwing kisses, the next kitchen knives ("It's as if they went nuts!"). One minute Alex is declaring her undying love for Dan, the next she is screaming that she wants him dead. This happens no more notably than when she leaves him a cassette tape recording. At first she is a woman in love, cooing, "I feel you, I taste you, I think you, I touch you." But Alex's monologue rapidly dissolves into a hate-filled diatribe as she graphically details what she imagines to be his sexual preference for other males. If he does not love her, it must be because he's a homosexual. At F. Scott Fitzgerald's garden party, a dashing young man who has made a bet that he could make her smile approaches Mrs. Parker. She dismisses him with a scathing remark. Still, he pursues her. She then interrupts his banter about his family's bird sanctuary with a long sloppy kiss and leads him into the topiary for a passionate quickie. She emerges, no longer amorous but instead acerbic. She tells him, "Don't worry, Roger. I don't review rehearsals," and then leaves him. Martha, too, can swing pendulously from scalding to freezing on a dime. One moment she tells George, "You make me puke," and the next she's leaping on him, girlishly begging for a wet kiss. "Once a month we get good," George says after finally being pushed to the limits of his endurance, when he has finally given up hope of ever finding the "girl beneath the barnacles, the little miss, that the touch of goodness will bring to bloom again." The relationships in which the Borderline becomes enmeshed can be exasperating. George simply has had his fill and declares a personal war.

The defenses of the Borderline Personality are very primitive. Their transferences are strong and anything but ambivalent. They idealize people, bequeathing unto them godlike virtue and power. Alex's attachment (though unearned) is unshakable. They may as quickly devalue others as weak and contemptible. Martha maintains an unceasing tirade against George and embarks on a spiteful quest to cuckold him, not so much for her own pleasure as for George's humiliation.

Borderlines also tend to shift their allegiance from one person or group to another with great ease and frequency. With Martha, George is History; the new professor is Biology. She devalues George: "I swear, if you existed I'd divorce you." She calls him, alternately and repeatedly, "cluck", "dumbbell", "simp", "muff monkey", "old bog", and "swampy." The new professor, nevertheless, is "good-looking, well built," and doesn't "need any props . . . no fake guns for him." She calls him "baby" and "stuff." But she is ruthlessly quick to do an about face, calling her once-idealized new friend "a houseboy" and George the "one man in my life that's made me happy." Mrs. Parker sobs when she loses her job at Vanity Fair: "I've wrecked my career. Kindly direct me to hell." She is so glorious a part of the Algonquin Round Table that she is its poster child; yet when asked of it later, she responds by claiming that they were "a bunch of loud mouths showing off . . . they're shit, really. A funny thing to say about your best friends . . . they should have called it the dingy decade." Her only true allegiance is to her own misery.

It aids understanding to imagine Borderline Personalities as often living in their own little impermeable bubbles of despair. Because of their tendency to polarize the world into the idealized or the devalued, they regularly appear to be always in a crisis, always in some sort of dilemma. George: "Unless you're carrying on like a hyena, you're not having a good time." Of Mrs. Parker: "Your passion for unhappiness is goddamned endless." Alex is a whirlwind, either taking Dan with her on a vertiginous weekend during which she cannot even get into an elevator without having sex, or stalking him—abducting his daughter and killing the family rabbit. There is no calm, except when she is left alone, and then her feelings of abandonment all but leave her catatonic with emptiness.

RELATIONSHIPS

The relationships of the Borderline are overwhelmingly patterned by instability. This is because of their habit of alternating idealization and devaluation. They pick you up, they throw you down. Simply put, they are exhausting to be around. "I'm numb enough that I can take you when we're alone," George tells Martha. But he is more patient (or more spineless) than most.

Borderline characters may be prone to panic when they get close to another person—they fear being engulfed, being totally controlled. Mrs. Parker's friends can see her predicament, perhaps with leveler heads than hers: "if a man pursued her, she wouldn't be interested, but let a man pursue another woman, and she will fall deliriously in love. Claws flashing, tears falling." Yet when they feel separate, they experience the trauma of abandonment. They feel both dependent and hostile, because they fear immanent abandonment whenever they do feel dependent. "George and Martha. Sad, sad, sad," Martha sadly muses. "Some night, some stupid liquor-ridden night, I'll push him too far, break his back or push him away, which is what I deserve." For her part, Mrs. Parker refers to herself as "Mrs. Parker" even though her marriage to Mr. Parker ended decades earlier. She cannot tolerate being a "Miss." Perhaps most telling in this case: "I could kiss you," she tells Benchley, "but I'm afraid I'd lose you."

Borderline Personalities cannot bear to be alone and usually are on a frantic search for companionship because being involved (no matter how unsatisfactory the actual relationship) is infinitely better than being left to themselves. Neither closeness nor distance is comfortable. Alex knew full well from the start that Dan was married, and even made him promise that he was discrete. She, of course, turned out to be anything but. She clings unreasonably and inappropriately to Dan, attempting everything from suicide to having his baby in order to get him to stay by her side. The Borderline Personality often takes in strangers as friends (*Leaving Las Vegas, The Man With the Golden Arm, The Lost Weekend*), or they are frequently promiscuous (*Blue Velvet, Fear, Fatal Attraction*). Whether friends or bed partners (most often both), they form frighteningly strong connections to people they have just met. Martha lures the biology professor: "encourage me," she begs him, shaking her already shaky physique. She eventually beds him and, like clockwork, emasculates him: "You're certainly a flop in some departments." Mrs. Parker seems to have found the root of all her problems: "I wish I'd never learned to take off my clothes." Their relationships are brief but intense. They tend to begin sexual conduct early in dating (if they haven't already taken care of it after the first "hello"). Mrs. Parker takes one look at Charles MacArthur and declares, "I may have him mounted."

The Borderline's black and white outlook applies likewise with love. There is nothing of courtship or the falling into it. Borderline characters are either in love or in hate. Alex is honestly surprised when Dan wonders why she is trying to hurt him—this after she has assaulted, threatened, and deceived him. She genuinely has no idea what he's talking about: "Why are you so hostile," she says. "I'm not your enemy. I love you." Mrs. Parker announces (quite accurately): "I'm going to wear my heart on my sleeve like a wet, red stain." She falls impulsively and tempestuously in love. "Would you like a drink before I kiss you?" she says to Charles MacArthur when she meets him. The next morning she announces to the Round Table that they are engaged, yet she derides him almost immediately after consummating their passion. She calls MacArthur, "Mr. Vomit." Her husband, Alan, is referred to as "a queer."

This denigration is usually automatic. It is a primitive devaluation. Little, if any, thought goes into the impulse or the consequences of it. These personalities readily find faults and flaws in others, especially mates (or prospects thereto), to bolster their own low sense of self-worth. They find it important to program failure from the start so as not to be blamed or surprised when they yet again crawl from the wreckage of a spoiled relationship: a "vicious circle" of abandonment/engulfment/salvation/annihilation.

DIMINISHED SENSE OF SELF

Borderline characters perceive the population as being either nurturing (attachment figures) or, by default, as being hateful. If hateful, others are seen as sadistic creatures bent on depriving them of the security Borderlines need and representing the dark, foreboding thunderhead of the always looming abandonment they so fear. Again a polarization into all good, all bad. This incapability to observe the complexity of others is mirrored in their views of themselves. They have difficulty with their identity integration, which is to say their experience of themselves is likely to be full of inconsistency and discontinuity. They are at a loss, generally, when they are asked to describe themselves. Alex is truly shocked when her spite and violence are not seen as signs of love. Martha describes herself as an Earth Mother when she is in fact the farthest thing from the nurturing, fecund symbol of enveloping warmth. Annie (*Misery*) does not understand why her guest/prisoner Paul Sheldon is so ungrateful at her need to take a sledgehammer to his feet and crush them. She is, after all, only trying to help him be a better writer.

The Borderline Personality is repeatedly incapable of complex, ambiguous emotions or unconditional love. When asked to describe important people in their lives, they can only manage some sort of global, reductive description. Mrs. Parker says of her mother: "I suppose she loved me, kept me warm, fed me roughage. Truth is, I can never remember being loved." Her psychiatrist tells her, "It's good remembering." She shoots back, "I'm not remembering. I'm guessing." Both Martha and Alex treat their respective objects of obsession alternately as omnipotent figures—the life's blood of their lives—or as worthless, ineffectual, impotent weaklings.

Borderlines are hard pressed to manage an evocative, humanizing description, because they cannot perceive it. Being unable to grasp the innate complexity of people (especially their own complexity) causes them to react with hostility if the subject is ever broached. They have unstable and distorted self-images, and their ability to acknowledge their own pathology is limited. They may seem resistant to offers of help because they don't see a need for help. They see no reason to perform any soul searching or changing of their ways because they simply don't see a problem. In fact, they perceive offers of help as attacks, or at the very least, as criticism. They have never known differently, never had a different character type with which to compare normalcy. They lack the emotional concept of empathy and have no idea what mature defenses must feel like. They see no ambiguity in their environment, and the ability to defer gratification is not one that would occur to them. They simply do not see what all the fuss is about. In fact, they may look on those who don't share these personality traits as abnormal.

The instability and mercurial volatility of their perception of others is reflected in the control they exhibit over

186 | Howard M. Gluss, Ph.D. with Scott Edward Smith

their impulses. They have little of it. They are prone to sudden and startling mood swings and their behavior is erratic and unpredictable. Some of the greatest and most startling moments in the history of film are the result of such frenzy: Annie and her mallet, Alex's "I won't be ignored," Joan's "No more wire hangers," Dorothy Vallens and her S/M lovemaking. When it is anger, it is intense and almost always inappropriate (usually these outbursts are volcanic, but short-lived). Such impulsive behavior is potentially damaging, and not just socially or amorously—like their lack of control over anger, Borderlines similarly lack control over impulses related to eating, alcohol, drugs, and sex. They are fond of binges, which fits in well with their penchant for self-destruction. In nearly all the films involving Borderline Personalities, the characters are shown as having tried or about to try suicide (razor, bottle, pills, whatever) if not homicide. Their self-destruction is a way of life. Both Mrs. Parker and Martha drink whiskey by the tumble full. Mrs. Parker only wants enough money "to keep body and soul apart." As for sex, Martha is on the biology professor like a poodle on a stew bone. Mrs. Parker can't be bothered waiting for a bedroom—she drags men into the bushes at a garden party. Alex cannot wait to get Dan into the bedroom and sexually engages him over a sink of dirty dishes.

GUILTLESS

It is important to keep in mind when creating Borderlines that they are in fact Borderline and not psychotic. An important difference here is that Borderlines do have a hold on reality, albeit perhaps distorted. Though both make plausible lethal killers, there is a good deal of psychological terrain between Alex (*Fatal Attraction*) and Hannibal Lecter (*Silence of the Lambs*). A significant difference is that Borderlines usually do not find anything wrong

with their behavior. Though they are aware of their pathology, they think that it's justified. Mrs. Parker is not
unaware of her behavior, and laments: "the years I've wasted being a party girl and a smart ass." Martha is also aware
of who she is: "I'm loud and I'm vulgar and I wear the
pants in the family 'cause someone's got to. I'm not a monster." Alex is only too aware of her actions. She keeps insisting that she will play fair if Dan will. Her spiraling into
psychosis leads her to believe that Dan is somehow avoiding his responsibility. She feels her escalating violence is
justified and forewarned. In contrast, Hannibal Lecter
knows very well that he is the personification of evil.

Because of this lack of flexibility or precision in their
thinking, Borderlines rarely lives up to their abilities and
potential. This too becomes a marked and defining trait—
the tendency to fail at careers. Martha does little but
harangue and decry her lot in life, thinking that she has
blown the opportunity of a lifetime being the dean's
daughter and marrying a less than ambitious and stagnant
man such as George. Mrs. Parker also feels she could have
amounted to more: "I know better than to expect anything
from myself. . . . I fall in love with married men, but I do it
on purpose. I drink too much, because I'm thirsty."

BACKSTORY

Borderline Personalities learn the behavior that classi-
fies them early in life, from their families . . . families in
which catastrophe is a way of life, where no one pays attention unless you are threatening mayhem. Trauma, especially incest, is often now thought of as instrumental in the formation of the Borderline Personality (a strong case for why
women are diagnosed more often than men).

Clinically speaking, the Borderline Personality is fixated at the separation-individuation process. They are
trapped in the notorious "terrible twos." They have been

frozen at the time when a degree of autonomy has been attained, yet the individual still needs reassurance that the parents remain available and powerful. The mother figure may discourage separation out of fear of abandonment (most likely being Borderline or Narcissistic herself). Or she refuses to be there when the child needs to regress after some independence has been achieved. The mother has aggravated issues with her children growing up and this plight does not go unfelt by the child. As the child reaches for independence, it feels the fear of abandonment. The mother (consumed in her own Narcissistic or Borderline Personality) does nothing to create for the child an internal image of mother. And since this internal sense of motherhood (security) is vital to our growth as individuals—it leaves the borderline child ill prepared if not unable to face separation.

It is not surprising that regression comes easily to the Borderline Personality. Martha often reverts to *baby-speak* with George when she needs affection. She might be sitting on his lap just before throwing herself into a rage and declaring war unto the death. "Daddy knows how to run things," she says, still the spoiled daddy's girl. Annie (*Misery*) uses a similar baby-speak with phrases such as "Mister Man" when addressing Paul. Dorothy Vallens (*Blue Velvet*) exposes her moments of "lost little girl" in the middle of sex.

Ultimately, it is an issue of the child who becomes confused by the conflicting message of the mother who has difficulty with internalizing nurturing relationships. These states of confusion will oftentimes create a depressive reaction in the child coupled with intense feelings of emptiness, rage, and fear. Many times the child will experience psychotic fragmentation as it desperately attempts to ward off feelings of panic due to an internal terror of being annihilated or smothered. Unfortunately, the negative experience of one parent is seldom counterbalanced by a positive experience of the other. In addition to the mother's pathological behavior, the father is generally attributed with being distant, uncaring, and sadistic in his control. Purgatory appears to be the defining state for the Borderline child. Trauma-rich psychodynamic conditions of child rearing appear to be coupled with a high degree of child physical abuse, sexual abuse, psychological abuse, and neglect. The duration and intensity of the abuse will have a major impact on the development of pathology. As a result of developmental and abusive conditions, the development of the Borderline individual is one of extreme complexity with no one factor contributing the definitive psychological blow.

THE ARC OF A BORDERLINE FILM CHARACTER

In *Fatal Attraction*, we first meet Alex Forrest when Dan Gallagher first meets her—at a cocktail party given by the publishing firm that employs Dan as legal council and Alex as an associate editor. With her leonine mane, Alex is the picture of confident (if predatory) female ambition. At their second meeting, the sexual attraction between Alex and Dan becomes blatant, and it's not long before Alex seduces Dan (after he assures her that he is discreet) and they are copulating over a sink full of dirty dishes. Dan soon discovers that Alex may have a slight problem with abandonment issues. He leaves her apartment the next morning, prompting her to call him angrily: "What happened? I woke up and you weren't here. I hate that!" She manages to coerce him into spending yet another day together. "You just don't give up, do you?" he says. So he gives in, even at the expense of spending the day in the country with his wife, Beth. When Dan again tries to leave, Alex attacks him verbally and physically—literally kicking him out of her bed. Before he can leave, she falls sobbing into his arms with slashed wrists. The first cracks in Alex's fragile psyche have become apparent.

In Act Two, Dan tries delicately to extricate himself from the situation, but he has little luck. Alex shows up to his office uninvited. She is contrite and apologetic. She seems marginally lucid. She blames her self-destructive gestures on the fact that "it was a bad time and everything was coming to a crisis." She then invites Dan to the opera. He declines.

But Alex (as she proclaims later) "won't be ignored." She is increasingly falling across the line into psychosis. Her life is empty. She is becoming dangerously bitter and resentful. She has outbursts of (alternately) obsessive clinging neediness and violent, vitriolic tirades of undiluted rage. Her time at home is spent listening to *Madame Butterfly* alone and crying—that and repeatedly calling Dan's home number only to hang up when his wife answers. When she finally gets Dan to agree to see her, he asks her why she is trying to hurt him. She is honestly shocked at the accusation: "I'm not!" she says, "I love you!" When he demands that she put an end to their "imaginary affair," she plays her trump card: she tells him that she is pregnant.

Dan doesn't know whether or not to believe her, but he knows he must end all communication with Alex. He changes his phone number and refuses to see her at work. When Alex can't get the operator to give her the new phone number (despite her intimidating use of salty language), she infiltrates his home by posing as a prospective home-buyer and gets the new number from Beth. Dan counters this by moving out to the country. Alex matches him by dousing his car with acid and completely ruining it. She also gives him an audiocassette that telescopes her descent into madness, her crossing the Borderline into full-fledged delusions. She starts the tape by telling him how consumed she is by him: how she can feel him, taste him, think him. It's not too much later that she's calling him and telling him that she hates him—perfectly encapsulating the Borderline's inability to think in anything but extremes. They must either idealize or devalue.

In Act Three, Alex graduates to a full-blown psychotic. She breaks into Dan's home and cooks the family's pet rabbit. For dessert she abducts his daughter. Dan, finally having had enough, confesses to his wife and then goes to confront Alex. Things get physical right from the start and they brawl in Alex's apartment. She comes at him with a butcher knife and, though he manages to disarm her, he imprudently leaves the weapon with her.

With the police involved and Beth forgiving Dan his transgression, all seems on track for a return to a happy normal life for the Gallaghers. Unfortunately, the police can't find Alex, and she shows up as Beth is drawing a bath. Alex, absentmindedly self-mutilating her thigh with the aforementioned knife, has broken from reality. She questions Beth in her own home: "What are you doing here? Why are you here?" Alex's attempted homicidal rampage is cut short when Dan drowns her in the bathtub, and, when that proves not to be enough (she wasn't kidding about not being ignored), Beth shoots her dead.

THE BORDERLINE PERSONALITY
SUMMARY

Examples of the qualities and qualifications that define a person with a Borderline Personality:

- They show consistent patterns of instability in their relationships
- They commonly complain of depression and boredom
- They have very little control over their impulses
- They have a fragile and unstable self-image and affect
- They exert a lot of energy avoiding abandonment, whether real or imaginary
- Their relationships tend to be intense and short-lived
- They alternately idealize and devalue others, particularly their mates
- They suffer from Identity Disturbance (a distorted or disturbed sense of self)
- They are recklessly impulsive, which can prove harmful to themselves and others. They are prone to substance abuse, binge eating, shopping sprees, and careless sex
- They are prone to indulging in suicidal gestures and threats
- They are prone to self-mutilation
- They have violent, eruptive mood swings
- They are very reactive. The slightest stimuli can send them into intense bouts of irritability, depression, and anxiety
- They cannot control their anger. It is usually inappropriate and often quite intense

- They are prone to acting out physically (i.e., fighting)
- They are prone to paranoia
- They often have severe dissociative symptoms
- They make excessive emotional demands in close relationships
- They have difficulty tolerating ambivalence
- They have great difficulty with being alone
- They tend to be non-reflective
- They tend to lead chaotic lives
- They allow themselves to be used by others
- They may experience intermittent psychotic delusions
- They demand gratification
- They prefer action to verbalization and reflection
- Diagnosis is more common in females than in males
- They always seem to be in a state of crisis
- Their behavior is highly unpredictable
- They rarely live up to their potential (because their lives are too erratic)
- They tend toward promiscuity in an attempt to circumvent being alone
- They place people at polar extremes, either all good or all bad
- They tend to dismiss complexity in their and others' personalities
- They tend to globalize and minimize. They tend to reduce to a single characteristic
- They don't have the capacity to defer gratification
- They don't feel that they have a problem—it's the only reality they have ever known

NOTEWORTHY CHARACTERISTICS OF THE BORDERLINE PERSONALITY

SPEECH

Usually will reflect the mood swings of the individual. When highly depressed, they will have flat, undefined speech that is global in nature and non-specific in structure. With feelings of abandonment, they are loud, accusatory, and known to rage. When regressed, they are childlike. They can be manipulative in order to minimize abandonment issues. Sometimes they are psychotic in nature, forming loose associations that don't relate (*"The television is on, let's get married!"*).

PROFESSIONS

Difficulty with maintaining a professional life. Usually not reaching their potential. Artistic fields such as acting, painting, writing—jobs that are means to managing their mental stress and chronic boredom. Usually not found in scientific or engineering fields.

DRESS

Again, reflective of moods. Typical example: go out shopping, bored with what they buy, and returns it all the next day—or buys ten belts out of indecisiveness. Flamboyant or overstated. Can manifest depression.

HEALTH

Issues concerning Hypochondriasis. Unreal views about body. Eating disorders. Hysterical conversions. Substance abuse. Sexual addictions. Self-mutilating.

POPULAR CLICHÉS
ASSOCIATED WITH BORDERLINES

- Moody
- The Live Wire
- The Short Fuse
- The Slut
- The Nut Case
- Unreliable
- Fly by night
- Capricious
- Treacherous
- Unbalanced

SIMILAR PERSONALITY TYPES
TO THE BORDERLINE

- THE ANTISOCIAL PERSONALITY
- THE HISTRIONIC PERSONALITY
- THE PARANOID PERSONALITY
- THE NARCISSISTIC PERSONALITY

VIEWING SUGGESTIONS FOR
THE BORDERLINE PERSONALITY

Bad Lieutenant (1992)—Drama, 98, Rated NC-17.
For Harvey Keitel as the Lieutenant.

Blue Velvet (1986)—Mystery, 120, Rated R.
For Isabella Rossellini as Dorothy Vallens.

Drugstore Cowboy (1989)—Drama, 100, Rated R.
For Matt Dillon as Bob.

Fatal Attraction (1987)—Thriller/Romance, 119, Rated R.
Glenn Close as Alex Forrest. Close was Oscar nominated for acting, as was the screenplay.

Fear (1996)—Romance/Thriller, 95, Rated R.
Fatal Attraction for teenagers. Mark Whalberg as the loose cannon, David.

Grifters, The (1990)—Crime, 113, Rated R.
For signs of Borderline in Angelica Huston as Lily Dillon. Huston was nominated for an Academy Award as was the taut screenplay.

Leaving Las Vegas (1995)—Drama, 112, Rated R.
Nicholas Cage's Oscar winning perform-ance as Ben Sanderson. Oscar nominated for Figgis' writing.

Lost Weekend, The (1945)—Drama, 101, No rating.
Ray Milland as Don Brinman. Won an Academy Award for the writing.

Man With the Golden Arm, The (1955)—Drama, 119, No rating.

> Frank Sinatra as Frankie Machine. Sinatra was Oscar nominated for Best Actor.

Misery (1990)—Horror, 107, Rated R.

> Kathy Bates in her Academy Award winning role as Annie Wilkes.

Mommie Dearest (1981) —Biography, 129, Rated PG.

> For Faye Dunaway as Joan Crawford.

Mrs. Parker and the Vicious Circle (1994)—Drama/Biography, 125, Rated R.

> Jennifer Jason Leigh as Dorothy Parker.

Pulp Fiction (1994)—Drama/Crime/Comedy, 154, Rated R.

> Uma Thurman as Mia Wallace. Won the Oscar for writing.

Rose, The (1979)—Musical, 134, Rated R.

> For Bette Midler as Rose. Signs of both the Narcissist and the Borderline.

Under the Volcano (1984)—Drama, 109, Rated R.

> Oscar nominated Albert Finney as Geoffrey.

Who's Afraid of Virginia Woolf? (1966)—Drama, 129, No rating.

> George and Martha. Burton and Taylor were both nominated for Oscars, as was the writing.

Woman Under the Influence, A (1974)—Drama, 155, Rated R.

> Gena Rowlands as Mable Longhetti.

PRIOR TO READING THE NEXT CHAPTER
IT IS RECOMMENDED THAT THE FOLLOWING
FILMS BE VIEWED:

SAY ANYTHING
LOST IN AMERICA
AS GOOD AS IT GETS

A LIST OF FILMS PERTAINING TO THE
OBSESSIVE-COMPULSIVE PERSONALITY CAN BE
FOUND AT THE END OF THIS CHAPTER.

6

THE OBSESSIVE-COMPULSIVE
PERSONALITY

I haven't seen my analyst in two hundred years and . . .
he was a strict Freudian, and if I'd been going
all this time I'd probably almost be cured by now.
—Miles Monroe/Woody Allen, Marshall Brickman

IN *SAY ANYTHING*, Diane Court is a girl who (when introduced at her graduation ceremony by her teacher) is
summed up with the words, "history [*dramatic pause*],
oceanography [*dramatic pause*], creative writing [*big dramatic pause*], biochemistry . . . I think you know who I'm talking about." Diane *is* her achievements, and during her
speech she is a veritable orchard of apples of the collected
parents' eyes. Her greatest achievement is her role as her
father's daughter. This is more important to her than her
summer university courses, her after school job in the
Home for the Aged; greater than her fellowship to study in
England. She has succeeded academically beyond either of
their wildest dreams and devoted her life to her father's
rigid plan for success. What she had not planned for was
love. Enter Lloyd Dobler, a young man with far more hormones than dendrites. Dobler is prone to goofy adolescent

antics and has as his only goal in life being devoted to Diane (that and becoming a professional kick boxer). Diane's father worries, and bitterly notes, that what Diane is about to do with the less than ennobled Lloyd Dobler is lose her foothold in superior standing and "learn to champion mediocrity."

David Howard is an advertising executive agonizing over his hyper-responsibility so that he can get a promotion to the vice-presidency. David finds himself passed over yet again and spontaneously (uncharacteristically spontaneously) quits his job. He and his wife, Linda (likewise leading a careercentric life) decide to get *Lost In America*. David has calculated to the penny what their savings will allow for and what their house will bring on the market. After poring over enough information on motor homes to shame the Library of Congress, he and Linda head first to Las Vegas to renew their wedding vows before embarking on a free-spirited existence. Unfortunately, Linda has an unanticipated gambling problem. She leaves their heart-shaped second honeymoon bed in the middle of the night to gamble away their nest egg. They are left broke, forlorn, and perhaps a bit too free and unburdened for David's taste and disposition.

In *As Good As It Gets*, Melvin Udall is a writer of torrid, bodice-ripping romance novels. His personal life, however, is very different from his professional one as he keeps the world at a very safe distance. He successfully isolates himself by employing his abrasive personality—a personality he has carefully, over the years, fashioned into a blunt instrument. When a nubile fan gushes over his work and asks him how he writes women so well, he responds by telling her that he "[thinks] of a man, then I take away reason and accountability." He refers to his gay neighbor, Simon, as a "fag" who "nances" around. He clears his favorite table at a restaurant by telling the Jewish patrons that "[their] appetites weren't as big as their noses."

Melvin's life is one of intense ritual, orderliness, and control. He refuses to touch anything public, or let anyone touch him. While walking down a crowded sidewalk, he valiantly fights to not step on any cracks. He will go to great lengths in his need to remain ordered—lengths that include paying the medical bills for the ill son of the neighborhood restaurant waitress, Carol. An act of selfish generosity on his part, done for no other reason than to allow Carol to continue to serve him in the only restaurant in which he will eat. This, not surprisingly, leads to a shattering of his ordered world when, once he has let her in, he falls in love with her.

S. O. B.

Intense, inflexible, rigid, righteous, orderly, controlling, stubborn, miserly. The Obsessive-Compulsive Personality is all of these and more. Although this might make for a rigid and colorless person, it often makes for interesting (if not the friendliest) screen characters.

Be forewarned: the Obsessive-Compulsive can be (along with colorless and rigid) terribly annoying. To conceive and develop such a character runs the same risks. Hard-lining the diagnostic criteria for the Obsessive-Compulsive will most likely create a character few people are going to sit down and put up with. When the individuals involved are up to the challenge (as in the case of *As Good As It Gets*), the rewards can well be worth the tricky footing.

Other notable portrayals of the Obsessive-Compulsive Personality that have found their way to the silver screen occur in the drama/adventure *The Mosquito Coast* (in which an Obsessive-Compulsive character is driven to play God); Woody Allen's icy *Interiors* (also severely depressed and suicidal); and David Mamet's wonderfully edgy and poetic gambling tome, *House of Games*.

Of particular note here: gambling (as a compulsion) may be for many an addiction issue more than a personality trait, but it is also a central fixation with many Obsessive-Compulsives. Along with Mamet's steely story there are several extraordinarily well-drawn high-rolling tales. Take for example the 1974 Karl Reisz directed / James Toback scripted *The Gambler*—a story that starts off looking like a pure and simple study in character before it takes a surprising turn. That same year also gave us *California Split*. Robert Altman directs a script by Joseph Walsh and delivers one of the best takes on the nature of obsessions and compulsions.

Gambling and the seemingly uncontrollable essence of chance may seem an odd behavioral pattern for someone described as ridged, controlling, or miserly. Quite often it is, but it is important to remember that under the façade of lady luck, gambling—most card games—are not games of luck. It is a game of math, calculated moves, and defined perimeters—a set of scientific laws that are unequivocally set in stone. It is a precisely ordered world that the Obsessive-Compulsive individual can understand completely. Their success or failure is reliant only on their knowledge and ability to act on it. Luck has nothing to do with it. As the intensely realized 1998 gambling film, *Rounders*, points out: "If it's luck, how come the same men play for the world championship every year?"

OCP Vs. OCD

The Obsessive-Compulsive Personality (OCP) has, in the clinical world, a sibling. This psychological twin is known as Obsessive-Compulsive Disorder (OCD). OCD is a more serious condition specifically involving behavior that is excessively intrusive (sometimes life threatening) to daily life.

What exactly is the difference?

An **Obsessive-Compulsive Personality** has issues with such things as orderliness, control, and efficiency.

Pervasive thoughts, excessive worries, and repetitive behaviors (the counting, the checking, and the rituals) control the individual with **Obsessive-Compulsive Disorder.** David Howard (*Lost In America*) behaves frequently in the manner of an Obsessive-Compulsive Personality. At the other end of the playing field (some might argue another stadium) is Melvin Udall (*As Good As It Gets*). Melvin seems to be swimming toward the deep end of the pool (Obsessive-Compulsive Disorder). Debate could ensue here as to whether Melvin is or is not OCD. There is little doubt that Melvin's obsessive tendencies are more pronounced than the obsessive tendencies of a David Howard or a Diane Court. Melvin does display the repetitive behaviors (counting, checking, rituals), but he is far from disabled or impeded by his odd characteristics. True OCD would involve individuals who behave in such ways that they spend hours locking and unlocking a door, tying and retying shoes, circling a room in a specific pattern—unable to go about their daily lives in a truly functional manner. More serious may be the individuals who may actually harm themselves, as do people who wash their hands repetitively to the point of bleeding.

Although clinically the Obsessive-Compulsive Personality and Obsessive-Compulsive Disorder are distinct, for purposes of inspiring creativity, characteristics from both will be reviewed here in order to achieve a more practical understanding.

The name is fairly self-descriptive: **Obsessive** —they have persistent thoughts; and **Compulsive** —they perform persistent actions. For the Obsessive-Compulsive Personality, there is a pervasive preoccupation with orderliness (both the physical and the emotional), perfectionism, and mental and interpersonal control. This usually happens at the expense of flexibility, openness and efficiency. It can also be construed that this means at the expense of others as well. Friendships are usually in short supply. The Obsessive-Compulsive's excessive fear of physical harm or the desire to control anxiety leads to compulsive behavior. These behavioral patterns include such things as the constant washing of hands, hoarding, unnecessary and minutely precise cataloguing, the following of precise and torturous routes to prevent harm, magical thinking, and ritualistic behavior. With such ritualistic behavior the rituals must be completed in exact sequence and painstaking detail, such as the tying and retying of shoelaces or the specific-numbered circling of a room or object.

At one time or another, everyone is obsessive about something. Everyone has moments when they are compulsive. For the Obsessive-Compulsive Personality, the thoughts, impulses, or images are not simply excessive worries about real-life problems. Melvin Udall's (As Good As It Gets) repetitive behavior—the rituals, the obsession with cleanliness and order, the checking, the counting—consists of acts that are not connected in any realistic way with what they are designed to do or prevent. They are clearly excessive. Albert Brooks' obsessive character in Lost In America seems mild in comparison, displaying behavioral signs found more toward the fringe.

Perfectionist. Controlling. Obsessive-Compulsive Personalities love order and discipline and are organized around thinking and doing as opposed to feeling. They place high value on their abilities as problem solvers and their logical faculties. Say Anything's Diane is synonymous with the classes in which she excels. Allie Fox (Harrison Ford) in The Mosquito Coast obstinately believes he knows what is right for his family. He never bothers to discuss with his wife or children the fact that they are leaving the comforts of American civilization for the hardships of an untamed jungle. Obsessive-Compulsives feel they must exact extreme control over themselves or risk losing control altogether. They are consciously aware that they must impose rigid order to conform to the societal ideals of personhood: hardworking, morally unimpeachable, and responsible to the point of paralysis.

To do this (to overachieve, hyper-accomplish) they must ignore their intuition and impulse. By using sheer will and stymieing self-control, they regulate and proscribe that which cannot be controlled or proscribed. They regulate drives (sex), spontaneous emotions (love), as well as common, everyday, household impulses. This control also bleeds beyond the boundaries of their selves and into the environment. Here they also prefer to be in control—where they eat, where they walk, who they encounter. Thus, these characters are often realized as controlling and exacting. They want others to bend to their wishes and appear very unreasonable if such wants are not granted. They function very well at work, but have difficulty in their off hours and home lives, where the structure is less rigid. Eve (*Interiors*) offers to buy new cologne for her son-in-law so that she might change his scent to something she feels better suits him. Allie Fox (*Mosquito Coast*) forces his family—no questions asked—to an uncivilized jungle and buys himself a ramshackle town.

THE OVERSEER

Obsessive-Compulsives do not always see themselves as free agents. They often are saddled (as though with their own personal ghosts) with their own *overseer* who issues commands, demands, warnings, and admonitions. Consider this overseer the "Spirit of Proper Conduct Ever Present." A vital presence in their life that leads them to behave rigidly so it satisfies some objective necessity, some social imperative. We all, hopefully, have a voice in our head (our overseer) that tells us what is right from wrong. Still, those afflicted with this behavioral pattern rarely experience it in such absolute terms. This demanding over-seer phenomenology may be perceived as being internal or external to Obsessive-Compulsives, who feel they have no free will. Their free will has been given over to "the agent" so they might feel safe or successful. When this agent's commands become more bizarre and alien (such as the exotic counting, repeating, cleanliness), the Obsessive-Compulsive actually perceives them that way—bizarre and alien. They do not actually assimilate the commands. They are driven, all the same, to obey. Compulsively. The gambling buddies of *California Split*, Bill and Charlie (with highlight performances by George Segal and Elliott Gould), gamble on death itself, regardless of logic or safety. Mugged for their gambling money a second time, they proceed to challenge the mugger—they want him to bet against if they are telling the truth and have honestly given him all their money.

The Obsessive-Compulsive character tries not to offend the overseer. Instead, he must appease authority (be it parental, societal, religious, or political) in order to avoid retribution or censure. Allie Fox (*Mosquito Coast*) blindly forges ahead in the name of the "Great New World" he is creating. He is listening to a voice—clearly not that of family and friends. Melvin's rituals equal his success. Diane is the proud daughter. Not surprisingly, all of these particular dynamics are put to their individual tests. This retribution or censure would be the highest form of punishment of all. So he is submissive to authority, and authoritarian to subordinates. He is over-conscientious, scrupulous, and inflexible about matters of morality, ethics, or values. He is highly critical and apt to wield cruel power without guilt. Diane, worshipful of her father, does not hesitate to excoriate Lloyd for his lack of ambition and for his views, which she believes are "ageist." Allie Fox sermonizes, lectures; he babbles to himself, his family, and anyone passing by about the moral decay of America and the evils of modern civilization. This litany (never actually directed at anyone) obsessively pours out of him. It quickly takes on the disquieting feel of a lost, religious chant—a mass—being offered to a greater power. It is a mantra from which his strength and fortitude are born.

IN-CHECK

Obsessive-Compulsives have a surfeit of self-doubt and are mercilessly self-critical. They often display levels of perfectionism that interfere with task completion; they therefore are unable to complete a project because their own excessively strict standards are not met. It is easy for the viewer to understand why David Howard (*Lost In America*) is passed over for promotions. Although he may be next in line as far as longevity within the company, his timidity and indecision socially hobble him. He exhibits no leadership abilities, only a remarkable flair for second-guessing himself. "Is this normal?" Diane asks Lloyd when he attempts to teach her how to drive a car with a stick shift. She is worried that she might fail, or not succeed in a standard, approved way.

This self-doubt and self-criticism causes Obsessive-Compulsives to keep their lives highly organized. They prefer organization thrust upon them—then they return the favor to others—without the burden of the anxiety that the rules sprang from anything questionable within themselves. They are reluctant to delegate tasks or to work with others who do not submit to exactly their way of doing things. The building of Allie Fox's jungle utopia in *The Mosquito Coast* occurs because Allie believes that only he is the architect of their salvation. There is the clear impression from Allie that he believes the motivation for building this New World village is coming by way of decree from someone (something) bigger than himself. Be it hauling his family off to the ends of the earth, telling the natives to clear a dense jungle hillside, or an exhausting trek across the mountains to show off a giant ice cube—Allie's motives and reasoning are not to be questioned or challenged. Her daughter sums up Eve, the disciplined, manipulative mother in Woody Allen's *Interiors*: "She created a world around us that we existed in. Where everything had its place. An ice palace."

The pressure (and resultant tension) to do, feel, and think in the right and correct way is pervasive and constant. Not only does Diane (*Say Anything*) miss her vacations to take college courses, but her teenage room is decorated with maps and anatomical charts instead of posters of teenage idols. She keeps a model of a brain handy, as well as a massive dictionary in which she marks each word for which she looks up the meaning. To no surprise, every page has multiple marks.

These individuals often try to stay perpetually busy, cognitively and behaviorally. The reason for this is to inhibit any spontaneous thought or action. To do this they focus their attention narrowly and invest a great deal of their energy in details. When David Howard (*Lost In America*) is choosing the free and easy life that is afforded with the motorhome lifestyle, he first has to study the exact specifications of every mechanical detail of every vehicle—comparing all the options. He explores this trivia with such great zeal that an expert salesman would be stumped—all the while he completely ignores the most important consideration of such a purchase: is it fun and comfortable? This focus on detail is intense and sharp and unwavering. Unfortunately, there is often no priority given, and the Obsessive-Compulsive will bestow equal (and equally grave) importance on the tiniest of inconsequential matters as he will on the bigger considerations. Preoccupied with details, rules, lists, order, organization, and schedules, Obsessive-Compulsives often miss the major by focusing on the minor. Eve (*Interiors*) arranges and rearranges a series of bedside vases. First front to back, then back to front, and so on. All the while, her husband of thirty-some years is walking out of her life. In truth, she spends most of the film arranging and rearranging inanimate objects such as pictures and lamps—all the while her family's emotional core collapsing around her.

The fear of error and the anxiety over imperfection can keep Obsessive-Compulsives focused solely on the peripheral. They are kept busy, but may never attain success or completion. *Say Anything's* Diane is extremely involved with high achievement in her scholastic endeavors. When it comes to building a life outside of school, she says (in her speech to her graduating class), "I have glimpsed the future, and all I can say is . . . go back!" School is definitely a lot safer place to be with its strict rules and schedules. Equally, Diane has a fear of flying that is briefly played on in the story. It is as much about the fear of putting her future (safety) in the hands of others—a defining moment at the end of the film. A very nice touch—never over accentuated by screenwriter Cameron Crowe.

Obsessive-Compulsives often ruin things by overcorrecting. Their self-doubt leads them to check and recheck each and every detail. This pattern spurs them to become mired in a morass of unimportant specifics. Their insecurity over possible error or overlooked flaws—their need to insure that they remain proper in the eyes of all overseers and their compulsion to ensure that they stay out of trouble at all costs—can in fact lead them directly into trouble. Diane's constant and careful weighing of each situation and the innumerable pros and cons of each option often result in her being stymied, miserable, and impotent. Little is accomplished because there is excessive wavering and deliberation over the most arcane details. Diane has prided herself in being the perfect daughter and telling her father every detail of her life. So much so that she discusses the ins and outs of losing her virginity the night before to

212 | Howard M. Gluss, Ph.D. with Scott Edward Smith

Lloyd. One can easily imagine that it will somewhat complicate this particular triad. As much as David Howard (*Lost In America*) wants to organize every mile of their road to the future in the hope of avoiding pitfalls, he most assuredly creates the ones that snag him. In *As Good As It Gets*, Melvin agrees to a road trip with Simon and Carol and all the trouble that he is convinced will come with such an outing. Melvin realizes straying so far from his regimented routine is only courting disaster. Yet he does it, not to help out Simon, but because he seeks approval in Carol's eyes.

OUT OF SYNC

It is often the case that Obsessive-Compulsives gain more pleasure from being busy than from actually bringing something to fruition. For all their self-driving and blundered focus on working and doing, they oftentimes do not get much done. Also, completion means decision. It means potential judgment, potential failure. They may refrain from making any decision out of fear of making the wrong one.

The Obsessive-Compulsive's pattern of rigidity persists in the face of repeated failure or apparent absurdity. Melvin (*As Good As It Gets*) is absolutely aware of the ridiculous act of going to great lengths to avoid stepping on cracks. When Verdell the dog starts imitating him and doing likewise, Melvin gently scolds him: "Don't be like me. You stay just the way you are 'cause you're a perfect man." When the New World civilization along the Mosquito Coast is destroyed and Allie Fox has subjected his family to near death at the hands of starvation and hurricanes, he still insists on "going upstream! Only dead things go downstream!" Stubborn, obstinate, they will continually forge ahead with fruitless behavior merely because they are convinced that it's the correct and proper way of doing things.

The Obsessive-Compulsive is many times the easiest personality type to spot from a distance. Their rigidity of thought and behavior often can be seen in their posture and dress. They appear rigid, tense, implacable, and unapproachable. In her opening scene, Eve (*Interiors*) enters wearing a shapeless yet refined outfit that she says the designer refers to as "ice gray." Well chosen to describe both her disposition and the effect she has on those around her. On their first date, Diane wears an anachronistic white dress, ornate flower arrangement in her hair, and a white shawl. She wears this to go to a high school keg party. Her dress, like her life, is out of sync with everything around her. This self-restriction extends to all aspects of their being—not only posture, attire, and style are affected, but also their finances. They tend to be frugal, parsimonious. They hold themselves and their possessions tightly reined. They often adopt a miserly spending style toward both themselves and others. Money is viewed as something to be hoarded against future catastrophes.

Obsessive-Compulsives do not devote much time to what most people would call the pursuit of pleasure from things, because these activities are not rationally driven. They are exceedingly devoted to work and productivity to the exclusion of leisure activities and friendships. They do this because they do not trust the feelings this pleasure brings. They do not trust themselves. They fear freedom, especially the responsibility that freedom brings. When they are free of one concern, it is not unusual for them to immediately shift their focus to the next concern. Dr. Margaret Ford (*House of Games*) is admonished time and again by her wiser and older mentor, Dr. Littauer. She informs Dr. Ford that she needs to relax, enjoy life, and visit her friends. Good advice . . . none of which Dr. Ford heeds. It is not until the doctor suggests she begin writing a new book that Margaret Ford pays attention, doing exactly what the doctor ordered. Losing herself in work is something to which Dr. Ford can relate—anything but reflect upon her own self. Melvin begins to open up and he starts to care for those around him. First, he finds a soft spot in his heart for Verdell the dog. Soon after, there appears to be room for Carol and Simon. He becomes uneasy and a little frightened. He runs (uncharacteristically against his schedule) to see his psychiatrist. He is falling into irrational love and the attendant novelty and unstableness threaten to capsize his life.

Tight-Fisted Emotions

Obsessive-Compulsives must keep their lives tightly bound to avoid a surge of untoward and potentially harmful impulses—impulses are seen as damaging, baneful, and are to be nipped at the roots. Impulses are unacceptable, case closed. They include such normal, healthy responses as sexual urges, aggression, competitive and spontaneous emotions, and all the other railings that are contained within (and define) the human soul. Allie Fox (*The Mosquito Coast*) sadly proclaims at the end of his journey of ruin: "Nature's crooked. I wanted right angles, straight lines." The avoidance of irresponsibility is the adherence to sanctioned responsibility. The only way to deal with negative feelings is control. Because they distrust their feelings en masse, these characters must be designed to channel all of their attention into thinking and doing. They block their emotions and become righteous for it. Allie Fox, in order not to deal with his family's feelings about returning to the United States and the personal ramifications of what is going on, lies and tells them that America has been destroyed in a nuclear war. He is their only hope .Attention is focused on the abstract, strict rules of conduct set forth by morally irreproachable institutions, and they expound these principles and rules. This shifting is indicative of the way Obsessive-Compulsive Personalities think. They strive to live life at arm's length, to keep life organized and intellectualized. Genuine interest and joy are suppressed.

Play, fun, humor: Obsessive-Compulsives rarely take to them. These things lack boundaries. Feelings are childish, weak, and show a lack of control and organization. Recreation is a sign of weakness and displays a lack of fortitude. Allie Fox's young twin girls joyously show him the old bicycle they have uncovered in the jungle. Fox immediately turns it into a pedal-pushing device for an automated washing machine. Soon, pumping those pedals in true sweatshop fashion, are his carrot-top twins. Woody Allen's character Alvy Singer (*Annie Hall*) would appear to be a likely prototype of the overwrought, compulsive Eve of *Interiors*. Released a year prior to *Interiors*, Allen's *Annie Hall* was originally entitled *Anhedonia* (which means the lack of capacity for experiencing pleasure).

Common strengths of Obsessive-Compulsive characters are that they are dependable, reliable, practical, precise, and honest—brutally honest. Often apparent are their high standards and strict ethical values; that they are rational, detailed, and disciplined thinkers. The Obsessive-Compulsive Personality excels at exacting professions such as accounting, law, technology, and research—careers that focus on detail rather than creativity and intuition. Melvin Udall has finished his 62nd novel. Obviously, they are successful books, but how creative any of them are is never revealed. His novels (as with his rituals at his front door) are most likely a series of patterns that he performs over and over again—to considerable success and financial reward. The price paid for their precision and practical output is a sacrifice of the spontaneity and experience of creativity.

The most common emotion that the Obsessive-Compulsive Personality will display is anger. Their anger stems from their perceived oppression by external forces and rules, which they believe they must follow to the letter.

Anger is also one of those unpleasant, unnecessary things known as emotions. Thus, when they become aware of it, it serves as further proof to them that suppressed inside their very being is a seething cauldron of unpleasant impulses. Should those impulses find release, it could spell ruination. Anger is acceptable in Obsessive-Compulsive characters if seen as justified and reasonable. Melvin can be brazenly anti-Semitic, telling a "table of Jews" to "shampoo my crotch." He feels justified in this because they are sitting at his table. They have broken the rules of his rigid world and are guilty of transgression. Allie Fox's response to his young son's crying and desperate plea to leave their dangerous world is to bring down upon the youngster a zealot-like wrath. At the onset of a fierce tropical storm, he damns the child and orders the helpless boy to "get out and never return!"

These individuals usually hold themselves above others because they can keep their needy and lustful aggressive parts in check. There is little doubt that Allie Fox is playing God along the Mosquito Coast. He brazenly thinks he knows better than modern civilization—more than the jungle natives. Dr. Ford (*House of Games*) drives alone to a dark and seedy area of town and enters the world of con men and gambling with no fear of the consequences because she considers herself a superior human being. Fear would be an emotion, and she is smarter than that. Obsessive-Compulsives take pride and consider themselves special because of such stringent self-control. Unfortunately, what is warded off can eventually intrude. Hence, the Third Act plot turn is created for Mr. Mamet's hard-boiled gambling story.

It takes a great deal of psychic energy to keep emotions squelched inside oneself—a condition that results is constant tension and anxiety. The more Obsessive-Compulsives fear emotions, the more they ward off that aspect of themselves. Any energy they give to that suppression means more opportunities and possibilities for dramatic and tense crises. There is also insecurity over being able to maintain the compulsion. Sometimes these demonic emotions do intrude in the form of sexual or violent thoughts—such as the tragic turn of events in *The Mosquito Coast*, as well as Eve's (*Interiors*) icy embrace with the unforgiving sea.

The more compulsive the character, the more prone he will be to jump into action without considering alternatives. This happens through fear of idleness and through fear of censure for not accomplishing. When Allie Fox watches his greatest creation destroyed (the heart of his utopia), he exclaims, "I'm happy! We're free!" He immediately moves on, never looking back, never addressing the painful emotions the destruction of his God/child/monster has brought. This type of impulsiveness (which is rarely constructive or creative) is at the center of their self-esteem— and their self-esteem stems from doing. With those who are more obsessive, self-esteem comes from thinking.

RELATIONSHIPS

Relationships are problematic for Obsessive-Compulsives. Melvin Udall, Eve, Allie Fox, Dr. Ford, Diane Court—none of these characters are portrayed as having a single close friend. Obsessive-Compulsives are known to keep their relationships at a formal level, strictly coded. To this, they generally can be counted on to formally adhere. They also expect such adherence will be reciprocated. Emotionally, they are atrophied. They have carefully cultivated a restrained and constricted manner. Obsessive-Compulsives have so subsumed their access to emotions that genuine feelings are difficult to access. Their social behavior is often stilted, emphasizing only the proper, prescribed rules of conduct. They therefore can appear distant, pedantic, self-possessed.

A fine example can be found in *Say Anything*. Diane gives in to what she anticipates will be the needs of Lloyd on an upcoming date. Before she goes on the fateful date she has pre-analyzed the event. Theoretically, she knows the time has come in their dating process in which young Lloyd's burgeoning manhood can no longer be held off at a distance. Diane decides to give in to him, not wanting "any problems." In her role as the high school girlfriend, she is compelled to succumb. When Lloyd's hormones do mull over the possibility of "no," she in turn attacks him. Diane believes she must experience the teenage sexual angst for which the situation calls because that is what the situation traditionally entails. Therefore, that is what she will have. This is also a great example of feelings that have been kept bubbling inside—erupting more dangerously because they have been pressurized through denial.

The interpersonal relationships of Obsessive-Compulsive characters regularly reflect either submission to authority or authoritarianism over subordinates. These strictly proscribed roles are often imposed on the domestic circle as well. When Linda loses their hard-earned lifetime savings in a night of gambling, David behaves in the role of the angry father/husband. He has her write out one thousand times, "I lost the nest egg." On Melvin's trip to Baltimore, he has everything preprogrammed and arranged. His music is individually labeled with such instructions as "to use as ice breaker," and "to pep things up." After he has severely insulted Carol, he insists on playing a song that says, "I love you." She is definitely not interested in hearing it. Melvin insists. She insists back. Moments of spontaneous passion have to be planned and calculated well in advance.

Because of this need for proscribed roles, power struggles often characterize Obsessive-Compulsive relationships. This is particularly true where the rules of the role (and the allocation of roles) are unclear or when there is a disagreement about the respective roles. Those close to Obsessive-Compulsive Personalities often find them frustrating—not only due to their inflexibility, but also because they are unable to make meaningful connections or partake in real communication. The Obsessive-Compulsive character is usually played as non-demonstrative. They separate feelings from thoughts, generally in order to dispense with the feelings. Tender shows of affection are usually blocked, or, if shown at all, are expressed indirectly. Hostility is likewise expressed indirectly and sometimes emerges as intrusive sexual, violent, or sadistic thoughts. Love is to be avoided because it is fundamentally messy on all levels. Allie Fox lies to his wife and children about the fate of civilization and not only refuses to listen to their needs, but also uses brute force when they cry against him. Eve's obsessive design forced upon her family to fit into the colorless contours of an emotionless world has resulted in what is decried as "too perfect to live in the world. No room for any real feelings." All have relationships that are strained at best.

Obsessive-Compulsives tend to make great business partners—great investment planners—but are a lousy way to spend a marriage. For that matter, spending a vacation with them is something to be scrutinized. Having a one-night stand with them may also be equally disappointing because they also tend to have trouble with their sexuality. The animalistic core from which such matters emerge is as far from the frontal lobes as possible. When Melvin kisses Carol at the end of *As Good As It Gets*, he stops and tries it again, declaring, "I know I can do better than that!" The two most common variables are either (a) shyness about sex that exposes them as distant, awkward, or nervous or (b) if not shyness, then overblown anxiety to the point that the sex becomes a fitful erratic, bruising encounter.

By its very definition, love touches the human side. This side, focusing on the heart and not the mind, is unpredictable. Also, due to their primal experience with their parents, Obsessive-Compulsives tend to hate those whom they love. If they do not hate them, at the very least they resent them. They tend to equate love with repression, which then feeds hostility. It would be difficult for Obsessive-Compulsive characters to come to an understanding and realization of their emotions and its roots. Quite often in films they outright die because of this inability (*Interiors, Mosquito Coast*). Instead, they feel that it may perhaps be best to leave the whole love issue alone. Plainly speaking, when it comes to film characters, the Obsessive-Compulsive is downright bad at love. It seems to be against their nature. They try to rationalize love . . . and love is anything but rational. This is perhaps the single most important reason why it is rare to see the Obsessive-Compulsive Personality in a lead (heroic) character. Their unwillingness to love or be loved makes them cold and distant. It becomes an arduous task to care for or worry about their quest. Although Harrison Ford gives a riveting (and unheralded), stellar performance as the Obsessive-Compulsive Allie, it is an exhausting and often frustrating journey the viewer is asked to go on. There is only so much an audience will put up with. The result is that the individual sitting there in the dark becomes annoyed—pushed and tested to the breaking point. The victimized viewer experiences an uncontrollable (somewhat obsessive, somewhat compulsive) urge to reach up at the movie screen and throttle some sense into the character. Or, at the very least throttle some sense into the characters that are putting up with the bad behavior and not doing some throttling of their own. Interest is lost and the story will predictably crash and burn.

This convincing themselves that they hate what they actually love (called **reaction formation**) is a defense mechanism that appears very frequently in the repertoire of the Obsessive-Compulsive Personality. They often have one part of their lives that is messy. Freud believed that this signified a desire for irresponsibility, that despite their claims to virtue, they remain corrupt in at least one aspect. They would never allow this to happen in a formal, public setting, so this often occurs in their home life. Melvin keeps a side of himself hidden from those who know him—a turbulent, torrid, messy side: the Melvin who writes ravishing and passionate romances. He keeps this facet of himself tightly under wraps and only lets it breathe when closely guarded and sitting at his word processor. Eve, for all her self-control, has a nasty habit of trying to kill herself.

BACKSTORY

The childhood of the Obsessive-Compulsive is critical because the tie between it and adulthood is very clearly representative. Obsessive-Compulsive parents breed Obsessive-Compulsive children. The child interjects the rigid standards of the parents. He thus tries to deny his natural impulses and instead become the model of behavior that is expected of him. This blocks the organic expressions common in the human species and the Obsessive-Compulsive fosters a false self—ruled by the despotic other, the tyrannical overseer that dominates his later life.

The child Obsessive-Compulsive views (and quite accurately remembers) the parents as stern, exacting, rule bound. The child is rigid—similar to the parent he will become. The parents are put off by the free-spirited and animal-like behavior of children. They work hard to turn the child into the model of a perfect societal prototype, a diminutive gentleman: mannered, contained, and submissive. They seek (and succeed) in taming the wild child who continues to tame himself after he has been set free in the world.

With the Obsessive-Compulsive there is an intense parental bond. They need their parents' praise—or at the very least, their lack of criticism. At a party, Diane risks peer disapprobation when she breaks away to call her father. Being the ideal daughter is far more important to her than having friends her own age. Her father (clearly the Obsessive-Compulsive mold from which Diane was cast) likewise values highly his public perception. When his credit card is declined, he is so humiliated by the idea that such a respectable person could be seen publicly in such a disreputable light that he runs home and cowers, fully dressed, in the bathtub. In the same fashion, Eve believes it will mean the end of the world to confront the humiliation that her husband has been speaking about the state of her mental health with her doctor behind her back.

Often the parents offer only qualified praise. The child may have done well, but the parents will offer insight on how he or she could have done better. The offspring, instilled with a fear of punishment or of love withheld, learns to be rigid and tends toward isolation. He learns to be a perfectionist. Dr. Margaret Ford (*House of Games*) is a famous author/psychologist, Allie Fox a genius inventor with multiple patents, Melvin Udall a successful writer. Diane Court is a national fellowship winner.

This personality generally is seen to develop later in childhood, when the child has matured enough intellectually to comprehend a moral system—a strict regime of what is right and what is wrong. Diane, forever self-sacrificing, is livid over Lloyd's flippant attitude toward the elderly, to whom she has devoted her non-studying hours. Allie Fox quotes Scripture by heart, yet threatens to kill the missionaries who try to bring God to his Utopia. Obsessive-Compulsives make the grave error of mistaking their opinions for absolute truths.

Though the parenting may be flawed, Obsessive-Compulsive parents try to do things as perfectly (as prototypical, as classically) and as best intentioned as possible. By sticking to the anemic rulebook of proper behavior they do not allow for spontaneity and, more vitally, intuition. There is not an overabundance of empathy in their technique. They do not have allowable margins for each child's inherent idiosyncrasies. They don't enjoy surprises. They afford no indulgences. They deny hostility (much as they do in themselves). Denying hostility is not the healthiest thing to do to a child, where hostility and obstinate behavior (another no-no) are only too natural and necessary for the healthy development of a young psyche. There is little lenience given to the child's developmental phases, and the parents do not encourage the disorderliness of play unless it's proper and prescribed play. We are not talking about terrifically fun parents.

Effusive displays of love and affection are likewise rarely encouraged and considered embarrassing. Sublimated expressions of love (when it can be communicated at a safe distance) are eminently more acceptable. The child is taught that the way to love the parents is to obey them. For the child, love may become synonymous with the loss of autonomy. Therefore, in later life, to feel love is to feel obligation. Certainly as an adult it is understandable that he may be reluctant to do so.

Childhood is also the root of the Obsessive-Compulsive character's self-debasing guilt. They are not good enough for their parents. Deep inside they feel they have failed to be perfect children and to live up to what was expected of them. Children with Obsessive-Compulsive Personality Disorder appear to suffer from parental upbringings that manifest in self-doubting, guilt-ridden behavior. The distant parental figures were oftentimes cold and aloof, creating obsessive behavior in the child that attempted to bring them attention, love, and admiration. Unconscious rage toward the parent(s) is usually a result of the child reacting against the aloofness of the parent. The Obsessive-Compulsive child grows up with powerful fantasies of being cared for, but a terrible disdain for the emotions that being cared for would manifest. This unconscious bind creates a need for strong control, both internally and externally. By controlling the external environment the child feels that he or she has pleased the parent and avoided own abandonment. By controlling their internal world, these children have protected themselves from their uncomfortable emotional state—the longing for loving nurturing attachment and the murderous rage directed at the parents for not receiving it. They strive for an idealistic view of themselves and chronically feel that they must always do more and always be better. This constant self-disapproval and striving for grandiosity and perfectionism sets the stage for depression. When needs cannot be met—when unrealistic goals supersede logic—the Obsessive-Compulsive is fraught with feelings of hopelessness and, in extreme cases, suicidal behavior.

To break the cycle of obsession-compulsion, sufferers must willfully challenge their tight defenses and gradually learn to accept and express their disavowed drives, effects, and thoughts. Melvin knows this all too well, actually confirming that very treatment with his own doctor. David Howard has to learn to open up a bit, that it's okay to get *Lost In America*. Diane learns to fly. It is not surprising that (at the core of stories such as those cited) the basic theme is about the ability to feel emotions . . . to experience love. Perhaps most important is taking on the responsibility of feeling those emotions.

THE ARC OF AN
OBSESSIVE-COMPULSIVE FILM CHARACTER

In *As Good As It Gets*, we are first given a series of scenes that catalogues Melvin Udall's Obsessive-Compulsive behaviors. It almost functions as a primer for the personality style. He is obsessed with cleanliness (sterility) to the point that he wears leather gloves whenever he goes outside. He disposes of them after a single use. He uses two fresh bars of soap to wash his hands. He is the victim of magical thinking (he has an elaborate toe-tapping ritual to put on his bedroom slippers), he has to lock and relock his door five times upon entering the house, and he is petrified to tread on any cracks in the sidewalk. He also visits only one restaurant—must do so precisely at the same time each day and sit at precisely the same table—and he must only be served by an entirely all too patient waitress named Carol. But what is most striking about Melvin is his Obsessive-Compulsive need for isolation—a need he satisfies extraordinarily well through his acerbic personality. Melvin is obnoxious to the point of being toxic. The first time we meet him he is shoving his gay neighbor's adorable little dog down a garbage chute.

Act One sets up the character of Melvin and his behaviors. Near the end of the first act, Melvin's gay neighbor, Simon, is beaten faceless. Melvin has thrust upon him temporary ward-ship of the dog, Verdell. He is horrified at first. "You can't do this," he tells Simon's friend, Frank. In no uncertain terms, Frank makes it clear that he can.

Melvin protests: "No one's ever been in here before!" Act One ends with Melvin's hermetic world being breached.

In Act Two, we see that fissures are starting to form in the aegis of his carefully organized world and the fortifications of his self-imposed exile begin to crumble. First is the dog. Against his will, he begins to fall in love with the furry little mug. When the time comes to return Verdell to Simon, Melvin can barely hold back the tears. He says to his psychiatrist that he realizes he must begin by changing one pattern in his life. Unfortunately, he is soon hit broadside by the changes outside of his control or resistance. Things begin to tumble in—most significantly in the growing intimacy between him and Carol, his waitress. He inadvertently provokes a confrontation that breaches the impersonal distance between the two of them when he makes an offhand comment about her son's health. With that he has crossed the line and Carol will not ignore it. She confronts him and won't back down, forcing him to acknowledge that he has erred. Things plummet when Carol is forced to leave her job to care for her son and Melvin, without Carol's intervention, is kicked out of the restaurant. "I'll be quiet," he pleads. "Just let me stay here. Just get Carol." But it is no use. After calling Carol's replacement "Elephant Girl," he has pretty much sealed his own fate. The exile of Melvin receives a standing ovation from the other patrons.

The routines of his life rapidly are dismantled. In efforts at self-preservation, he is forced to allow access into his life to people he previously has denied. He enters into Carol's personal life when he starts paying her child's medical bills so that she can return to work and wait on his table. He also befriends Simon because he needs to remain close to Verdell. Melvin gradually breaks free of his rigid patterns and begins to take his place in the world around him. He notices for the first time that the decor in his doctor's office has been changed . . . though it's been two years since it was changed. What's startling is that he is beginning to take in data from outside the sphere of his own frame of reference. The point of no return occurs when Melvin actually falls in love (this disrupts everything he's so carefully managed). As he confides to Simon, "I haven't been sleeping, I haven't been clearing my head or felt like myself. I'm in trouble."

Nearing the end of Act Two, Melvin is again strong-armed by Frank to do a favor for Simon—this time, take him to Baltimore. Repelled at first, Melvin soon sees this as an opportunity to get close to Carol, whom he invites to come along. He plans the trip down to the smallest of details, packing his suitcase using a clipboard. Act Two ends in Baltimore, when Melvin severely insults an amorous Carol—his obnoxious behavior, his pushing people away has long since become so entrenched that he does it almost reflexively. He realizes then that his mode of behavior is no longer working for him and stands in the way of his happiness. He is in love—isolation has become anathema. Carol has told him that she doesn't want to see him again.

In Act Three, we watch Melvin progress rapidly. First off, he welcomes Simon into his home as his roommate. This is a huge step, not only because it is an act of inestimable generosity and kindness, but also in the fact that he is opening his previously highly guarded sanctum to someone that he formerly despised. He is then convinced that he must court Carol, seek forgiveness, make himself available. When he heads out to visit her in Brooklyn, he is bolstered by the fact that he had forgotten to perform his ritual of repeatedly locking the deadbolts on his door and no harm had befallen him. In Brooklyn, he tells Carol that he's better. By all accounts he is. Not cured, just better. When he kisses her he puts his last remaining vestiges of perfectionism to good use. After a faulty first attempt he tells her, "I can do better than that." And he does.

THE OBSESSIVE-COMPULSIVE
PERSONALITY SUMMARY

Examples of the qualities and qualifications that often define a person with an Obsessive-Compulsive Personality:

- They tend to be preoccupied with orderliness
- They strive for perfection
- They have a need for intellectual, unemotional control
- They are often inflexible and stubborn
- They frequently lack spontaneity
- They tend not to be open or forthcoming
- They sometimes sacrifice efficiency for attention to the smallest and most insignificant of details
- They follow rules and schedules
- They are excessively devoted to work and productivity
- They allow themselves little or no time for friends and leisure activity
- They tend to be inflexible when it comes to proper behavior and moral conduct
- They may not be able to ever throw anything away, even if it holds no sentimental value
- They tend to be reluctant to delegate tasks but prefer to complete them themselves
- They view money as something that is to be hoarded in case of future calamities. They tend to be miserly
- They seldom display emotions. When emotions are displayed, anger is the most common. Anger is acceptable to them if it is justified. Righteous indignation is therefore admired
- They tend to be rigid in both manner and appearance
- They have difficulty working with others

- They are overly disciplined
- They are highly non-adaptive
- They are dependable and reliable
- They succumb to ritualized behaviors
- They hold themselves up to impossibly high expectations. They feel shame when they fall short
- They consider emotions and feelings to be weak, childish, disorganized, and messy
- They tend to convert emotional situations into intellectual situations
- They keep the aggressive, lustful, needy parts of themselves strictly in abeyance
- They tend to worry needlessly and a lot
- They do not make choices easily; difficult ones can paralyze them
- They tend to isolate. Isolation is their favorite defense mechanism
- They are preoccupied with cleanliness and may exhibit an abject fear of contamination, and therefore a compulsion to wash
- They may have an obsession with doubt, and therefore a compulsion for checking
- They often have intrusive and unwanted thoughts. They have the desire to ignore or suppress such intrusive thoughts with action
- They often have a childhood characterized by harsh discipline
- They tend to lack a sense of humor, taking everything seriously
- They tend to be unwilling or unable to compromise
- They tend to alienate people
- They are eager to please those that they perceive as being more powerful than they are

NOTEWORTHY CHARACTERISTICS OF THE OBSESSIVE-COMPULSIVE PERSONALITY

SPEECH

Mechanistic. Factual. Logical. Rational. Unemotional. Non-spontaneous. Extremely articulate. Detail oriented. An often-rambling speech style.

PROFESSIONS

Oftentimes law, high tech, or research. It would be extremely rare to find this type of personality in jobs requiring creativity, intuitive action, or public and excessive social interaction.

DRESS

Often reflective of their secretive, tightly held personality. Colorless and non-specific in statement. Nothing that would draw attention to itself. Certainly nothing that would indicate a creative or expressive nature inside the individual.

HEALTH

General worrisome attitude about health. Clean. Fastidious.

POPULAR CLICHÉS ASSOCIATED WITH OBSESSIVE-COMPULSIVES

- The Workaholic
- The Worry Wart
- The Control Freak
- The Dark Cloud
- By The Books
- Penny Pincher
- Perfectionist
- Fussy
- Strict
- Demanding
- Scrupulous
- Exigent
- Difficult
- Hard to please
- Imperious

SIMILAR PERSONALITY TYPES
TO THE OBSESSIVE-COMPULSIVE

- THE ANTISOCIAL PERSONALITY
- THE NARCISSISTIC PERSONALITY
- THE SCHIZOID PERSONALITY

VIEWING SUGGESTIONS FOR THE OBSESSIVE-COMPULSIVE PERSONALITY

As Good As It Gets (1997)—Comedy, 139, Rated R.
Jack Nicholson's Oscar winning perform-ance as Melvin. Favors heavily the Obsessive-Compulsive Disorder, nonethe-less a great film for inspiration and exam-ples brilliantly conveyed.

California Split (1974)—Comedy, 108, Rated R.
Robert Altman's look at two obsessive gam-blers, Bill and Charlie.

Crossfire (1947)—Crime, 86, No rating.
For Robert Ryan's performance as the obses-sive, isolated Montgomery—an anti-Semitic killer. Also interesting for the Paranoia Chapter. John Paxton's writing was Oscar nominated.

Gambler, The (1974)—Drama, 111, Rated R.
Robert Altman returns to the gambling theme—this time with an obsessive James Caan in the lead role.

Hard Eight (1997)—Drama, 101, Rated R.
Fascinating take on the gambling scene by then newcomer Paul Thomas Johnson.

House of Games (1987)—Crime, 102, Rated R.
Lindsay Crouse as Dr. Margaret Ford—author of a book about obsessive-compul-sive behavior—finds her life becomes the real thing.

Interiors (1978)—Drama, 93, Rated PG.
Geraldine Page in a pristine performance (as well as Academy Award nominated) that offers great examples and insights. Oscar nominated for the writing.

Lost In America (1985)—Comedy, 91, Rated R.
Albert Brooks' obsessive-compulsive version of *Easy Rider.*

Mosquito Coast, The (1986)—Adventure, 117, Rated PG.
Dark portrayal of the obsessive-compulsive world. A good example of why lead characters rarely demonstrate this personality type. The hardship for an audience to care for these people . . . even when portrayed by Harrison Ford.

Say Anything . . . (1989)—Drama/Comedy, 100, Rated PG-13.
For the primary female character, Diane.

PRIOR TO READING THE NEXT CHAPTER
IT IS RECOMMENDED THAT THE FOLLOWING
FILMS BE VIEWED:

FIVE EASY PIECES
POWDER
SILENT RUNNING

A LIST OF FILMS PERTAINING TO THE
SCHIZOID PERSONALITY CAN BE FOUND
AT THE END OF THIS CHAPTER.

7

THE SCHIZOID PERSONALITY

If you wouldn't open your mouth,
everything would be just fine.
—Robert Dupeau/Adrien Joyce (Carol Eastman)

B OBBY (IN BOB Rafelson's marker film, *Five Easy Pieces*) is inarguably a genius. He's gifted—he excels at everything he tries—be it playing an etude by Chopin or bowling a winning game down at the local lanes. Yet despite these seeming advantages, he chooses to work on oil rigs (that is, when he can get a job). He spends his spare time drinking beer out of a can, listening to country music on a jukebox, and flirting with low-rent beauty parlor habitués. He shares a bed with a woman, Rayette Dipesto, who is so inappropriate for him that he can't bring himself to calling her by her first name. He addresses her (when he must), with no small note of condescension, as simply "Dipesto." Bobby fled his comfortable, affluent home (a veritable nest of musical geniuses) in the Pacific Northwest for a life of tenuous manual labor and the company of undereducated, less than ambitious crackers. He abandons his potential and the expectations of society for a world he never has to fear fitting into.

The titular Powder, from the movie *Powder*, is a hairless (he has an innate capacity for self-electrolysis), painfully pale (he's an albino), sensitive young man who is saddled with having to go through life as a semiconductor. He was emotionally abused as a child by an angry father and then by distant grandparents. He has never been allowed any interaction with the outside world due to the familial embarrassment his odd appearance might cause. He is found in the basement of his grandparents' house after the grandfather has died, and ushered, begrudgingly, into society. Powder has only contempt for the outside world—he is bullied for being physically different, misunderstood for being mentally superior, and vilified for his unusual ability to conduct electricity (be it lightning or brain waves). He only wants to return to his basement, to be left alone, harassed by no one. "I don't want to be anywhere that's not home," he tells a well-intentioned social worker. "Home" means in his farmhouse cellar, surrounded by books.

In the outer space of *Silent Running*, Freeman Lowell is stationed in orbit around the Earth. He tends to a vast botanical garden that represents all the species of plant life that the barren earth has become too polluted to sustain. Freeman is a solitary figure, dressing in a natural fiber tunic instead of the regulation space suit, eating fresh cantaloupe instead of tubes of synthetic space food, and letting his hair grow wild. He is an object of derision for his fellow, tour-of-duty astronauts, but he doesn't care. He is happiest when alone, isolated, tending his plants and nurturing lost ecosystems. He is an iconoclast, self-absorbed and focused on his personal mission. While his comrades race around in utility vehicles, bored, biding their time as they wait to return home, Freeman Lowell has no desire to ever return home. He is happiest in orbit—the sole occupant of his own little world while below him the planet for which he has little concern spins away, on a fast track to self-destruction.

THE OUTSIDER

The term "schizoid" refers to the defensive tendency to withdraw, to pull back from the complex and confusing tangles of interpersonal relationships. It is a need to retreat to an inner world in which the rules and expectations they adhere to are solely of their own devising. The Schizoid Personality is the ultimate outsider, standing at a distance from the rest of the world—a casual, dispassionate observer of the human condition.

Schizoids are not considered psychotic and should not be confused with those diagnosed with *Schizophrenia*, which is an organic malady marked by delusions and hallucinations. They may seem peculiar and eccentric, but they have no severe oddities in behavior or perception. They are often described as "sensitive" or "gentle." Unlike the Antisocial (whose self-esteem comes from gaining power over others) or the Narcissistic Personality (whose self-esteem comes from the admiration of others), Schizoid individuals (at least in outward appearances) don't care what other people think. Regardless, they do face a tug-of-war between a fear that their own neediness will harm or drive away others and a fear that others will consume their identity. On the continuum of personality disorders, some Schizoid individuals may just seem introspective, whereas others may be socially disabled. An interesting delineation of the Schizoid is that generally they are much less fearful of abandonment than they are of being consumed.

As a result of this tug-of-war, the outward and the inward life for the Schizoid exist mostly in a state of contradiction. They are rarely sure of who they are. It will come as no surprise then that the films and stories that represent these individuals will also appear as an eccentric mixed bag. Here is a personality that includes both a teenager with an affection for killer rats (the horror luxury *Willard*) and a painfully shy woman dominated by her tyrannical father in 1850s New York City (William Wyler's exquisite interpretation of *The Heiress*). There is the dispassionate wiretapper, Harry Caul (*The Conversation*); the introverted Harold (the small marvel *Harold and Maude*); and sundry mad scientists (*The Fly*). Some are wealthy and some are poor. Some lived in centuries past and others live far in the future. Some are powerful and strong and some are terribly weak. What they do have in common is that they are all misfits. Oddballs, to say the least. They all share the inherent traits of being removed, unemotional, aloof, eccentric, loners, and (to varying degrees) asexual.

The most apparent aspect of the Schizoid is his disregard for social conventions and expectations. Freeman Lowell (*Silent Running*) forgoes the macho roughhousing for his pursuit of pastoral serenity; Bobby (*Five Easy Pieces*) turns his back on an expected career in music for the itinerant life of the road; Powder scoffs at the attempts to socialize him and heads back to the farm.

The Schizoid Personality shows a strong degree of detachment. They tend to involve themselves in solitary activities, and (often very intelligent) to excel at them. Freeman, for example, is a brilliant botanist, and Powder can memorize an entire library. Harry Caul (*The Conversation*) is considered the best electronics bugger in the business. Seth Brundle (*The Fly*) is a brilliant scientist, a man so focused on himself that his wardrobe is entirely made up of black clothes so as to avoid wasting time on choices. Such things might distract him from his own desires. Schizoids will withdraw socially. They isolate themselves and they tend to have very few close friends. Freeman (*Silent Running*) prefers the company of drone robots; Bobby (*Five Easy Pieces*) chooses friends (and mates) who are far beneath his intellectual level and are incapable of proving interesting or challenging to him. Peter Miller (*Dressed to Kill*) prefers to stay locked up in his bedroom with his invented gadgets (it is not until his mother is viciously murdered that he steps into the outside world).

Catherine Sloper (*The Heiress*) rarely leaves 16 Washington Square. An interesting backstage side note concerns Montgomery Cliff, who played Catherine's suitor. Cliff was considered bright, aloof, and a bit of a loner (some might say, schizoid). Despite this being what many consider his finest performance, he was unsure of himself in the role. He was apparently in fear of being "consumed" by the legendary talents of William Wyler, Ralph Richardson, and Olivia de Havilland. Cliff found his own schizoid tendencies playing forth and, during the course of the film, he reportedly refused to speak with other cast members or come out of his trailer except for his scenes.

ME AGAINST THEM

Because of this self-distancing, Schizoids often seem aloof, contemptuous. They tend to have an emotional frigidity, a flattened affectivity. They are not forthcoming with their feelings. They don't believe that others could be capable of comprehending what they are feeling and, quite honestly, they don't care if they do. For this reason, they have difficulty with aggression and hostility—bottling it up instead of releasing it. They see themselves apart from the world—disengaged observers—and are therefore not unduly affected by it. Praise or criticism from the world at large means nothing to them. *Five Easy Pieces'* Bobby sneers at Catherine Van Ost, a protégé of his father's, when she tells him how beautifully he has played. He dismisses her by saying that it had no feeling in it whatsoever, that he's played it by rote since he was a child. When Powder is told that his superlative mind might be the next step in the evolution of man, he replies, "So what?"

Unlike the Borderline Personality, who splits the world into all good and all bad, the Schizoid splits the world into himself and everyone else. He is seen as living in two worlds at once—or in his own world bubbled within the larger one (in the case of Freeman Lowell, *orbiting* around the larger one). The outer world is perceived as consuming, distorted, and a threat to the security and individuality of the Schizoid. So he turns inward, creates his own world— Freeman's floating greenhouse, Bobby's lonely sage in a land of fools. He perceives with his own unique vision— Powder's telepathic ability to empathize. He doesn't care whether or not the world misunderstands him.

Because these are inward turning souls, it is not surprising that the Schizoid Personality gravitates to such reflective and self-analytical enterprises as literature, art, and philosophy. On the other end of the spectrum, they are also found in careers that require minimal human interaction such as computers, engineering, and mathematics. Because establishing themselves as separate, distinct entities is central to the Schizoid, they end up appearing as eccentric—authentic in the extreme. Though Bobby shuns the opportunity of individual creative expression of being a pianist for the unstable life of a migrant worker, he is in fact a distinctive individual. Stemming from this result of being separate, the Schizoid Personality is often extremely self-critical, self-effacing. They have only the highest expectations of themselves and they can be very harsh in their self-judgment if the mark is not hit. Powder shrugs off all the amazement at his encyclopedic knowledge; Freeman kills himself because he feels he failed as the protector of the plants. They carry the rare burden that it is not easy to pleasantly surprise oneself—to create something original when the sources and the mysteries of that creation are intimately known and the resultant self-castigation can be scathing. They tend to intellectualize in order to understand the world. They use their high intelligence as a defense and the most adaptive use of this defense is a withdrawal into their creativity. Young Peter Miller (*Dressed to Kill*) has more concern over inventing a gadget that might nab his mother's killer than experiencing any grief over her death. The Schizoid individual is often seen as misunderstood or under-appreciated—geniuses, the special child that everyone failed to recognize. This is precisely because they do not seek recognition or admiration—they walk away from it and hide from it when it is offered.

The Schizoid tends to have a deep interest in non-human pursuits. Peter (*Dressed to Kill*) has his inventions, Seth (*The Fly*) his morbid science, Catherine (*The Heiress*) her embroidery work. Harold (*Harold and Maude*) has managed to morph the concept of non-human pursuits into an attraction to funerals and the dead (people, but dead).

Some Schizoids have a tendency to form strong attachments to animals.

Willard Stiles (*Willard*) is a man who cannot find his place in the world, and he doesn't care. He shares a rambling, musty house with his nagging, manipulative mother and her intrusive friends. At work he is routinely and publicly humiliated by his boss, Mr. Martin, who is the man who stole the business from Willard's father and has set out to destroy the entire family. As Willard retreats from the outside world and isolates himself, he finds at last a suitable set of companions. Queenie, Socrates, and Ben are rats that he was ordered by his mother to kill—instead they become the only creatures to whom he truly opens his heart. With a little training and a lot of love the rats are soon able to destroy Willard's enemies with but a signal from his hand.

THE STORM WITHIN

The Schizoid Personality has difficulty promoting their self-expression. They see no point in making their feelings (pleasure or displeasure) known. They care little that anything they could ever do or say would make any difference to the outside world, which exists as another sphere entirely below the threshold of their concern. When Willard's mother dies he reacts to the news without dropping a tear or uttering a word of regret, or remorse, or love. He takes the news so dispassionately in fact that his mother's ubiquitous friend feels the need to take up the slack and go into a mourning frenzy. For Willard, it is only in his regard for his creative endeavors that he shows any strong emotion at all. When Willard's favorite rat, Socrates, is bludgeoned to death, Willard reacts first by openly sobbing and then, when alone with his surviving rat, Ben, by becoming stricken with guilt and berating himself for his powerlessness to stop the killing.

The Schizoid Personality is not overtly hostile or aggressive and can seem to lack any defenses at all. But this may be a case where placid waters can hide a wicked undertow. The Schizoid can feel hostile and does so often. The fear of being consumed (and the perceived annihilation of their individuality) can incite intense anger. But showing it, exhibiting it, can be dangerous for them. Unlike the Borderline Personality, who directs his hostility outward, the Schizoid directs it inward. It shows up in their unduly harsh criticism of themselves. Witness Freeman Lowell, who takes self-criticism as far at it can go—which means suicide. Very commonly the anger and hostility they feel emerges in their violent fantasies. Willard lies down and takes whatever abuse Mr. Martin feels like serving him—from making him work weekends without overtime to stealing his house out from under him. Though he doesn't defend himself against Mr. Martin, when Willard is alone he enacts all manner of miniature scenarios with his rats that feature aggression and destruction.

The Schizoid also tends to be hypersensitive, which is to say they are over-stimulated by people. This hypersensitivity can also be to light, motion, or noise. Any external stimulation can seem overly intrusive to the acutely interior world of the Schizoid (hence the perception that they are sensitive). This excess stimulation causes them to become more insular or retreat into greater fantasy. Bobby, when faced with Rayette's nagging need for recognition of her talent (or her very existence), merely zones out, damning her singing with faint praise. Catherine Sloper (*The Heiress*) will eventually lock out the world (literally and figuratively) and carry upstairs her single lamp of dimming light into a dark abyss.

The Schizoid customarily seems to hold the knowledge that the world is spiraling unstoppably into catastrophe. So, really, why bother? This fatalistic worldview has actually come to fruition in *Silent Running*, thereby justifying Freeman's derision. Powder, too, doesn't seem to hold much fondness for the outside world—a world that kills deer for sport. He wants to go back to his basement. Mr. Ripley, his insightful math teacher, can't help but agree with him. He tells him that the horror he has witnessed in books can't come close to what goes on in the real world. Powder declines Mr. Ripley's invitation to become part of the solution.

RELATIONSHIPS

Considering all this, the Schizoid's major font of problems is in the sphere of interpersonal relationships. Social settings present times of great discomfort for them. They feel awkward and fraudulent. They have little capacity or patience for idle social chitchat. At the family dinner table, Bobby can only roll his eyes contemptuously at the forced civility of the situation. At his own birthday party, Willard is at first annoyed and then openly disgusted at the banter of his mother's friends that is meant to encourage him. Finally he takes his piece of cake and, without a word of explanation or apology, leaves the house.

Schizoid individuals take pleasure in few if any social activities, and, being ill at ease, their attempts at humor come off as forced or inappropriate. Most of their anxiety centers on keeping their life safe and differentiated. Social activities, by definition, demand fitting in with and becoming part of the greater whole. This is the utter opposite of what the Schizoid wants. When forced into such situations, the Schizoid's defenses are triggered. They isolate themselves and the result is that they are then perceived as aloof, snobbish, superior.

But, being human beings first and Schizoid second, they also desire love and closeness. They want the bonding, the attention, but are very uncomfortable (and may even panic) when they get it. There exists a real fear that their needs will send others away. In *Five Easy Pieces*, Bobby chooses a mate with whom he has absolutely no common ground, intellectually or socially. This prevents him from ever getting too close to her. She's a body in the bed next to him, but he couldn't care less if she leaves him or stays. When Bobby's familial problems are at last put to rest and he is on the road again with Rayette and it looks as though that may be all he has left, he abandons her. With not so much as a kiss goodbye, he hitches a ride with a logger while she is in the restroom of a gas station. Catherine Sloper (*The Heiress*) uses the outward projection of her insecurities (the desire/fear of being loved) to ward off suitor after suitor.

Relationships become an emotional tug of war with the Schizoid, both internally and with their partners. The Schizoid, in non-threatening situations—or at least before intimacy has become an expectation—may seem gentle, intimate, honest. But the situation must include insurmountable walls protecting the Schizoid in order to make him feel safe enough to let down his guard. Powder is sincere and affectionate with a young girl from school (Lindsey), but society has enforced a distance between them. Bobby is very sincere and forthcoming with Catherine Van Ost, but both she and Bobby know that he is unavailable. The Schizoid can be very genuine, even needy, as long as the line that prevents others from getting too close is not crossed. That line is crucial. It protects his uniqueness (his essence) from the threat of being subsumed by the other person. Harry Caul (*The Conversation*) recites a list to a woman he believes is falling in love with him. It is a list of all the negative attributes a man such as him has to offer—a damning self-criticism. Harry asks her if she would stay with such a man if all he could offer her were that he said he loved her. The woman responds, "How would I know he loved me?" To which Harry sadly concedes, "You would never know."

The Schizoid is generally not the most sexual of people. They regularly remain detached and removed when in the act. They may be perfectly orgasmic, but they rarely abandon themselves to the ecstasy of the moment. They tend to save their sensual intensity for their creative endeavors. Schizoids are commonly lovers at a distance. Bobby only acquiesces to Rayette's incessant pleas for declarations of love with a contemptuous monosyllable when her whining threatens to interfere with his sleep. Powder returns Mr. Ripley's advances of friendship with a curt, "I don't need a friend." On one level, they crave closeness and complain of alienation and loneliness (even though it is self-imposed). They are sincere, sensitive, and disarmingly honest because they have no time or interest in the maze of social games and pretensions. They are blunt, forthright, and real—their paucity of social skills serves them well in this area and can make them very attractive. But the push/pull of love and fear makes them very trying as mates. No sooner do they attract others—which they may well have wanted to do—than they must force them away out of their own pathological sense of self-preservation. The attention required by a mate, the conjoining of identities called for in a relationship, is stifling. For this reason the Schizoid rarely marries.

BACKSTORY

The Schizoid is viewed developmentally as being fixated at the oral stage, at around the time of the "terrible twos." There is an early decision made to isolate. Quite often this self-imposed exile occurs because there has been a failure to receive what they need from the mother (sometimes the father). This rejection means that they can make no further attempts to receive what they need from others later on in their lives. It is also not uncommon for the child to interpret their neediness as the cause of the parent seeming to be driven away from them. Later, they will deny wanting from others for fear it will drive them away as well.

The childhood of the Schizoid can go one of two very different ways.

The primary caregivers (or the childhood environment) may be intrusive or domineering. The parents are often overinvested or over-involved with the child. They may transgress the personal boundaries, through being either overprotective or hypercritical. Bobby's siblings and father are all noted musicians and the expectation that he would follow in the family footsteps are tangible. He could play Chopin at the age of 8. No child, no matter how gifted, can do that without a strict regimen and discipline. Bobby has musical greatness thrust upon him, and his reaction was to turn his back and flee. When Catherine Van Ost asks him why he wasted his life, he is surprised, saying that in no way does he consider his life wasted. This child then escapes to an inward world of imagination and exclusion in order to form a healthy ego.

Conversely, the childhood of the Schizoid may be one of loneliness and relative neglect. Powder is rejected and abused by his father and subsequently banished to the cellar by his grandparents (ostensibly to keep him from frying them). Dr. Sloper (*The Heiress*) holds his daughter Catherine accountable for the death of his wife. All of her life, Catherine has been dictated over and punished. In this scenario, the child will retreat into a fantasy world to create a safe, nurturing environment: a place where he feels accepted; a place where the only type of parenting available to him will be a symbolic one—one that he must supply for himself.

THE ARC OF A
SCHIZOID FILM CHARACTER

Harry Caul in Francis Ford Coppola's early showing of film making power, *The Conversation*, is a surveillance expert who is a genius in his business of covertly recording the business of others. He is excellent at his job because he is, by the necessity of his profession, detached from the world—a dispassionate observer and cataloguer of behavior. He is detached, removed, unmoved. He is presented to us as an almost prototypical Schizoid. Coppola's filming emphasizes these qualities—he wears a translucent wrinkled raincoat at all times, in all weather, a shield through which he can see the world but is nonetheless protected from it. He is also frequently filmed using long shots and a static, mounted camera—this conveys how dwarfed he is by his surroundings, how easily engulfed he is, and how impersonally he moves through the world, even his own home. His very name is symbolic—a caul is the veil of tissue over a newborn infant's face; again a mask, a separation that keeps Harry and the world apart (although he can still observe it). To emphasize this, throughout *The Conversation* Harry is filmed as though through a caul. He is shot with his face covered by a sheer curtain, through an opaque shower door. When his rival surveillance man, Bernie Moran, confronts him about his responsibility in the deaths of former clients, Harry secludes himself behind a translucent scrim before responding.

Harry prides himself in not letting anyone in. When his landlady surprises him with a birthday gift left in his apartment he upbraids her, demanding to know how and why she has the keys to let herself in. She explains that she needs them in case of an emergency. Harry responds that he would rather have all of his personal things burn up in a fire because, as he tells her, "I don't have anything personal." He also tells her that he's getting himself a post office box for his mail from that day forward—one with a combination: "No keys."

As is often the case with the Schizoid, Harry is exquisitely talented in one area, an area that luckily happens to be his livelihood. "Harry's the best," Moran grudgingly admits. It is by no coincidence that Harry's job requires no personal interaction.

In Act One, we see that Harry has a relationship (of sorts) with a girl named Amy. It is a relationship that places no undue pressure on him for commitment, one that is not threatening because it is of such little importance (not unlike the relationship Bobby has with Rayette Dipesto in *Five Easy Pieces*). Amy is sweet, cherubic (if not perhaps a little thick), and so malleable that it is easy for Harry to keep her at arm's length. She doesn't know where Harry works, where he lives, or anything remotely personal about him. Their entire relationship can be summed up in that he visits her at night and pays her rent. She asks him questions because, she claims, she wants to know him. He responds to her inquisition by telling her that he doesn't "want people asking me a lot of questions." Then he leaves. His privacy is of paramount importance and any intrusion into his private life is anathema to him—interesting because his lucrative career is based on violating the privacy of others.

Act One ends with Harry, isolated and alone, riding a bus and haunted by the fates of the young couple, Ann and Mark, whose conversation he has recorded for a high paying client known only as "the Director."

In Act Two, Harry Caul's entrenched Schizoid behavior is severely challenged. Because he is feeling dangerously empathetic with Ann (the woman on whom he spied), he lashes out at Stan, his colleague, when Stan questions him on the nature of the tapes. "It's curiosity," Stan shrugs, "You ever hear of that? It's human nature." "I don't know about human nature," Harry yells at him. "That's not part of what I do." In life as well as work, it would seem. He also lashes out at Moran who, in an effort to impress him, secretly plants a microphone in Harry's lapel. This breach of Harry's privacy sends him reeling and he explodes in such volcanic ire that his guests shrink away, frightened and alarmed.

We learn through Moran that his callus, disinterested ways led to the killing of three people in New York. Haunted by the guilt of that incident, he begins to humanize the very people to whom he should retain an utmost professional distance, Ann and Mark. Although he would be loath to bring himself to reach out from the protective bubble of his self-imposed isolation, he realizes that history could repeat itself—Ann and Mark could be killed as a result of his actions. He forces himself to care, to get involved, and to take action. He withholds the incriminating tapes from the Director. When the tapes are stolen from Harry's workshop, he goes to the hotel where the murder will occur to try and somehow stop it.

Also in Act Two, we are given a brief peek into the childhood of Harry Caul when he has a dream and warns Ann of the impending threat to her life. He tells her a little something about himself, which is typical of the formative years of the Schizoid Personality. He tells Ann about being ill as a child, so ill that he was paralyzed and had to be washed by his mother—circumstances forcing her into the role of doting mother. It is not inconceivable that this kind of incident would blur the lines of privacy for the growing child's emerging selfhood. Harry also recalls how once his mother had to answer the phone in the middle of a bath. Helpless, young Harry began sinking into the water, the fear of being consumed taking a very tangible turn.

In Act Three, Harry takes decisive action. Despite having already accepted the money for the tapes, and despite the very real physical danger, he goes against all of his tendencies to isolate and heads to the hotel where he believes the Director will kill his young wife, Ann. Once in the adjacent hotel room, Harry goes through a Schizoid's waking nightmare. He hears the screams and violence in the next room but he is unable to make himself leave the physical cocoon of the room—mirroring the isolation he imposes on himself emotionally. He wants to break out, reach out into the world, but he finds that he is unable. His isolation that was once his sanctuary is now his prison. It is at this point that Harry (up until now a perfectly functional Schizoid) crosses over into psychosis. The line separating healthy suspicion from abject paranoia becomes blurred—real and imagined dangers become indistinguishable. We become uncertain as to what Harry is seeing: an actual murder or delusions. When it turns out that a murder did take place, but that the victims (or so Harry presumed) turned out to be the perpetrators, Harry is told that he is being watched. He knows who the real murderers are, and they know that he knows. When they let him know that his privacy has been breached, he goes on a rampage and completely tears apart his home—obsessively, methodically slashing up and destroying not only all of his belongings, but the walls and floor as well.

THE SCHIZOID PERSONALITY SUMMARY

Examples of the qualities and qualifications that define a person with a Schizoid Personality:

- They exhibit a pervasive need to detach from any social situation
- They tend to be loners with few close friends or confidantes (if they do have friendships, it is usually just one close friend)
- They are usually not close to their families
- They are not joiners
- They tend to be unemotional or at least undemonstrative
- Though they may be sexually functional and orgasmic, they tend to show very little interest in sex with other people. If they do, the sex tends to be perfunctory
- They tend to gravitate toward solitary activities and pursuits
- They don't seem to take pleasure in any activities *except* for their solitary pursuits
- They are often perceived as being aloof, distant, or frigid
- They often appear to others as being eccentric, lonely, isolated
- They are not usually garrulous, and almost never volunteer personal information
- They seem indifferent to either the praise or the criticism of others
- They tend to be severely self-critical
- They seldom marry or, if they do, the union is usually passionless

- They exhibit discomfort in social situations
- They gravitate toward jobs that are solitary and require little interaction with people
- They show little concern for the day to day lives of those around them
- They are usually unable to express anger directly
- They tend to invest a lot of their energy in non-human interests, such as academics and science
- They can become very fond of and deeply attached to animals
- They often find it difficult to maintain eye contact for very long periods
- They tend to be good at pursuits that involve theory, philosophy, or the arts
- They are usually non-confrontational and therefore usually seem passive
- They usually have a disregard and contempt for conventional social expectations
- They usually have a fear of being subsumed or obliterated by others
- They generally are much less fearful of abandonment than they are of being consumed

NOTEWORTHY CHARACTERISTICS
OF THE SCHIZOID PERSONALITY

SPEECH

Representative of isolation from society. Simplistic or highly evolved vocabulary—it lacks influence from society.

PROFESSIONS

Drawn to careers such as literature, art, and philosophy. Or on the other end of the spectrum, careers that require little human interaction such as computers, engineering, and mathematics.

DRESS

Eccentric, odd, non-compliant with societal norms. Not highly influenced by fashion.

HEALTH

Not particularly obsessed with matters of health. Absence of stress-induced illnesses. Not particularly affected by stresses of the world.

POPULAR CLICHÉS
ASSOCIATED WITH SCHIZOIDS

- Weirdo
- Oddball
- Misfit
- Sensitive
- A Prodigy
- Stuck up
- Snobbish
- Spinster
- Eccentric
- Leper
- Pariah
- Droll
- Duck

SIMILAR PERSONALITY TYPES
TO THE SCHIZOID

- THE PARANOID PERSONALITY

VIEWING SUGGESTIONS FOR
THE SCHIZOID PERSONALITY

Conversation, The (1974)—Drama, 113, Rated PG.
For Gene Hackman as Harry Caul. Assuredly one of his finest performances. Oscar nominated for Best Picture and for the Original screenplay by Coppola.

Dressed to Kill (1980)—Thriller, 105, Rated R.
Keith Gordon as Peter Miller, the "nerd" son of razor victim Angie Dickinson.

Five Easy Pieces (1970)—Drama, 98, Rated R.
An instant classic performance by Jack Nicholson as Robert. The film was nominated for Best Picture. Nicholson was Oscar nominated for his performance. Adrien Joyce and Bob Rafelson were nominated for writing one of the most remarkable scripts of any decade.

Fly, The (1986)—Horror, 100, Rated R.
For Jeff Goldblum as creepy, crazy scientist Seth Brundle—well on his way to never having to interact with the human species again. Careful what you wish for. NOTE: this is a remake of a 1958 horror film and errs (at least for the first half) a little more on the human/psychological side of the character. Once the fly becomes the fly, director Cronenberg can't resist the gross-out horror value and all bets are off.

Harold and Maude (1972)—Comedy, 90, Rated PG.
Bud Cort as Harold. Wonderful, brilliant
examples of the Schizoid. Forever a classic.

Heiress, The (1949)—Drama, 115, No rating.
Olivia de Havilland as Catherine.
Unquestionably her finest work. Not surprisingly, she took home the Oscar. Perhaps
one of the finest films ever made. So many
people at the top of their form. Nominated
for eight Academy Awards—oddly though,
not for the exceptional writing that got
everyone there.

Powder (1995)—Fantasy/Drama, 111, Rated PG-13.
For Sean Patrick Flanery as Powder.

Silent Running (1971)—Science Fiction, 89, Rated G.
For Bruce Dern as Freeman.

Willard (1971)—Horror, 95, Rated PG.
For Bruce Davidson as Willard.

PRIOR TO READING THE NEXT CHAPTER
IT IS RECOMMENDED THAT THE FOLLOWING
FILMS BE VIEWED:

WELCOME TO THE DOLLHOUSE
SWINGERS
SUGARBABY

A LIST OF FILMS PERTAINING TO THE
MASOCHISTIC PERSONALITY CAN BE FOUND
AT THE END OF THIS CHAPTER.

8

THE MASOCHISTIC PERSONALITY

All the time I keep feeling the need to destroy it.
—Bree Daniels/Andy & Dave Lewis

DAWN WEINER, in *Welcome to the Dollhouse*, is a prepubescent girl who goes through life so deflated that she can no longer summon up enough gumption to do battle with the epithet, "Weinerdog." It is a chorus that echoes through the school corridors whenever she passes. She falls victim to the belief that she is not smart enough—certainly not when compared to her older brother, Mark; not pretty enough—especially when compared to her little sister, Missy; and not special enough to merit any concern, let alone love . . . even parental love. Though she longs for the affection of a high school stud named Steve, the only attention that she gets from boys is the promise of rape by the school bully, Brendan. Dawn learns the tough lesson that, even when she is stranded alone in New York City, her parents can't tear themselves from their ministrations to sister Missy to come to the phone. Dear little Missy who has only to don a ballerina outfit to become her parents' little princess.

Mike, a reluctant swinger in *Swingers*, is a scrambling actor and denizen of LA's seedy-chic hipster world of borderline poverty—a world in which poverty is not a source of denigration, but the status quo. Despite his friend Trent's claim that he is "money" and that the "beautiful babies" are ripe for his plucking, he feels otherwise. He moons over his old girlfriend who he left behind in New York. He will leap at any opportunity to whine and moan over his own self-induced pathetic plight.

Munich's own Marianne (*Sugarbaby*), whose girth is directly proportionate to her depression, works at the R.I.P Funeral Home, where she hauls caskets, dresses corpses, and in general chooses to live her life amongst the dead. In the living world, she is much less generous with her affections for life. She goes through life numb—a gray, expressionless slab responding to nothing that goes on around her. For fun, she floats, alone, in a pool. And she eats. She prepares huge trays of food to take to bed with her, and then she falls asleep watching television.

MORAL MASOCHISM

The concept of masochism usually brings to mind images of sexual deviation or, at the very least, someone who enjoys physical pain. Those who use physical pain in the pursuit of pleasure are masochist. The individual who needs pain to feel more alive—who cuts himself and relish at the sight of his own blood because it proves he is alive. These individuals enjoy feeling pain because it means that at least they are feeling something. Though these individuals can be considered masochists, of more importance here is the individual who displays what Freud labeled "*moral masochism.*" We are talking about the individual whose personality exhibits the need for suffering, complaining, self-damage, and self-deprecation. These people feel they need to live a life that is self-defeating, that they need to endure pain and suffering for their own greater good. Sexual masochists, on the other hand, are not necessarily self-defeating. They may only adopt masochism in carnal situations as a means of acting out fantasies. The reverse may also be true: a self-defeating person may not necessarily be masochistic during sex.

To note: Masochism is not technically considered a Personality Disorder (with regard to the DSM), but it is considered a personality style in psychodynamic literature. The reason for this variance is somewhat of a conundrum. Suffice to say the complex ideological opinions within the psychological community have placed the Masochist's titled status firmly in an interpretive world about as defined and specific as the nature of life itself. The Masochist presents, without a doubt, a perplexing and intriguing personality dilemma. More importantly, it shows up in some very good films. A great place to start encountering the Masochist: the canon of films regarding prostitutes. Hollywood and hookers have had a long love affair and you need go no further than a computer key-word search for "streetwalker" to encounter jaw dropping proof of a passionate liaison ("hooker" provided a list of some 750 films). From *American Gigolo* to *Whore* and from *Belle de Jour* to *Taxi Driver*, filmmakers return with a vengeance time and again to this tried and true persona.

A debate could boil over here about the true nature of the oldest profession in the world: that it has more to do with a male dominated (male oppressive) society rather than psychology. Nonetheless, where films are concerned, more often than not the stories portray these characters victimized by forces from without as well as struggling with their own demons within. To understand the latter aspect, a study of the nature of the masochistic persona and its related personality types will be beneficial.

The gal (or guy) with a heart of gold offers wonderful opportunities to see the manifestations of the masochist—

quite often in very bold, primal strokes. For the purposes of study, this is ideal. The ability to only feel gratified when they are victimized, the desire for punishment, the attraction to unhappy relationships, their sense of unworthiness, and the belief that it is better to be abused than to remain untouched and rejected—all appear regularly within the call girl psychodynamic. Two great standouts exhibiting signs of the masochist: *Leaving Las Vegas* and *L.A. Confidential*. Also, perhaps best known for going to this well on more than one occasion, is Shirley MacLaine. *Some Came Running, Irma La Douce*, and Bob Fosse's underappreciated *Sweet Charity* give us memorable portrayals. *Irma La Douce* got MacLaine the attention of the Academy, as did her character Fran in Billy Wilder's *The Apartment*. The "battered wife" genre also offers great viewing with such films as *Sleeping with the Enemy, The Burning Bed*, and *What's Love Got to Do With It?* Some give us interesting glances into the lives of teenagers exhibiting signs of this trait—John Hughes' touching *Some Kind of Wonderful* with Mary Stuart Masterson in a heartfelt performance as a young girl struggling with her sense of self.

The Masochist in film—the true Masochist—is often hard to find. Many characters in film embody certain characteristics of this psychological condition—observe Humphrey Bogart's character, Rick, in *Casablanca*; Ryan O'Neal's loony punching bag, Howard Bannister, in *What's Up, Doc?*; the put upon Thelma (Geena Davis) in *Thelma and Louise*; or Kathy Bates in *Dolores Claiborne*. These films offer sound examples. . . if somewhat abstract in their interpretation. It is rare for films to take on characters that embody the full manner. The Masochist appears weak by their traits, and weak characters at the center of a story can be terribly difficult to root for. This is not to say that psychotic killers are easy to love, but their irrational behavior becomes acceptable because they are seen as disturbed and irrational individuals. But a character that is a Masochist frequently appears to be a "normal" person in all other ways. When we experience their self-destructive tendencies, such as seen in an abusive relationship, common sense and logic cause the viewer to lose empathy. We shake our heads at these characters and wonder why they don't walk away from such a mess. Dolores (Kathy Bates in *Dolores Claiborne*) wins our appeal because her masochistic tendencies are mostly in the past. She has recently taken some definitive steps to dealing with her problem. A stellar performance by Jane Fonda as Bree Daniels (in *Klute*) as well as Carrie Snodgress' beautifully insinuated portrayal of Tina Balser (in *Diary of a Mad Housewife*) are further prime examples of a lead character that embodies the Masochistic Personality and pulls it off. Primarily this occurs for two reasons. First, there is the quality of the performances, but more importantly the stories are told specifically from their perspective; the view of the other characters is slightly askew—perhaps not the way we would see them, but the way the central character interprets them. When done to full effect and we witness the entire world through the eyes of the lead character (when our world becomes their world), it is nearly impossible not to develop some empathy and understanding for them and the journey they are on.

THE ACCIDENT WAITING TO HAPPEN

The self-defeating behavior of the Masochistic Personality goes against the belief that human beings are inherently pleasure seeking, at least in the obvious sense. Their habitual need for self-imposed suffering actually affords the Masochist a sense of moral triumph and they hold that triumph high. It can be a sense of penitence, a feeling of release that someone (themselves) is so inherently worthless that he or she is only getting what is due. There is also a martyrdom possibility—they get to feel special for being so constantly put upon. Although it certainly can't be pleasurable to be consistently taunted, Dawn Weiner (*Welcome to the Dollhouse*) is inarguably the most special girl in school. Her locker is decorated with highly ornate script proclaiming "Weinerdog" and "Woof Woof." She definitely gets more attention than do any of the other girls—certainly more than she herself gets at home from her parents. It is a behavior that provides an efficient way for Masochists to have their needs met. By being submissive, downtrodden, they can garner sympathy. Pain is a form of attention. Sympathy is better than nothing. In *Swingers*, Mike is constantly bemoaning his fate and his failure with girls. "Girls don't go for me the way they go for you," he tells Trent. But every time he does complain this invariably goads his friends into telling him how "money" he is. It is a constant Pavlovian source of attention, compliments, and positive reinforcement.

Masochists may also believe they are suffering pain and anguish (and are only too happy to do so) as a way of circumventing greater pain, such as that related to abandonment. Marianne (*Sugarbaby*) in Munich pines for the U-Bahn conductor known as Huber 133. She is lonely, emotionally atrophied, and she tortures herself by repeatedly playing a record of "Sugarbaby." It's their song, although Huber doesn't know it yet. Marianne raises herself up from the muck of despair and obsessively pursues Huber, knowing full well that he is a married man. She finally manages to seduce him. She then suffers devastating humiliation at the hands of Mrs. Huber, and she loses him. Her pain is excruciating. The lesson for the Masochists is that it is better to pine and moan (and suffer in hope) than to actually lose that which you want most. Hence, Dawn's attachment to high school heartthrob Steve Rogers in *Welcome to the Dollhouse* and Mike's attachment to Michelle (the girl he left behind) in *Swingers*.

The Masochistic Personality commonly feels that their lot in life is no fault of their own but rather is merely bad karma, a short straw drawn at reincarnation time, being born under some unlucky astrological trine. Masochists feel they deserve this lot in life. They believe they are essentially unworthy of better treatment. For Masochists, the whole world is against them. More importantly, the whole world is right. An interesting film that explores this is an odd little gem called *Such Good Friends*. It's worth viewing if for no other reason then to see the results of a collaboration between the seemingly humorless director Otto Preminger and comic writer Elaine May (using a pseudonym here). Dyan Cannon gives a polished performance as a housewife lost on a journey into self-abasement.

The Masochistic Personality tends to be passive, isolated, and demoralized. Huber's (*Sugarbaby*) wife bursts into the disco where Marianne has taken Huber for a night on the town. Pushing her way through the crowd to Marianne, she mercilessly pummels Marianne's head with her purse. Marianne stands there, unflinching, cowed—deserving. Dawn Weiner cloisters herself in her "Special People's Club," the only other member being someone more outcast than herself. They are also great practitioners of self-sabotage. They experience a constant attack on their self-esteem, security, or physical well being. In order to circumvent that, they take the initiative and launch the attack on themselves. Marianne's greatest hurdle on her path to a vibrant social life is her excess weight, yet the first thing that she does when she experiences rejection is to plow through a plate of pastries. Mike finally meets a girl with whom he might be able to forget his past girlfriend and somehow mend his broken heart. After getting her phone number, his friends (true swingers) advise him to wait a few days before calling her. Instead, Mike arrives home that night, well into the wee hours of the next day, and calls her. In an effort not to appear needy, he leaves repeated messages on her answering machine, trying to undo the pathetic damage he had done with each previous message. Only managing to dig himself deeper, he finally calls off the whole relationship before it has begun.

Such individuals will commonly feel that the punishment they constantly receive is in their best interest. The Masochist's unconscious need for punishment is based on guilt and leads to self-inflicted suffering via accidents, financial loss, failure, disgrace, and unhappy relationships. Marianne falls in love not only with a married man, but also with a beautiful one who does not acknowledge the space that she takes up. Dawn Weiner sets herself up for disappointment by falling in love with an older high school heartthrob who only has interest in beauty queens who have already developed sexually. Charity Hope Valentine, Cabiria, Sera, (*Sweet Charity, Nights of Cabiria, Leaving Las Vegas*) and their fellow working girls all have resumes of wrong men. They punish themselves by looking for love in all the wrong places.

Masochists often actively use their victimhood. After all, they assume the mantle of the victim to gain sympathy. They use victimization to gain love. The prostitute character Bree Daniels in *Klute* holds (through denigrating herself) a certain power over her customers. Because she knows she is at the bottom of the heap (as a hooker), there is nowhere to go but up; or, more importantly, she has the security of knowing that her life can't possibly get any worse. She's wrong, of course, and therein lies the play.

Masochists are often consumed by feelings of unworthiness and the subsequent rejection therefrom. But self-fulfilling prophecies may come into play here. They make themselves unworthy—they feed into what makes people reject them. Marianne feeds the problem that defeats her. Mike mopes, giving up before attempting, or willfully not playing it cool by heeding the advice of his sexually successful friends. Instead of waiting to call a girl, he calls her so much that it borders on stalking.

Masochists also exhibit a near constant sense of being incomplete. Something is always missing in their lives. What's missing is love. Hardly a surprise. They feel unappreciated, operating with the feeling that if someone would actually take the time, they would find something valuable, something to nurture. As it is, that *something* inside of them goes unrecognized. Instead of demanding their worth be appreciated, they jump on the bandwagon of taunting and hatred, often being the first to deride their own person. As they perceive attacks from others, they enthusiastically attack themselves. No one is more victimized than those who allow it, let alone encourage it. Few scenes in films can apprehend the heart and essence of a personality style as well as the shot from *Sugarbaby* in which Marianne, at work in the funeral home, holds hands with a corpse as if it were her boyfriend. Desperate for love, even if it's from the dead.

TRIUMPH OF THE UNDERDOG

Masochists may believe that those around them are inferior, yet they will do nothing to reverse the status of their own inferiority. Mike knows that he is sensitive, loving, and that his swinger friends show little consideration to women (if not outright contempt), but he is content to mope and wallow and condemn Trent's behavior. Meanwhile, Trent makes off with all the "beautiful babies." Dawn Weiner knows that her sister is a spoiled, manipulative, prancing caricature of a princess, but she bows down to her parents' adoration of her lesser siblings and humbly takes her place as the ugly handmaiden. As with Mike's mumbled complaints, Dawn only shows her displeasure in private. She finds an outlet for her rage by sawing off the heads of Missy's dolls (a scene for the audience that elevates Dawn to near Norma Rae status).

These individuals seem to enjoy their punishment and suffering and often they brag about it to others. Masochists seldom forgo the opportunity to gush about their misery and self-efface. They are the quickest ones to point out their own faults and shortcomings, even if none exist. They constantly beat themselves up, usually verbally, but also physically. What this pride in victimhood does for the Masochist is provide them with the triumph of the underdog. Their martyrdom belittles their attackers and because they exalt in their suffering—because their self-esteem is enhanced by it—they can outwardly appear grandiose, scornful. Dawn Weiner sneers at the gorgeous have-alls who, if not bullying her, ignore her. Marianne is fully aware of the withering glances she gets, not only for her occupation, but for her girth as well. Instead of cowering or being ashamed, she holds her head high. She seems almost haughty.

The Masochist can also suffer from a fear of success. Egocentric, they destroy everything good that happens to them. This is because their pattern of behavior has worked for them so far. Why change things? They have managed to get the desired attention and sometimes even sympathetic affection. They have come up with a method of behaving that has produced results. If they ever became winners they would lose their status as martyrs—they would be introduced into a new and alien circumstance in which they would not know how to operate. They might be noticed, and then they would lose the comfort of anonymity. They would lose the ability (and hence the reassuring leisure) to fail. With success comes a standard they must live up to. With success comes pressure to promulgate that success, or fail more miserably. The fall doesn't hurt as badly when you're already as low as you can go. But perhaps the most compelling cause of the fear of success is the Masochist's deep-rooted feelings of unworthiness. Masochists feel that they don't deserve success or love,and if they achieve or receive it, they feel that sooner or later they will be exposed as frauds.

To ensure avoiding such scenarios, the Masochist uses a host of defense mechanisms. Chief among these defense mechanisms:

- Denial

- Reaction Formation

- Deflection of Guilt

- Immoralization

- Projection

- Acting Out

- Repetition Compulsion

Denial—this denial is most recognizably seen in the previously mentioned belief that they themselves are not responsible for their suffering that it is instead due to the workings of outside, malignant forces. They take little responsibility for their own abject misery. They are victims of "God's ill humor."

The Masochistic Personality also uses a great deal of **re-reaction formation**. They adopt behavior that is diametrically opposed to what they fear. They fight back by not fighting back.

Along with this is **deflection of guilt**. Fickle, unjust, mean-spirited fates are responsible for their plight. In relationships, this deflection carries over to the partner (*"See how you've hurt me? I'm in pain because of you"*). In *Swingers*, Mike moons over his old girlfriend. She has shattered his life, yet he is the one who left her and moved to Los Angeles.

Immoralization is also a common defense. Masochists want to justify their behavior through moral victory. Suffering is an only too common requisite of the righteous.

But these individuals have the unconscious belief that they are intrinsically bad, intrinsically deserving of their misery. They therefore get others to validate this belief; they get others to be guilty of greater moral wrongs than they believe themselves guilty.

This is **projection**, another defense mechanism. They project their self-defeating behavior outside themselves so as not to have to take responsibility.

The Masochist also defensively **acts out**, which is to say that they take the initiative when it comes to doling out the harm. They will feel anxiety over the notion that someone (such as an authority figure) is set to do them harm, or they are secure in the knowledge that someone eventually will do them harm, so they expect it. In order to relieve this anxiety they punish themselves first in anticipation. They may also exhibit behavior of extreme provocation. Again, they will force others to harm them to relieve the anxiety of the inevitable. Dawn secures punishment at the hands of her mother in the surest way possible—targeting Missy.

This also leads to **repetition compulsion**—trying to resolve early childhood trauma through constantly repeating the past. Though the Masochist may be responsible for their ill treatment (it may actually come at their own hands), they still see themselves as the victims because the punishment is seen to have come eventually from others.

RELATIONSHIPS

It is common in relationships for Masochists to be overly dependent, submissive, and malleable in the extreme. They function best as victims, so victims they become. Their self-defeating behavior also emerges in their choice of relationships. Often they will choose to associate or align themselves with others who are bullies or, in the case of love and marriage, with partners who are distant, uninterested, or totally inappropriate. They manage to find someone eager to serve as a generator of abuse. They gravitate toward those who will validate their low sense of self-worth and recreate relationships in which they are pummeled with either abuse or insensitivity or sadism.

Attachment to others may be in the form of having pain inflicted on them, either emotionally or physically. Pain, for the Masochist, is love manifested. Masochists find that in their relationships their self-defeating behavior pays off. They get what they want and need—it's called protection. If they don't get the attention through sympathy, they will get it through provocation. The more they suffer the greater the response. Dawn Weiner longs for unavailable men, but settles for abusive Brendan—a boy with the longest and most secure history of abusing her. Mike pines for a girl after he has made sure that there is 3000 miles between them. In the wonderful little independent thriller, *Apartment Zero*, Adrian LeDuc takes in a boarder, Jack Carney, a young rouge who is as sensually handsome as he is sexually mysterious. Clearly a bad choice from the start, Adrian can't help himself and the results turn disastrous—this, despite his own intelligence and a remarkable knowledge of films that unfold this way.

Common to their thinking is the belief that if they can only get someone to feel sorry for them, they won't be abandoned emotionally. One of the great fears of the Masochist is that of abandonment—in many cases it supersedes the fear of bodily harm or death. "Don't leave me or I'll kill myself," is an expression of this extreme. Mike is given an opportunity to have sex with a girl in a trailer park in Las Vegas. The scene is set. The girl is willing and any qualms as to the purpose of the excursion to the trailer are allayed by the fact that Trent and his girl are already going at it behind a folding screen. Instead of seducing the girl—which in this instance would take little time or talent—Mike regales her with the story of his shambles of a love life. Instead of kisses and petting, he offers her whines and complaints. But he achieves what he wants: the girl is all but reduced to tears of sympathy and takes him to her (purely figurative) maternal breast and coddles him.

Masochists often appear subdued. "Doormats" would probably serve as the appropriate colloquialism here. They are victims waiting to happen . . . weaklings slouching around wearing hangdog expressions that make them look easy to hurt, ready and willing targets. This often evokes exasperation in those around them, which can only further encourage the Masochist. Exasperation from others is almost as good as abuse. Exasperation often leads to anger in the partner. Their mates may become infuriated by having to constantly save their masochistic mates. It is very hard to remain neutral in a relationship that is so out of balance. For the sake of love (or for the sake of hanging onto someone and not being abandoned) the Masochist will forfeit all of his personal power and self-esteem. Dolores (*Dolores Claiborne*) will withstand many years of abuse before she strikes out. They take the submissive role—they are the helpless, rain-battered orphans —and need to be taken care of. They will constantly demonstrate their suffering so as to elicit their partners' attention. People in contact with Masochists will be persuaded to save and comfort them because they wholeheartedly live their roles as victims threatened by life's ugly improprieties and dangerous situations.

BACKSTORY

The childhood of the Masochistic Personality is often mirrored in their adult behavioral patterns. Masochists often spend their formative years as victims of abuse or abandonment. In the former instance, the reductive worldview of the child equates abuse with love. The child's primary bond is to the parent, and the parent is the sole font of affection. If the parent abuses the child, the child's early logic confuses the two . . . mistakes one for the other. When the developing Masochist seeks love and attention, he therefore seeks an abusive relationship. The ground rules have been set. The logic is in place. In *Welcome to the Dollhouse*, the only attention that Dawn Weiner receives is negative. Her attention comes in the form of degradation. She surreptitiously meets Brendan, who, against his better judgment and peer pressure, is attracted to her. Yet Dawn makes it known that it is perfectly acceptable for him to degrade her. It is what she knows, what she is equipped to handle.

The Masochist who experiences abandonment early on tends to use this early experience as a template for adult relationships. They tend to seek out remote, distant partners who will not be able to provide for their emotional needs. By doing so they satisfy that elusive love that they never attained as children. They seek to right old wrongs, heal old wounds. *Sugarbaby*'s Marianne was overfed as an infant because she was a runt. From then on she equates feeding with love. She feeds Huber just like she fed her mother when she was withering away toward death.

Lessons learned early in their development include the idea that the punishment they receive is often in their best interest. Why else would their role models (and parents *are* omnipotent) behave as they do? They must be justified in their actions and the justification falls squarely on the intrinsic guilt of the budding Masochist. Young Masochists also believe that it is better to be beaten than neglected, because neglect equals abandonment, which equals death. So the Masochist will learn a pattern of provocation. In order to avoid abandonment, he will incur wrath.

The Masochist may say that their parents assaulted them a great deal, either physically or verbally, yet they seem to relish in the act of telling their manifold sorrows. This tendency, likewise, is seen in the adult. The Masochist is a victim, but gains a great deal of satisfaction in being so, and thus is eager to relate any and all ill treatment that he receives. These individuals usually emerge from childhood with unresolved dependency issues and the fear of being alone. This is easily understood because the roots of the Masochistic Personality are in the lack of nurturing or the improper nurturing that they receive.

THE ARC OF A MASOCHISTIC FILM CHARACTER

When we first meet Mike in *Swingers* we see him in the role that he is all too accustomed to playing, one that he is comfortable with, one that is overly familiar to his friends. He is the victim, the self-proclaimed loser who stews in the misery and attendant loneliness of life without his girl-friend—a girlfriend he left behind, but whom he feels betrayed by when she doesn't call. So entrenched and habitual is this sulking and whining that he feels he has to apologize for continually harping. "I'm sorry," he tells his friend, Rob. "We always talk about the same thing all the time." Trent (another friend) tells him that he not only has to get over his girlfriend, but he has to get out of his stuffy apartment as well. So, in yet another valiant effort to lift Mike from his mire of self-pity, Trent takes him to Las Vegas.

But Mike manages to fail in Vegas as well—the prime directive of swingers being, presumably, to score with the "beautiful babies." Mike aborts his seduction of a casino cocktail waitress (in the process thwarting Trent's more urgent attempts at doing likewise). He regales her with his well-hashed whining about his ex-girlfriend, extinguishing all passion in the room more effectively than bathing in saltpeter. He circumvents failure by admitting defeat before the battle's waged. How can he be dumped when he's already in such a self-imposed state?

Act Two begins as the pair head back to Los Angeles and Mike resolves to "get back out there, not make any more excuses for myself."

But back in LA, Mike quickly backslides and glumly goes through the days of an actor-slash-comedian. He frequents parties and bars where he strikes out with any number of those beautiful babies. He assumes the mantle as the easy butt of his friends' jokes—and an easier mark to spring for pizza. Meanwhile, Trent and the others have no problem making time with innumerable women, counseling Mike that he can't be weak (the eternal victim). He has to newly imagine himself as the aggressor, as the victimizer. But as Mike watches how his friends carry on, he expresses umbrage at their behavior. He takes the moral high ground. Sure, he's a victim, but at least he's righteous. From this position of moral infallibility, he chastises Trent and his other friends for their poor treatment of women, for using them for sex and discarding them, for scamming phone numbers at parties only to tear them up in full view of everyone assembled.

When Mike has words with his friend, a boy named Sue, Sue tells him that he is, "a whiny little bitch." It makes no difference if he got a phone number or not because he would only screw it up anyway. Sue knows this because Mike never shuts up about it. This shoves Mike into a true depression and he holes himself up in his apartment. His friend Rob comes over and convinces him that he is only a victim because he chooses to be: "You don't look at the stuff that you have, you only look at the stuff that you don't have. She won't call because you left. It's like you miss the pain like you miss her."

Act Three begins as Mike crawls out of his misery, out of his submissive position as an emotional spittoon for women. He ventures back into the world on newly confident, yet somewhat wobbly, legs. Sue apologizes and Mike tells him that he needed "a good kick in the ass. We're better friends for it." When he goes out to swing again with the boys, he meets a lovely woman with whom he has something in common and a mutual attraction. When she tells him that she'll see him around, he tells her that that's not good enough, that he wants to make definite plans to see her. When he is at last able to hang up on Michelle to take another phone call, right when she is in the middle of saying "I love you," he has truly arrived. He is finally a master of his own domain. Trent is delighted. "My little baby's all grown up," he marvels as he does a dance on the table among their breakfasts. Mike stops being a victim when he stops acting as though he were one.

THE MASOCHISTIC PERSONALITY
SUMMARY

Examples of the qualities and qualifications that define a person with a Masochistic Personality:

- They tend to exhibit a depressive mood
- They tend to complain about being the victims of fate
- They tend to feel that malevolent people are somehow involved in their prosecution
- They usually experience early childhood fears of rejection and abandonment
- They usually have sadistic tendencies. Sadistic and masochistic feelings are usually always linked. The guilt of having these sadistic feelings turns inward to self-sadism, or masochism
- This personality usually emerges early in childhood
- They usually only feel gratified when they are victimized
- Their desire for punishment is usually subconscious
- They tend to manifest failure in their lives
- They are usually accident prone
- They tend to find or place themselves in positions in which disgrace is inevitable
- They seek out unhappy relationships or derail the ones that are good
- They tend to be resistant to therapy. They don't want to give up their suffering
- They tend to undermine pleasurable experiences
- They seek out maltreatment, even when better options are presented
- They usually feel that they are unworthy of any good things that come their way

- They usually respond with guilt when things do go their way
- They tend to invite rejection, then feel hurt, defeat, or humiliation
- They tend to provoke others to anger
- They tend to self-sacrifice to a harmful degree, and this is usually unsolicited and discouraged by others
- They tend to avoid situations that would make them happy
- When they do enjoy themselves, they are reluctant to admit it
- They usually fail to complete tasks, even when they are able to, because that would mean success
- They tend to reject or ignore people who treat them well
- They tend to harbor a sense of moral triumph through self-imposed suffering
- They tend to believe that by enduring pain they are preventing some greater anguish (such as abandonment)
- They tend to have constant sadness and unconscious guilt and may feel anger and resentment toward others for their torment
- They tend to store up and harp on injustices done to them, rather than to try and correct them
- They tend to feel that it is better to be beaten than untouched, abused rather than rejected
- Unlike Paranoid Personalities, Masochists need people around them onto whom to transfer their sadistic tendencies.They need victimizers in order to be victims
- They tend to live in a state of dread . . . dread that people will observe their shortcomings and reject them

NOTEWORTHY CHARACTERISTICS
OF THE MASOCHISTIC PERSONALITY

SPEECH

Self-defeating. Self-deprecating. Abusive and demeaning (toward themselves).

PROFESSIONS

Professions that may have a demoralizing stigma attached to them, such as prostitutes. Actors. Comedians. A subservient role in business, such as the secretary that is overqualified for a job but never leaves.

DRESS

Similar to speech, it is self-deprecating. Not unusual to dress in a manner that will give credence to their belief that they are unattractive.

HEALTH

Their love of pain might create an over exaggeration of symptoms. Constant health problems due to terrors of pleasure. Stress-related illnesses. Headaches. Gastrointestinal. Back pain.

POPULAR CLICHÉS
ASSOCIATED WITH MASOCHISTICS

- The Stick-in-the-Mud
- The Complainer
- The Punching Bag
- The Accident Waiting to Happen
- The Sourpuss
- The Crank
- The Grouser
- The Kvetch
- The Martyr
- The Zealot
- Doormats
- Weaklings
- Scapegoat
- Victim
- Sucker
- Dupe

SIMILAR PERSONALITY TYPES
TO THE MASOCHISTIC

- THE NARCISSISTIC PERSONALITY
- THE BORDERLINE PERSONALITY

VIEWING SUGGESTIONS FOR
THE MASOCHISTIC PERSONALITY

Apartment, The (1960)—Drama/Comedy, 125, No rating.
Shirley MacLaine's Oscar nominated performance as Fran. Winner of five Academy Awards, including one for the skillful writing.

Apartment Zero (1988)—Thriller, 124, Rated R.
For a terrific performance by Colin Firth as the doomed Adrian. The film (lost in a Hollywood storm) is a great character study and a thrill of a ride.

Burning Bed, The (1984)—100, No rating.
Farrah Fawcett in a career-changing performance as a battered wife.

Casablanca (1942)—War/Drama, 102, No rating.
Subtle, interesting displays of masochistic tendencies from Humphrey Bogart. A great example of how to use the characteristics without drowning in the personality. Among many other Oscar awards, one for the legendary writing.

Cinderella Liberty (1973)—Drama, 117, Rated R.
Marsha Mason in her Oscar nominated performance as a hooker.

Diary of a Mad Housewife (1970)—Drama/Comedy, 103, Rated R.
Carrie Snodgress in her Oscar nominated performance as the mentally abused housewife, Tina Balser.

Dolores Claiborne (1995)—Thriller/Mystery/Drama, 131, Rated R.
> A seamless and stunning performance by Kathy Bates as an abused wife. Perhaps one of the best movies ever made that captures the essence of psychology and storytelling.

Klute (1971)—Crime, 114, Rated R.
> Jane Fonda as call girl Bree Daniels. She won the Oscar. It was also nominated for the tough-as-nails writing.

Leaving Las Vegas (1995)—Drama, 112, Rated R.
> Elizabeth Shue in a riveting performance. Shue was nominated for Best Actress, as was Mike Figgis for the writing and the directing.

Nights of Cabiria (1957)—Drama, 110, No rating.
> Fellini's glorious take on prostitute life. Winner of Best Foreign Film. The basis of the American musical, *Sweet Charity*.

Some Kind of Wonderful (1987)—Romance, 93, Rated PG-13.
> A terrific and rare look at a teen masochist. Mary Stuart Masterson as Watts. John Hughes offers some of his best writing.

Such Good Friends (1971)—Comedy, 100, Rated R.
> Great performance by Dyan Cannon as a self-abased woman. Truly one of the oddest Director/Writer collaborations ever: Otto Preminger and Elaine May (using a pseudonym).

Sugarbaby (1985)—Drama/Comedy, 87, No rating.
Touching performance by Marianne Sage-
brecht as Marianne.

Swingers (1996)—Comedy, 96, Rated R.
A strong twist that gives us a modern male
version of a masochist.

Tommy Boy (1995)—Comedy, 96, Rated PG-13.
Funny and very broad telling of a male
masochist. Chris Farley as Tommy Callahan.

What's Love Got to Do With It? (1993)—Musical/
Biography, 119, Rated R.
Interesting look at the real-life masochistic
tendencies of a superstar.

What's Up, Doc? (1972)—Comedy, 94, Rated G.
Great screwball comedy with Ryan O'Neal
as the put-upon Howard Bannister.

Welcome to the Dollhouse (1995)—Comedy, 88, Rated R.
Very dark comedy about a young girl suffering from masochistic tendencies. Great
viewing of tough subject matter.

II

THE MENTAL DISORDERS

Listed by category, the major Mental Disorders, as defined by the American Psychiatric Association's Diagnostic and Statistical Manual of Mental Disorders (the DSM).

ADJUSTMENT DISORDERS

Adjustment Disorder

The fundamental feature is the development of clinically significant emotional or behavioral manifestations to an identifiable, psychologically stress-related disturbance (except bereavement). Symptoms last for no more than six months. Associated features may include a depressed mood, sexual dysfunction, guilt, and obsession.

ANXIETY DISORDERS

Panic Disorder

A discrete period of intense fear or discomfort.

Agoraphobia

Anxiety about being in places or situations from which escape might be difficult.

Social Phobia

A marked and persistent fear of one or more social or performance situations in which the person is exposed to unfamiliar people or to possible scrutiny by others.

Specific Phobia

Distinguished and chronic fear that is extreme or irrational, set off by the presence or expectation of a situation or thing such as flying, heights, animals, receiving an injection, or seeing blood. Anxiety in the presence of a specific stimuli.

Obsessive-Compulsive Disorder

Either obsessions or compulsions causing a clinically significant distress that is time consuming or significantly interferes with a standard routine (such as occupational, social, and personal activities).

Post-Traumatic Stress Disorder

A person has been exposed to a traumatic event in which the traumatic event is persistently re-experienced and causing marked difficulties in social, occupational, or other important areas of functioning.

Generalized Anxiety Disorder

Extreme anxiety and concern—and difficulty in controlling the worry—for more days than not over any number of occurrences (such as occupation).

Acute Stress Disorder

An individual is exposed to a traumatic event (which is persistently re-experienced). It is similar to Post-Traumatic Stress Disorder but must occur within a four-week period of the event and be resolved within a four-week period.

CHILDHOOD DISORDERS

Attention-Deficit Disorder

A consistent inability to give specific attention to fine points or makes careless errors in areas of life such as education, work, and personal activities. Signs of persistent hyperactivity/impulsivity. Developmentally inappropriate for the age of the child.

Autistic Disorder

Delays or abnormal functioning in social interactions, with marked impairments in communication.

Conduct Disorder

A recurrent and chronic pattern of behavior in which the basic rights of others are violated (such as aggression to people or animals, destruction of property, theft, or deceitfulness).

Oppositional Defiant Disorder

A pattern of negativistic, hostile, and defiant behavior toward authority.

Separation Anxiety Disorder

Developmentally unsuitable and extreme distress concerning separation from home and/or persons.

Tourette's Disorder

The marked presence of both aggregated motor and vocal tics.

Rett's Disorder

More specific patterns of deficit than Autism, beginning at age five months. Conditions include decelerated head growth, loss of hand skills, and impaired language development. Reported in females only.

Childhood Disintegrative Disorder

After the age of two and before age ten, there is a loss of previously required skills in two or more areas (such as language, social, or motor). In Autism the developmental abnormalities are evident earlier, in the first year after birth.

Asperger's Disorder

Qualitative impairment in social interaction and restricted repetitive and stereotyped behaviors, interests and activities. In contrast to Autism, there is no delay in language development.

Mental Retardation

Significantly sub-average intellectual functioning (IQ = 70 or below); impairments in adaptive functioning; and onset before eighteen years of age.

Borderline Intellectual Functioning

The person's IQ is in the 71 – 84 range.

Learning Disorder

As opposed to all areas, achievement in one specific area (such as reading, math, or language) is substantially below average.

COGNITIVE DISORDERS

Delirium

Diminished ability to maintain attention to outside stimulation and to appropriately shift attention.

Vascular Dementia

Damage in short-and long-term memory affecting such things as abstract thinking and judgment in a stepwise and patchy progression. Caused by Arteriosclerosis or Cerbovascular disease.

Dementia (Alcoholism)

Impairment in short-and long-term memory due to a prolonged and/or heavy ingestion of alcohol.

Dementia (Alzheimer Type)

Damage in short-and long-term memory with personality change and irritability. Gradual onset of symptoms and a slow progressive decline beginning usually around age 65.

Dementia

Gradual impairment in short-and long-term memory in which the person is usually unaware of the impairment.

Amnestic Disorder

Impairment in the ability to learn new information or to recall previously learned information or past events. A general medical condition or substance abuse causes it.

CONVERSION
DISORDERS

Conversion Disorder

Symptoms that suggest a serious neurological or other medical disorder (paralysis, blindness) but for which no medical explanation can be found. Conversion Disorders have two characteristics:

Primary Gain – keeping an inner conflict out of consciousness.

Secondary Gain – Avoiding an activity or obtaining support.

SOMATOFORM
DISORDERS

Somatoform Disorder

Physical symptoms that suggest a medical condition, but that are not fully explained by a medical condition, the effects of a substance, or another mental disorder. The symptoms are not voluntarily produced.

EATING
DISORDERS

Anorexia Nervosa

A fierce panic at gaining weight or becoming fat, even though underweight. There is an unwillingness to maintain body weight at or above a normal weight for age and height.

Bulimia Nervosa

Ongoing and extremely inappropriate compensatory behavior in order to prevent weight gain and experienced through such behavior as self-induced vomiting or misuse of laxatives, diuretics, enemas, or other medications.

MOOD
DISORDERS

Major Depressive Disorder

The marked appearance of an abnormally depressed mood. The sorrow is often described as despondent, forlorn, broken hearted. Depressed mood for a majority of time as indicated by such things as poor appetite, overeating, low energy, fatigue, low self-esteem, poor concentration, difficulty making decisions, or feelings of hopelessness. There is a markedly diminished interest or pleasure in all, or almost all, activities.

Dysthymic Disorder

Chronically depressed mood, which is present most of the time for at least two years in adults and one year in children.

BIPOLAR MOOD DISORDERS

Bipolar Disorder

The presence of at least one or more Manic or Mixed Episodes with or without a history of a Major Depressive Episode.

Bipolar II Disorder

In contrast to Bipolar I Disorder, there are no Manic or Mixed Episodes.

Cyclothymic Disorder

Fluctuating hypomanic symptoms and numerous periods of depressive symptoms for at least two years in adults or one year in children or adolescents.

PERSONALITY DISORDERS

Paranoid Personality

A pervasive distrust and suspiciousness of others such that their motives are interpreted as malevolent.

Schizoid Personality

A pervasive pattern of detachment from social relationships and a restricted range of expressions and emotions with regard to interpersonal settings. Beginning by early adulthood and present in a variety of contexts.

Schizoitypal Personality

A pervasive pattern of social and interpersonal deficits marked by acute discomfort with, and reduced capacity for, close relationships as well as by cognitive or perceptual distortions and eccentricities of behavior, beginning by early adulthood and present in a variety of contexts.

Antisocial Personality

A pervasive pattern of disregard for and violation of the rights of others. Most significant is the substantial lack of remorse for the crimes that they commit. They also often exhibit an inability to control their violent impulses. They erupt without warning.

Borderline Personality

A pervasive pattern of instability of interpersonal relationships, self-image, affects, and marked impulse behavior. Beginning by early adulthood and present in a variety of contexts.

Histrionic Personality

A pervasive and excessive emotionality, theatricality, self-dramatization, and attention-seeking behavior. Beginning by early adulthood and present in a variety of contexts.

Narcissistic Personality

A pervasive self-centeredness—an all-encompassing grandiosity about themselves, their achievements, and their place in life. Along with this exalted self-centered behavior, there is also a discernible lack of empathy and a sense of entitlement that blinds them to all needs except their own. Beginning by early adulthood and present in a variety of contexts.

Avoidant Personality

A pervasive pattern of social inhibition, feelings of inadequacy, and hypersensitivity to negative evaluation, beginning by early adulthood and present in a variety of contexts.

Dependent Personality

A pervasive and excessive need to be taken care of that leads to submissive and clinging behavior and fear of separation, beginning by early adulthood and present in a variety of contexts.

Obsessive-Compulsive Personality

A pervasive pattern of preoccupation with orderliness, perfectionism, and mental and interpersonal control at the expense of flexibility, openness, and efficiency. Beginning by early adulthood and present in a variety of contexts.

SCHIZOPHRENIA & OTHER PSYCHOTIC DISORDERS

Schizophrenia

A preoccupation with delusions or frequent auditory hallucinations. Characteristic symptoms include disorganized speech and/or disorganized behavior, a flat or improper sway in their person, physical immobility or excessive activity, marked instances of extreme negativism, and idiosyncrasies in intentional movement as demonstrated by their posturing.

Delusional Disorder

Non-bizarre delusions (those involving situations that occur in real life, such as being followed, poisoned, infected, loved at a distance, or deceived by spouse or lover or having a disease). Characteristics include a grossly disorganized or catatonic behavior.

Brief Psychotic Disorder

Symptoms occur shortly after and apparently in response to events that, singly or together, would be markedly stressful to almost anyone in similar circumstances in the person's culture. Characteristics of delusions, hallucinations, disorganized speech, and grossly disorganized or catatonic behavior.

Schizoaffective Disorder

An uninterrupted period of illness during which, at some time, there is either a Major

Depressive Episode, a Manic Episode, or a Mixed Episode concurrent with symptoms that meet the criteria for Schizophrenia.

Shared Psychotic Disorder

A delusion develops in an individual in the context of a close relationship with another person(s) who has an already established delusion. The delusion is similar in content to that of the person who already has the established delusion.

DISSOCIATIVE
DISORDERS

Depersonalization Disorder

One or more episodes of depersonalization (feeling of detachment or estrangement from oneself), with reality testing left relatively intact.

Dissociative Amnesia

One or more episodes of an inability to recall important personal information that cannot be attributed to ordinary forgetfulness. The gaps in memory are often related to a traumatic event.

Dissociative Fugue

Abrupt, unexpected travel away from home or work with an inability to remember some or all of one's past and confusion about one's personal identity or a partial or total assumption of a new identity.

Dissociative Identity Disorder

The existence of two or more distinct identities or personality states in which each has its own pattern of perceiving, relating to, and thinking about the environment and self.

DYSSOMNIA & PARASOMNIA DISORDERS

Dyssomnias

Sleep disorders characterized by disturbances in the amount, quality and timing of sleep.

Parasomnias

Sleep disorders involving behavioral or physiological abnormalities during sleep or in the sleep-wakefulness transition.

SEXUAL
DISORDERS

Paraphilia

A Sexual Disorder in which intense, recurrent sexual urges, fantasies, or behaviors involve either non-human objects, the suffering or humiliation of oneself or one's partner, or children or non-consenting partners. Examples include Fetishism, Pedophilia, and Voyeurism.

TRANSVESTISM & GENDER
IDENTITY DISORDERS

Transvestism

In a male, recurrent, intense, sexually arousing fantasies, sexual urges, or behaviors involving cross-dressing.

Gender Identity Disorder

Involves a strong persistent cross-gender identification and discomfort with one's sex or a sense of inappropriateness in the gender role of that sex.

SEXUAL DYSFUNCTION &
SEXUAL RESPONSE DISORDERS

Desire Phase Dysfunction

Includes sexual fantasies and desire for sex.

Excitement Phase Dysfunction

Includes physiological changes related to arousal.

Orgasm Phase Dysfunction

The culmination of sexual pleasure, with release of sexual tension.

SUBSTANCE-RELATED DISORDERS

Substance Abuse

A maladaptive pattern of substance use involving clinically significant impairment or distress as manifested by the presence of at least one symptom during a 12-month period.

Dependence

Involving the continued use of a substance despite significant substance-related problems, as evidenced by the presence of at least three characteristic symptoms during a 12- month period. Dependence may or may not involve tolerance and withdrawal (physiological dependence). Substance Dependence is more serious than Substance Abuse.

Substance Withdrawal

Autonomic hyperactivity, hand tremor, insomnia, nausea or vomiting, transient illusions or hallucinations, anxiety, psychomotor agitation, and/or agitation following a period of prolonged or heavy use.

The Dependence Disorders

The Disorders for Substance Abuse, Substance Dependence, and Substance Withdrawal are:

- Alcohol Dependence Disorder
- Amphetamine Dependence Disorder

- Cannabis Dependence Disorder
- Cocaine Dependence Disorder
- Hallucinogen Dependence Disorder
- Inhalant Dependence Disorder
- Nicotine Dependence Disorder
- Opioid Dependence Disorder
- Phencyclidine Dependence Disorder
- Sedative Dependence Disorder

III

THE WORKPLATES

CHARACTER DEVELOPMENT
QUESTIONNAIRE

The following is a series of questions designed to stimulate the creative process and offer guidance in understanding and developing solid, well-rounded, and believable characters.

By going to our website, you can answer these questions on-line and print out a "workbook" profiling your characters.

Visit at: www.keylightcompany.com/reel_links.htm. Scroll and click on the "Screenplay Systems" logo.

THE
HISTORICAL
WORKPLATES

THE HISTORICAL
WORKPLATES

DEFINING THE BASICS

1. What is the character's name?
2. Is the character male or female?
3. How old is the character?
4. What is the character's birthday?
5. What is the character's height?
6. What is the character's weight?
7. What is the character's hair color?
8. What is the character's eye color?
9. What is the character's racial orientation?
10. What is the character's religion?

THE HISTORICAL
WORKPLATES

DEFINING THE PHYSICAL

1. Does the character have any disabilities?

2. What is the character's physical build?

3. How is the character's posture?

4. Is the character graceful or awkward?

5. Is the character comfortable with his/her body?

6. Is the character attractive? Does he/she think so?

7. Does the character have an accurate physical self-image?

8. Is there any part of the character's physicality that he/she is ashamed of?

9. Is there any part of the character's physicality that they are proud of and perhaps flaunt?

THE HISTORICAL
WORKPLATES

DEFINING THE PAST

1. Where was the character born?
2. Are his/her parents still alive?
3. How old were the parents when the character was born?
4. Was the character adopted?
5. Are there any brothers or sisters?
6. What is the birth order of the children?
7. Did the character have his/her own room while growing up?
8. Where was the character raised?
9. Did the family have a habit of relocating?
10. Was the character close to his/her mother when growing up? How about the father?
11. How close is the character to his/her mother now? Father?
12. Did the character suffer abuse (physical, emotional, sexual) at the hands of either parent?
13. Did the character suffer abuse from any of the siblings or other family members?
14. Are the parents still married? Was this their first marriage?
15. Were there any deaths in the family while the character was growing up? Any significant illnesses or accidents?
16. What illnesses did the character have as a child?
17. How religious were the parents in the upbringing?
18. What was the role of religion in the character's life?
19. What hobbies did the character have when he/she was growing up?
20. What was the family's financial situation when the character was growing up? How did he/she feel about it?

THE HISTORICAL WORKPLATES

DEFINING THE PRESENT

1. Does the character live in the city or in the country? Where exactly?

2. In what environment does the character live (a house, an apartment, a military base)?

3. Does the character live alone? If not, with whom does he/she live?

4. Is the character married? (see RELATIONSHIPS WORKPLATE)

5. Does the character have any children? If so, what are their sexes and ages?

THE HISTORICAL
WORKPLATES

DEFINING EDUCATION

1. How far did the character go in school? Did he/she go to college?
2. How was the character's scholastic performance?
3. Did they like school?
4. What were their favorite subjects? Least favorite?
5. What, if any, extracurricular activities did they engage in?
6. Was the character involved in athletics?
7. Were they popular in high school? College?
8. Did the character have any learning difficulties (attention deficit, conduct problems)?
9. Did the character have any problems with teachers or authority?

THE HISTORICAL
WORKPLATES

DEFINING WORK

1. What was the character's first job?

2. At what age did the character start working?

3. What is the character's present job?

4. Does the character's occupation satisfy him/her?

5. Describe the character's financial situation.

6. Did the character choose this occupation, or was it thrust upon him/her?

7. Does the character do his/her job well?

8. Does he/she work extra hours?

9. Does any other part of the character's life (the home life) suffer due to devotion to the job?

10. Is there a possibility of advancement in the character's career?

11. Are the demands of the character's job intellectual?

12. Do they take their work home with them?

THE HISTORICAL
WORKPLATES

DEFINING HEALTH

1. Does the character smoke?
2. Does the character exercise? How often and what kind?
3. What is the family history with regard to illness?
4. Is the character afraid of illness and disease?
5. Does the character take precautions against any diseases?
6. Does the character suffer from any allergies?
7. What are the character's eating habits?
8. Does the character have any eating disorders?
9. Does the character have a problem maintaining his or her weight?
10. Is the character on any medications? If so, what kind and for what ailment?
11. Does the character have any problems sleeping?
12. Does the character drink alcohol?
13. Does the character have a problem with alcohol? (see DRUGS & ALCOHOL)
14. Does the character take any illegal drugs? (see DRUGS & ALCOHOL)

THE HISTORICAL WORKPLATES

DEFINING SPEECH

1. Does the character have a speech impediment?
2. What is the character's native language?
3. What was his/her parents' native language?
4. Does the character speak with an accent?
5. Is the character articulate?
6. Does the character use slang?
7. Is the character's speech excessively formal?
8. Does the character think before speaking?
9. Does the character speak inappropriately, either using swear words or endearments?
10. Is the character loud? Is he/she soft spoken?
11. Does the character listen well?
12. Does the character monopolize the conversation?
13. Is the character's voice deep or high?
14. Does the character have a sense of humor?
15. Does the character ever have a joke at someone else's expense?
16. Is the character's humor always appropriate?
17. Is the character sarcastic? Silly? Playful?

THE HISTORICAL
WORKPLATES

DEFINING COGNITION

1. Can the character keep a train of thought, or is he/she easily distracted?
2. Is the character's IQ high? Low?
3. Does the character display a logical progression of thought?
4. Is the character stymied by any religious restrictions?
5. Is the character prone to daydreaming?
6. Does the character tend to think in concrete terms or abstract?
7. Is the character prone to fanciful thought or language?

THE
PSYCHOLOGICAL
WORKPLATES

THE PSYCHOLOGICAL
WORKPLATES

DEFINING PERSONALITY TYPE

1. What personality type does the character most represent?

   - Narcissistic
   - Borderline
   - Histrionic
   - Antisocial
   - Schizoid
   - Masochistic
   - Obsessive/Compulsive
   - Paranoid
   - Other Mental Disorder (see list)

2. What aspects of that specific personality type does the character seem to adhere to?

3. How might the character's childhood have contributed to his specific personality type?

4. What personality types might the character's parents have been?

5. What type of relationships is the character attracted to?

THE PSYCHOLOGICAL
WORKPLATES

DEFINING BEHAVIOR

1. Is the character more outgoing or reflective?

2. Does the character accept responsibilities readily, or does he/she avoid them?

3. Is the character harshly self-judgmental?

4. Is the character uncritical of his/her own behavior?

5. How would you rate the character's impulse control?

6. Does the character tend to be superficial?

7. Is the character decisive? Does he/she weigh and consider all options before acting?

8. Is the character honest?

9. Does the character trust others? Do others trust him/her?

10. Does the character find starting a conversation easy?

11. Who does the character find easiest to converse with? Who is the hardest?

THE PSYCHOLOGICAL
WORKPLATES

DEFINING A SENSE OF IDENTITY

1. Does the character possess the ability to distinguish between what is internal? And what is external or is there a pattern of delusional behavior?

2. Does the character express his/her fantasy life in a realistic fashion?

3. Does the character defend against his/her sexual or aggressive desires?

4. Is the character driven by impulses to the point where there is danger to self or others?

5. Can the character possess the ability for judgment and adequately anticipate the consequences of his/her actions?

6. Does the character see problems as having an internal origin or are all difficulties externalized and blamed on others?

7. Is the character utilizing such defense mechanisms as repression, projection, or denial?

8. Does the character espouse realistic ideals or is his/her driven by unreachable fantastic goals?

THE PSYCHOLOGICAL WORKPLATES

DEFINING A SENSE OF SELF

1. Is the character in possession of a durable sense of self? Or is it prone to fragmentation in response to the smallest slight from a friend or family member?

2. Does the character need to be in the spotlight? Does he/she need to continually receive affirming responses from others?

3. Does the character possess the ability to create long-term relationships?

4. Is the character capable of a stable lifestyle?

5. Is the character conscious of different social boundaries? Body boundaries?

6. Is the character capable of industry and enthusiasm? Or is he/she subject to feelings of inferiority and inadequacy?

7. Has the character found "meaning" in his/her life and is he/she able to express this sense of meaning in his/her relationships or vocation?

8. Does the character exhibit a defensive manner at the possibility of being observed and judged? Or is the character open to criticism?

9. How aware is the character of his/herself?

10. Does the character continually seek the approval of others?

11. Does the character seek stability in his/her life? Does he/she avoid it?

12. Does the character ever experience a separation of mind and body?

13. Does the character ever feel inadequate? When?

THE PSYCHOLOGICAL
WORKPLATES

DEFINING HOPES AND DREAMS

1. What is the worst thing that ever happened to the character?

2. What is the best thing that ever happened to the character?

3. What does the character do to relax?

4. What does the character do for a good time?

5. What are the character's life goals?

6. Does the character ever take risks? Does he/she ever take dangerous risks?

7. How realistic or achievable are the character's goals?

8. Who is the character's hero? Why?

9. Does the character ever wish he/she were someone else? Who?

10. What superstitions does the character have?

11. Does the character believe in destiny?

12. How would the character imagine a perfect life?

13. Is the character's life as he/she imagined?

14. Does the character think that he/she has lived up to his/her parents' expectations?

15. Does the character remember his/her dreams?

16. Is the character an optimist or a pessimist?

17. Is the character confidant or shy?

18. If the character had three wishes, what would they be?

19. Have the character describe him/herself.

THE PSYCHOLOGICAL
WORKPLATES

DEFINING EMOTIONS

1. How aware is the character of his/her feelings?
2. How aware is the character of the feelings of others?
3. How comfortable is the character in expressing his/her feelings?
4. How does the character express his/her feelings?
5. What particular emotions is the character most comfortable with?
6. What particular emotions make the character uncomfortable?
7. What makes the character depressed? How often is he/she depressed?
8. What makes the character anxious?
9. Does the character cry easily? What would make the character cry?
10. What is the character afraid of? Is this a valid fear, or is it a phobia?
11. Is the character conceited or vain?
12. Is the character openly affectionate?
13. Do people tend to believe the character, or is he/she seen as a phony?
14. Is the character kindly?
15. Does the character have an emotional support system? If so, who?
16. How does the character take care of his/her emotional needs?
17. Is the character self-indulgent?
18. Is the character impulsive?

THE PSYCHOLOGICAL
WORKPLATES

DEFINING SOCIAL SKILLS

1. Are the antisocial aspects of the character realized?
2. Is the character capable of starting a conversation?
3. Is the character capable of completing a conversation?
4. Does the character choose the appropriate time and place when engaging in conversation?
5. Does the character pay attention when someone else is talking?
6. Does the character pay attention to instructions and carry them out appropriately?
7. Does the character appreciate things that others have done for him/her?
8. Does the character tell others they are sorry after doing things that are wrong?
9. How does the character dress?
10. Which of the character's attributes does he/she accentuate? Which does he/she hide?
11. Is the character sloppy or neat?
12. Does the character dress appropriately for his/her age? For the situation?
13. Describe the character's personal style.

THE PSYCHOLOGICAL WORKPLATES

DEFINING EXPRESSION OF FEELINGS

1. Is the character aware of his/her feelings?
2. Does the character appreciate the feelings of others?
3. Is the character capable of expressing feelings in a socially acceptable manner?
4. Does the character figure out the reasons for failing in particular situations?
5. What defenses does the character rely upon to hide his/her feelings?
6. Is the character critical of others?
7. How does the character respond to criticism?
8. Does the character tend to seek approval?
9. What does the character refuse to think about?
10. Who does the character hate and why?
11. What does the character do in uncomfortable situations?
12. Does the character have any habits?
13. Does the character engage in any repetitive behavior?
14. Does the character tend to avoid eye contact?

THE PSYCHOLOGICAL WORKPLATES

DEFINING ASSERTIVENESS

1. Does the character assert his/her rights by letting others know where he/she stands?
2. Does the character offer help to others who may need or want it?
3. Does the character tell others when he/she is responsible for creating a particular problem?
4. Does the character work toward a fair solution to someone else's complaint?
5. Is the character capable of controlling his/her temper?
6. Does the character carefully consider another person's position?
7. Does the character decide on his/her own what to do when others pressure him/her to do something?
8. Can the character communicate feelings and ideas assertively rather than aggressively?
9. Does the character effectively communicate his/her opinion on an issue?
10. Is the character fair when it comes to handling a dispute?
11. How persuasive is the character? What does he/she do to persuade others to come around to his/her way of thinking?
12. Is the character rash in making decisions?
13. Is the character realistic in judging his/her own abilities?
14. How much does the character think ahead and plan?
15. To what degree does the character act spontaneously?

THE PSYCHOLOGICAL
WORKPLATES

DEFINING HOW A CHARACTER
PROBLEM SOLVES

1. Is the character capable of deciding which of several problems is most important and should be dealt with first?
2. Does the character consider alternatives and make decisions in his/her best interest?
3. Does the character realistically decide what he/she can accomplish before beginning a task?
4. Does the character make those preparations that will help get the job done?

THE PSYCHOLOGICAL
WORKPLATES

DEFINING A CHARACTER'S ANGER

1. Can the character include anger as part of his/her personality and allow anger to be expressed naturally?

2. Is the character able to express anger in a direct fashion?

3. Are the character's feelings of anger exaggerated or unreasonable?

4. Can the character appropriately communicate anger to others?

5. Can the character communicate feelings assertively rather than aggressively?

6. Can the character regulate his/her feelings of anger?

7. When does the character get angry?

8. Is the character's anger always reasonable? When isn't it?

9. Does the character have a problem showing anger?

10. How does the character release his/her aggression?

11. How does the character show his/her anger indirectly?

12. Has the character ever solved a problem through violence?

THE PSYCHOLOGICAL
WORKPLATES

DEFINING MENTAL HEALTH

1. Is the character able to manage his/her anxiety? If unmanageable, is it expressed in a hysterical manner or a fixated phobic reaction—like agoraphobia?

2. Is the character living his/her life? Or are they in a depressed state of mind?

3. Does the character suffer from delusions, hallucinations, paranoia, or catatonia?

4. Is the character an alcoholic or substance abuser? If so, is his/her abuse impacting his/her life? (see DRUGS & ALCOHOL)

5. Does the character suffer from any sleep problems that are impacting his/her life?

6. Are there any medical problems that are affecting the character's mental health behavior, such as Dementia, Cancer, or AIDS?

7. Has culture, social economic status, gender, sexual orientation, or genetics had a major impact on the character's development?

8. Has the character been a victim of child abuse, elder abuse, domestic violence, or self-abuse, including suicide attempts?

9. Is there any major life factors (such as divorce, marriage, death, or job displacement) that have had a role in determining the character's well being?

THE PSYCHOLOGICAL
WORKPLATES

DEFINING DRUGS & ALCOHOL

1. What drugs does the character take? How often?
2. Has the character ever been in an alcohol or drug treatment program? Should he/she be?
3. When does the character use drugs or drink?
4. What prompts that indulgence?
5. Does the character's friends and family use drugs or drink too much?
6. Does the character ever lie about how often they use drugs or alcohol?
7. Does the character ever use drugs or alcohol to overcome shyness or gain confidence?
8. Does the character feel he/she should quit using drugs or alcohol, or at least cut down on the frequency of doing so?
9. Does the character drink too much at the wrong time?
10. Does the character ever drink or do drugs in the morning?
11. Are drugs or is drinking causing the character to have problems with his/her family?
12. Are drugs or is drinking causing the character to have problems at work or in school?
13. Does the character ever drink or do drugs to escape his/her problems?
14. Has the character ever been told that he/she drinks too much or has a problem with drugs?
15. Does the character hide his/her drinking or drug taking from family and friends?
16. Has the character ever been in trouble with the police because of alcohol or drugs?

17. Has the character ever required medical attention because of drinking or drug taking?

18. Does the character have to keep using or drinking once he/she starts?

19. Does the character ever have a blackout?

20. Does the character drink or do drugs at a particular time every day?

21. Do either of the character's parents have a problem with drugs or alcohol?

22. Has the character ever unsuccessfully tried to stop using drugs or alcohol?

23. Does the character drink or do drugs when he/she is alone?

24. Is the character getting a bad reputation because of drugs or alcohol?

25. Is the character's health suffering due to drinking or taking drugs?

26. Does the character ever go to work or school under the influence of alcohol or drugs?

27. Does the character ever feel guilty or sad because of drinking or drug taking?

28. Does the character have money woes because of drinking or drug taking?

29. Does the character have problems sleeping because of drinking or drug taking?

30. Does the character put him/herself in dangerous situations because of drugs or alcohol?

THE
RELATIONSHIPS
WORKPLATE

THE RELATIONSHIPS
WORKPLATE

DEFINING A CHARACTER
IN RELATIONSHIPS

1. Has the character developed the capacity for healthy relationships?

2. Has the character developed the capacity for intimacy with an appropriate aged partner or is the character still bound to satisfying parental needs?

3. Do the parent's marital problems play a factor in the character's personality?

4. Is the character always taking care of others who are less functional and more in need of care taking?

5. Is the character repeating an old relationship?

6. Is the character behaving like the person that he/she wished to be in his parent's eyes?

7. Does the character view others as being all good or all bad?

8. What is the character's sexual orientation?

9. Is the character very sexually driven?

10. How often does the character have sex?

11. Does the character find sex satisfying? Why and why not?

12. Does the character have any fetishes or peccadilloes?

13. Is the character dating anyone?

14. Is the character in love?

15. Is the character married?

16. Is the character's marriage reflective of his/her parents' marriage? Are the same problems repeating?

17. Is the character capable of sustaining long-term relationships based on commitment?

18. What does the character find attractive in another person?

19. What are the character's most attractive qualities?

20. Does the character have problems with intimacy?

21. Is the character monogamous?

22. Is the character jealous? Possessive?

23. Has the character ever abused a mate? How?

24. Has a mate ever abused the character? How?

25. Why did any previous relationships fail?

26. Is the character trying to be the person he/she thinks that his/her parents want them to be?

27. Who are the most important people in the character's life?

28. Does the character tend to avoid people?

29. Does the character hate to be alone?

30. Does the character have a problem with meeting people and making friends?

31. Is the character comfortable in social situations?

32. Is the character the life of the party?

33. Does the character have a lot of friends?

34. Who are the character's friends?

35. Who is the character's best friend?

36. Who is the character's hero? Why?

37. Does the character tend to enter into relationships in which he/she must take care of the other person?

38. Does the character choose partners and friends who are harmful or manipulative?

39. Does the character ever display masochistic tendencies in relationships?

40. Is the character usually a victim?

41. Does the character tend to be self-destructive?

Index

Symbols

A